Anonymous

Hand Book of the Builders' Exchange of San Francisco, Cal., 1895-6

Anonymous

Hand Book of the Builders' Exchange of San Francisco, Cal., 1895-6

ISBN/EAN: 9783337118235

Printed in Europe, USA, Canada, Australia, Japan

Cover: Foto ©ninafisch / pixelio.de

More available books at **www.hansebooks.com**

ESTABLISHED IN 1874

Golden Gate Plaster Mills

HOME INDUSTRY

215 and 217 MAIN STREET, Bet. Howard and Folsom, San Francisco

LUCAS & COMPANY

MANUFACTURERS OF

. CALCINED . PLASTER .

PLASTER PARIS

MARBLE DUST, LAND PLASTER, ETC., ETC.

H. T. HOLMES, PRES.   E. K. HAWKINS, SEC'Y.   WM. JONES, TREAS.

H. T. Holmes Lime Co.

INCORPORATED AUG. 1889.

—— IMPORTERS OF ——

Portland . Cement, . Plaster, . Fire Brick,

TILE, FIRE MATERIAL, Etc.

Manufacturers of Santa Cruz and Alabaster Lime

SOLE AGENTS FOR

Higginson Newburgh Plaster and Marble Dust

22-24 Sacramento St., - - San Francisco, Cal.

HAND BOOK
OF
THE BUILDERS' EXCHANGE
OF
SAN FRANCISCO, CAL.
1895-6.

CONTAINING THE

Articles of Incorporation, By-Laws, Rules, Regulations and Classified List
of the Members of the Builders' Exchange of San Francisco, Cal.
The Building and Fire Ordinance of the City and County
of San Francisco, Lien Law of the State with Reference Abstract and form of Lien and other
matter invaluable to Architects,
Builders, Contractors and
Owners, with a Full
and Complete
List of

ARCHITECTS OF THIS CITY,

—AND—

Classified Directory of Kindred Trades
of Building Industries.

PRICE, $2.00

L. H. COSPER & CO., Publishers

Received Highest Award, Gold Medal and Diploma
Midwinter Fair, 1894

J. R. POOL
House Mover and Raiser

RESIDENCE: 1224 Mission Street   **YARD:** 1130 Mission Street

—: ESTIMATES GIVEN :—

Box 217 Builders' Exchange, New Montgomery and Mission.

BOX 122   **L. SANTINI**   TEL. MAIN, 5110

Manufacturer of
Plaster Decorations, Center Pieces,   **Sculptor**

BRACKETS AND MOULDINGS

Outside Staff, Cement, Carton Pierre and Plastic Composition

Modeling of any kind and Jobbing of any kind Promptly Executed

Office: Builders' Exchange,   New Montgomery and Mission Sts.,
San Francisco, Cal.

PREFACE

In the preparation of this, the first volume of the "Hand Book" of The Builders' Exchange of the City of San Francisco, we have endeavored to collect for those engaged in the various branches of building, as well as for the dealers in and manufacturers of building materials, such information as would tend to establish the usefulness of the book as a handy and valuable reference, thereby securing that constantly sought for object of a business publication, viz: A closer business relationship between purchaser and seller, whereby an increased trade may be assured.

In connection with the above will also be found a complete list of the Architects of the city, and an alphabetical list of the members of The Builders' Exchange, a classified Business Directory, together with the Lien Laws of the State, with Reference Abstract and Form of Lien, and the Building and Fire Ordinance of the City and County of San Francisco.

With thanks to our patrons, and trusting that you will find the Hand Book complete and useful,

We are, yours truly,

L. H. COSPER & CO.,

SAN FRANCISCO, 1895. Publishers.

B. RANSOME   J. J. LEONARD   R. KEATINGE

Keatinge, Leonard & Ransome

Concrete and Twisted Iron

(Ransome's Patents)

ROOMS 1–12 NUCLEUS BLD'G

Box 13, Builders' Exchange

Room 9, Columbian Bld'g
Portland, Oregon

Telephone, Main 5748
San Francisco, Cal.

EDWARD B. HINDES & CO.

411 MISSION ST.

HILL'S PATENT   **Inside Sliding Window Blinds**

Venetian Blinds

Hindes' Perfection Fly Screen

SELF=COILING FIRE, and BURGLAR=PROOF

Steel Shutters

(NOISELESS)

HINDES' ROLLING PARTITION

For Schools and Churches

Box 174   -   -   -   Builders' Exchange

INDEX TO CONTENTS.

Architects, San Francisco..181-183
Builders' Exchange, The
   Articles of Incorporation..61
   By Laws...69
           Directors 1895-6, Illustrations
     Anderson, W. B..51
     Brady, O. E., Vice Pres..33
     Butcher, Thos. W...47
     Dunlop, Chas..43
     Elam, Thos..39
     Hayes, John T...49
     Kendall, A..45
     Lewis, Oscar, President...31
     McInerny, Jas..41
     Sibley, L. B., Treasurer...37
     Wilson, Jas. A., Secretary...35

     Cobb, Wm. H., Att'y..53
     Larsen, L. A., Asst Rec. Sec'y...57
     Meaddows, J. F., Doorkeeper..59
     North, S. D., Fin. Sec'y...55

     Exchange Building..29
     First President, C. C. Terrill, deceased...................................26
     First Vice President, W. N. Miller...26

   Members, Alphabetical list...159
   Officers 1890-1...27
   Officers 1891-2...25
   Officers 1892-3...23
   Officers 1893-4...21
   Officers 1894-5...19
   Officers 1895-6...17
Builders' Association of Cal., The..165
   By-Laws..171
   Constitution...165
   Executive Committee, Illustration..173
   Members, Alphabetical list...177-178
   Officers, Illustration...169
Building and Fire Ordinance..81
Classified Business Directory...185
Form for Mechanics' Lien..157
Index to Advertisers..11-13-15
Index to Lien Law..153-155
Mechanics' Lien Law of Cal...137
Preface...7
Title...5

TELEPHONE, MAIN 1927

OFFICE
327 MARKET STREET
SAN FRANCISCO

SOLD AT COMPETITIVE PRICES AND IN ANY QUANTITY

J. D. Spreckels & Bros. Co.

SOLE IMPORTERS

"GILLINGHAM"

London

Portland Cement

ENDORSED BY ALL LEADING ARCHITECTS ENGINEERS AND CONTRACTORS

INDEX TO ADVERTISERS.

Ackerson & Patterson; contractors and builders.................................... Page 40
Adams, Chas.; tailor.. 151
Alpine Wall Plaster Co.; (E. L. Snell, S. F. Agent)....................................... 36
Alum Rock Orchard Co.; real estate... 192
Ambrose, Wm. F.; concrete.. 54
Ammerup, G.; paints, oils, etc... 20
Anderson Bros.; contractors and builders... 50
Architectural Iron Works; O'Connell & Lewis.. 30
Barbich, A. E.; restaurant... 118
Bassett, T. R., & Bros.; contractors and builders....................................... 48
Bass-Hueter Paint Co.; paints, oils, etc... 82
Bell, Frank C.; contractor and builder... 184
Blumenthal, M., & Co.; wines liquors and cordials.................................. 118
Brady, M. V.; mason and builder... 58
Brady, O. E.; mason and builder... 32
Brennan, M. & Son; contractors and builders... 151
Brennan & Fraser, plasterers... 42
Bridge, H. S., & Co.; tailors... 65
Brown, B. Allen; architect... 98
Budde, Jos.; sanitary appliances.. 194
Building News & Review; (Geo. H. Wolfe)... 138
Butler, Thos.; mason and builder.. 58
Butterworth, Thos. C.. 22
California Art Glass Works... 6
California Paint Co.; paints, oils, etc... 12
California Sandstone & Contracting Co... 74
California Title, Insurance & Trust Co.; (L. R. Ellert mang'r).................... 110
Central Lumber & Mill Co.; lumber and planing mill............................. 86
Chatham, Wm.; contractor and builder.. 186
Cienega Lime Co.; O. M. Tupper, manager.................................. Back cover
Clark, N., & Sons; terra cotta, fire brick, etc... 68
Clawson, L. E., & Co.; patent chimneys............................... Inside front cover
Cobb, Wm. H.; attorney.. 52
Coghlan, Frank; plasterer... 151
Conlin & Roberts; metal roofers... 12
Cosper, L. H., & Co.; printers and publishers.. 150
Cowell, Henry, & Co.; lime, cement, etc............................... Inside back cover
Cronan, Wm.; Eagle Sheet Metal Works... 14
Cushing-Wetmore Co.; concrete and artificial stone............................... 136
Daniels, Gus. V.;.. 24
Davies, E.; plasterer... 42
Davis, Geo., & Son; house movers.. 28
Day, Thos. H., & Sons; contractors and builders...................................... 190
Depew, Chas. M.; planing mill.. 158
De Solla-Deussing Co.; boiler covering, etc... 180
Diggins Bros.; street contractors... 74
Dillon, David; teamster and contractor.. 60
Doe, B. & J. S.; doors, sash and blinds, mill work................................... 4
Doyle, R., & Son; contractors and builders.. 188
Dunlop, Chas.; plasterer.. 42
Dwyer, L. J.; painter and decorator.. 82
Dyer Bros.; Golden West Iron Works... 96
Eagle Sheet Metal Works (Wm. Cronan).. 14
Elam, Thos.; contractor and builder... 38
Fennell, Martin, & Son; masons and builders... 122
Field, Wm. J.; contractor and builder... 186
Forderer Cornice Works, pat. skylights, roofing &c................................ 30
Foster, John; contractor and builder.. 188
Fuller, W. P., & Co.; paints, oils, &c... 18
Furness, John; contractor and builder... 40
Gillespie, G. G.; contractor and builder... 184

Telephone Main 1798

Conlin & Roberts

METAL SLATE ROOFERS

Galvanized Iron and Copper Cornices

SKYLIGHTS and VENTILATORS

Patent Terra Cotta Chimney Pipes

—

720-730 MISSION STREET

JOHN REID

Merchant Tailor

907 Market Street
Near Fifth
Under the WINDSOR HOUSE

SAN FRANCISCO,
Cal.

California Paint Company

AVERILL AND RUBBER MIXED PAINTS

Agents — Santa Cruz Gilsos, Dealers in Varnishes, Etc.
Colors Ground in Oil and Pure Linseed Oil Putty

Office and Factory
22 JESSIE STREET   ... San Francisco

INDEX TO ADVERTISERS.

Gilletti, Secondo; artificial stone	54
Gillogly, G. & R.; teaming	82
Gladding, McBean & Co.; arch. terra cotta	98
Golden Gate Lumber Co.; lumber and planing mill	156
Golden Gate Plaster Mills; calcined plaster	3
Golden West Iron Works (Dyer Bros)	96
Goodman, Geo.; artificial stone, etc	54
Grant, W. J.; contractor and builder	38
Gray Bros.; art. stone and concrete work	80
Griese, Carl; art. stone and concrete	54
Griffin, P.; contractor and builder	168
Hammond, J. D.; printer	52
Hammond, Philip, metal roofer	30
Hanavan, J. H.; mason and builder	34
Hansen, A.; planing mill	188
Hansen, F. L.; contractor and builder	190
Hansen, M., & Co.; planing mill	56
Harrison, Fred., mason and builder	34
Hayes, John T.; contractor and builder	48
Healy, M. J.; stone contractor	74
Herring, R.; office fittings, mill work, &c	56
Herrmann, C., & Co.; hatters	122
Hetty, L. B.; electrician	Front cover
Hindes, Edw. B., & Co.; inside sliding blinds	8
Hock, T., & Son; masons and builders	180
Holmes H. T., Lime Co.; lime	3
Huber, Frank; doors, sash and blinds	22
Ingerson & Gore; contractors and builders	184
Jacks, Henry; contractor and builder	38
Jack, Wm. R.; contractor and builder	110
Jackson, P. H., & Co.; illuminating tiles	152
Jordan, D., & Son; masons and builders	182
Keatinge, Leonard & Ransome; concrete work	8
Keefe, J. H.; painter and decorator	24
Kelleher, M.; house mover	189
Kendall, A.; Pacific Coast Lumber & Mill Co	44
Kenney & Wells; inlaid floors	155
Kent, S. H.; contractor and builder	50
Knowles, Wm.; contractor and builder	38
Knox & Cook; contractors and builders	186
Kuss, P. N.; painter and decorator, paints, etc	110
Larsen, H. H.; mason and builder	46
Leprohon, P.; steam and hot water heating	182
Leibert & Hoffman; masons and builders	46
Level, A.; boots and shoes	20
Logan, J. F.; adjuster and builder	190
Lucas & Co.; calcined plaster	3
Lutgens, A. C.; architect	98
Lyons, Chas.; London tailor	192
Maguire, A. B.; lime, plaster, cement, &c	158
Mangrum & Otter; heating, &c., furnaces	179-185-187-189-191-193
McDonald, John A.; contractor and builder	186
McGowan, M.; mason and builder	32
McInerny, Jas.; contractor and builder	40
McLachlan, T. M.; contractor and builder	40
McLeod, J. C., plasterer	182
McMurray, J. P.; plaster decorations	182
Merchant & Nickels; paints, oils, etc	Back edge cover
Miller & Beck; masons and builders	34
Miller & Hamilton; planing mill	151
Montague, W. W., & Co.; mantels, tiles &c	46
Moore, G. Howard, contractor and builder	188
Moorehouse, J. J.; plasterer	42
Morrell, Frank D.; Norton door check	28

ALSEN'S PORTLAND CEMENT (GERMAN)

THE STRONGEST
FINEST GROUND
And MOST UNIFORM
CEMENT
IN THE WORLD

The Largest Works
— AND —
Greatest Production

212 COMMERCIAL STREET
LOS ANGELES, CAL.

U. S. Office 143 Liberty Street, New York

WILLIAM WOLFF & CO.
California Agents
327-329 Market St., SAN FRANCISCO, CAL.

TELEPHONE S. 224

EAGLE SHEET-METAL WORKS
WM. CRONAN
MANUFACTURER OF

ORNAMENTAL, GALVANIZED IRON and COPPER **Cornices**

G. I. Skylights, G. I. and Copper Gutters and Conductors
Tin, Iron and Slate Roofing, Cast Zinc Work
Roofs Repaired and Painted   General Jobbing Attended to

GENERAL AGENT FOR

THE POPULAR LINE OF "Superior" Warm Air Furnaces

STEAM AND HOT WATER HEATING
POWER FANS for HEATING and VENTILATING WORK

1213 & 1215 Market Street, SAN FRANCISCO

Estimates for heating Dwellings, Schools, Churches, or Buildings of any size with warm air, hot water, steam or hot blast.

INDEX TO ADVERTISERS.

Mulville, D. F.; plasterer	Page 180
Niehaus, Edward F., & Co.; hardwood lumber	56
Norton Door Check	28
Oakland Metal Works; (Philip Hammond)	30
O'Brien, Jas. J.; contractor and builder	184
O'Connell & Lewis; architectural iron works	30
Office Specialty Mfg. Co.	135
Osborne, R. F., & Co.; builders' hardware	114
O'Sullivan, D.; mason and builder	60
Pacific Coast Lumber and Mill Co.	44
Pacific Refining & Roofing Co.; roofers &c.	94
Palace Hardware Co.; builders' hardware	168
Paraffine Paint Co.; paints, roofers' and building paper	80
Patent Brick Co.; brick	58
Pavert, R. J.; contractor and builder	156
Peacock & Butcher; masons and builders	46
Petersen Brick Co.; original red pressed brick	96
Pettitt, J. G.; elevator works	28
Pollock, Geo.; boots and shoes	130
Pool, Jas. R.; house mover	6
Powers, Daniel; contractor and builder	190
Ralston Iron Works	151
Raymond Granite Co.; stone work	66-67
Reichley, Geo.; contractor and builder	50
Reid, John; tailor	12
Reigle & Jamieson; whitewashing	Front cover
Remillard Brick Co.; brick	58
Rocklin Granite Co.; stone work	79
Sacramento Transportation Co.; brick	78
Sanborn, A. J.; stairbuilder	22
San Francisco Photo. Eng. Co.	52
San Francisco Towel Co.	20
San Joaquin Brick Co.; brick	96
Santini, L.; plaster decorations	6
Schroeder, Wm.; art glass works	6
Schulze, Henry A.; architect	98
Scott & Van Arsdale Lumber Co.; lumber	56
Sibley, L. B.; teamster, grading, &c.	36-86
Smith & Young; building supplies	90
Snell, E. L.; lime, plaster, &c	36
Sorensen, Chas. M.; tailor	108-158
Spreckels, J. D., & Bros. Co.; cement	10
Steiger, A., Sons; arch. terra cotta	68
Stevens, P. M.; patent chimneys	104
Sullivan, J. F.; painter and decorator	24
Swain, Edward R.; architect	98
Tay, Geo. H., & Co.; plumbers' supplies	132
Tobin, J. R.; plasterer	60
Trotter, John; contractor and builder	48
Tuttle, John; teamster, plasterers' supplies	158
Union Lumber Co.; lumber	44
Wagner, Henry F.; painter and decorator	24
Wagner, J. Ferdinand; mason and builder	46
Walsh, Thos. J.; wines and liquors	32
Weiss, Fredrick K.; florist	118
Western Granite & Marble Co.	74
White Bros.; hardwood lumber	168
Wickersham, W. H.; contractor and builder	50
Williams, F. A.; contractor and builder	98
Wilson, James A.; mason and builder	34
Wilson, J. H.; mason and builder	122
Wright, F. W.; builders' hardware	108
Wolfe, Geo. H.; Building News & Review	138
Wolff, Wm., & Co.; cement	14

W. W. MONTAGUE & CO., San Francisco Los Angeles San Jose

WARM AIR, HOT WATER AND STEAM

HEATING APPARATUS

For Warming Dwellings, Halls, Churches, School-Houses and Public Buildings.

Artistic Brass, Bronze, Steel and Iron **Fire Place Trimmings**

W. W. MONTAGUE & CO.

SAN FRANCISCO—LOS ANGELES—SAN JOSE

MANTELS · GRATES · TILES ·

Wrought, Steel Ranges and French Ranges
For Hotels, Restaurants, Clubs and Boarding Houses

COMPLETE KITCHEN OUTFITS

Manufacturers of Corrugated Iron Roofing and Riveted Sheet Iron Water Pipe

W. W. MONTAGUE & CO., San Francisco Los Angeles San Jose

Officers, 1895-6.

OSCAR LEWIS, *President.*
O. E. BRADY, *Vice President.*　　JAS. A. WILSON, *Secretary.*
L. B. SIBLEY, *Treasurer.*

DIRECTORS.

OSCAR LEWIS,　　　　　　　　　O. E. BRADY,
JAS. A. WILSON,　　　　　　　　L. B. SIBLEY,
W. B. ANDERSON,　　　　　　　A. KENDALL,
THOS. ELAM,　　　　　　　　　CHAS. DUNLOP
THOS. W. BUTCHER,　　　　　　JOHN T. HAYES
JAS. McINERNY.

COMMITTEES.

ROOMS.
THOS. ELAM,　　JAS. McINERNY.　　L. B. SIBLEY.

MEMBERSHIP.
CHAS. DUNLOP,　　THOS. W. BUTCHER,　　A. KENDALL.

ARBITRATION.
JOHN T. HAYES,　　O. E. BRADY,　　JAS. A. WILSON.

FINANCE.
A. KENDALL,　　W. B. ANDERSON,　　THOS. W. BUTCHER

W. H. COBB, *Attorney,*
S. D. NORTH, *Financial Secretary.*
L. A. LARSEN, *Recording Secretary.*
J. F. MEADDOWS, *Doorkeeper.*

W. P. FULLER & CO.

...DEALERS IN...

PLATE AND WINDOW GLASS

PACIFIC COAST AGENTS FOR WIRED GLASS FOR SKYLIGHTS

MANUFACTURERS OF...

PIONEER WHITE LEAD
PIONEER RED LEAD .
PIONEER COLORS . .
MIXED PAINTS . . .
LUBRICATING OILS . .
MIRRORS . . . . .

LARGEST STOCK ON THE PACIFIC COAST

COR. PINE AND FRONT STS.

Tel. Main 516

SAN FRANCISCO

Officers, 1894-5.

C. C. TERRILL, *President.*
OSCAR LEWIS, *Vice President.*   M. J. DONOVAN, *Secretary.*
ANDREW WILKIE, *Treasurer.*

DIRECTORS.

C. C. TERRILL,	M. J. DONOVAN,
OSCAR LEWIS,	L. J. DWYER,
C. C. MOREHOUSE,	W. B. ANDERSON,
JAS. McINERNY,	THOS. ELAM,
H. WILLIAMSON,	S. H. KENT,

ANDREW WILKIE.

COMMITTEES.

ROOMS.
L. J. DWYER,   JAS. McINERNY,   ANDREW WILKIE.

MEMBERSHIP.
C. C. MOREHOUSE,   M. J. DONOVAN,   THOS. ELAM.

ARBITRATION.
S. H. KENT,   OSCAR LEWIS,   ANDREW WILKIE.

FINANCE.
W. B. ANDERSON,   H. WILLIAMSON,   S. H. KENT.

S. D. NORTH, *Financial Secretary.*
L. A. LARSEN, *Recording Secretary.*
J. F. MEADDOWS, *Doorkeeper.*

G. AMMERUP

DEALER IN

1314 ✻
Market Street

Opposite Seventh   SAN FRANCISCO

...Paints

OILS, GLASS, VARNISHES
WALL PAPERS, Etc.

Agent for J. L. McCloskey & Co's Liquid Royal Wood Filler

J. F. VOGLER
Practical Glazier
16 POST STREET

Box 47   OR   BUILDERS' EXCHANGE
Telephone 5110   SAN FRANCISCO

46 MARKET STREET

Estimates Given on all kinds of Glass and Glazing

The San Francisco Towel Co.

(CALIFORNIA TOILET CO.)

116 DAVIS STREET

Give us a Trial   We are not a **cheap** Towel Company, but give a perfectly **CLEAN** service at reasonable rates

---

A. LEVET

Manufacturer of and Dealer in.... **BOOTS AND SHOES**

REPAIRING PROMPTLY ATTENDED TO   **638 Market St.**
                                       (BASEMENT)
Men's Soleing - 50c.
Ladies' Soleing - 40c.   Bet. Kearny and Montgomery Sts.
                                          Opp. Palace Hotel

Branch, 181 Minna St

Officers, 1893-4.

C. C. TERRILL, *President.*
W. N. MILLER, *Vice President.*   M. J. DONOVAN, *Secretary.*
WM. YOUNG, *Treasurer.*

DIRECTORS.

C. C. TERRILL,		M. J. DONOVAN,
W. N. MILLER,		WM. YOUNG,
C. C. MOREHOUSE,		J. P. M. PHILLIPS,
J. F. RILEY,		WM. CRONAN,
J. W. LUCAS,		J. K. FIRTH,
	OSCAR LEWIS.	

COMMITTEES.

ROOMS.

WM. CRONAN,	J. P. M. PHILLIPS,	J. W. LUCAS.

MEMBERSHIP.

M. J. DONOVAN,	C. C. MOREHOUSE,	J. P. M. PHILLIPS.

ARBITRATION.

W. N. MILLER,	OSCAR LEWIS,	WM. YOUNG.

FINANCE.

OSCAR LEWIS,	J. F. RILEY,	J. K. FIRTH.

BOX 185   BUILDERS EXCHANGE

A. I. SANBORN

STAIR BUILDER AND TURNER

MECHANICS' MILL

Corner Mission and Fremont Streets   —   San Francisco

FRANK HUBER

Manufacturer

Sash, Blinds and Doors

ALL KINDS OF HARDWOOD WORK

561-563 Brannan Street   San Francisco, Cal.

Officers, 1892-3.

C. C. TERRILL, *President.*
W. N. MILLER, *Vice President.* M. J. DONOVAN, *Secretary.*
A. W. STARBIRD, *Treasurer.*

DIRECTORS.

C. C. TERRILL, M. J. DONOVAN,
W. N. MILLER, A. W. STARBIRD,
WM. CRONAN, C. C. MOREHOUSE,
J. F. RILEY, J. P. M. PHILLIPS,
OSCAR LEWIS, J. K. FIRTH.

T. W. PETERSEN.

COMMITTEES.

ROOMS.

WM. CRONAN, J. P. M. PHILLIPS, C. C. MOREHOUSE.

MEMBERSHIP.

M. J. DONOVAN, J. P. M. PHILLIPS, C. C. MOREHOUSE.

ARBITRATION.

W. N. MILLER, OSCAR LEWIS, A. W. STARBIRD.

FINANCE.

OSCAR LEWIS, J. K. FIRTH, J. F. RILEY.

BOX 1　　　　　　　　　　　　　　TELEPHONE MAIN 5110

J. F. SULLIVAN

HOUSE SIGN AND FRESCO PAINTER

—— OFFICE ——
BUILDERS' EXCHANGE
New Montgomery and Mission Streets

J. H. KEEFE

TELEPHONE GRANT 199

PAINTER AND
INTERIOR DECORATOR
317 SUTTER STREET
SAN FRANCISCO

GUS. V. DANIELS

Painter, Polisher and Decorator

OFFICE

BUILDERS' EXCHANGE
NEW MONTGOMERY AND MISSION STREETS

TELEPHONE MAIN 5110　　　　　　　　　　SAN FRANCISCO

BOX 277　　　　　　　　　　　　　TELEPHONE MAIN 5110

BUILDERS' EXCHANGE

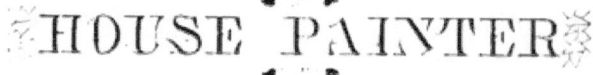

HENRY F. WAGNER....

HOUSE PAINTER

Polishing and Interior Decorating

—— OFFICE ——
635 CALIFORNIA STREET - - - SAN FRANCISCO, CAL.

Officers, 1891-2.

C. C. TERRILL, *President.*
W. N. MILLER, *Vice President.* M. J. DONOVAN, *Secretary.*
A. W. STARBIRD, *Treasurer.*

DIRECTORS.

C. C. TERRILL,	M. J. DONOVAN,
W. N. MILLER,	A. W. STARBIRD,
E. R. SHAIN,	OSCAR LEWIS,
A. HOSMER,	C. C. MOREHOUSE,
WM. CRONAN,	T. W. PETERSEN,

M. C. KEAN.

COMMITTEES.

ROOMS.

A. HOSMER, WM. CRONAN, T. W. PETERSEN.

MEMBERSHIP.

C. C. MOREHOUSE, M. J. DONOVAN, A. HOSMER.

ARBITRATION.

W. N. MILLER, A. W. STARBIRD, OSCAR LEWIS.

FINANCE.

OSCAR LEWIS, M. C. KEAN, E. R. SHAIN.

C. C. TERRILL, Deceased
First President Builders' Exchange

Officers, 1890-1.

C. C. TERRILL, *President.*
W. N. MILLER, *Vice President.*   M. J. DONOVAN, *Secretary.*
A. W. STARBIRD, *Treasurer.*

DIRECTORS.

C. C. TERRILL,	M. J. DONOVAN,
W. N. MILLER,	A. W. STARBIRD,
JOS. R. WILCOX,	C. C. MOREHOUSE,
J. F. RILEY,	A. HOSMER,
J. K. FIRTH,	WM. CRONAN,

GEO. F. DUFFY.

COMMITTEES.

ROOMS.

| J. R. WILCOX, | A. HOSMER, | WM. CRONAN |

MEMBERSHIP.

| C. C. MOREHOUSE, | M. J. DONOVAN, | A. HOSMER. |

ARBITRATION.

| W. N. MILLER | A. W. STARBIRD, | J. K. FIRTH. |

FINANCE.

| J. K. FIRTH, | GEO. F. DUFFY, | J. F. RILEY |

"THE NORTON"
Door Check and Spring

Will Close Your Doors Without Slamming

IT IS ALMOST HUMAN!

It is the BEST, simplest and most durable. Strictly an AIR CUSHION CHECK. Automatically charged when door opens. All nickel-plated and guaranteed. All others in market are liquid checks. Applicable to EITHER SIDE of any size or shaped doors. R or L hand. In ordering, give size of door hinge side or opposite, state how much, if any, casing projects over door, when a bracket extension will be sent to fit. Duplicate parts in stock. The Palace Hotel, Crocker and Chronicle Buildings are using this check.

YOU TRY THEM

Frank D. Morrell — 503 Mission Street, near Second
SAN FRANCISCO, CAL.

GEO. DAVIS & SON, House Movers, Residence and shop, 31 South Park, bet. 3d and 4th, Sts. Box 251 Builders' Exchange, San Francisco. Buildings Moved Raised and Lowered. All orders promptly attended to. Raising Moving and Holding Up Brick Buildings a Specialty.

J. G. PETTITT

Telephone 555

✹ Millwright and Elevator Works

...ESTIMATES FURNISHED...

Manufacturers of all Classes of Hydraulic, Steam and Hand Power Elevators, and the sole right to build **HINKLE'S** Improved Patents for Automatic Safety Clutch and Sidewalk Elevator Frames.

No. 325 Mission Street, Corner of Fremont, San Francisco, Cal.

THE BUILDERS' EXCHANGE
NEW MONTGOMERY AND MISSION STREETS, SAN FRANCISCO

DANIEL POWERS,
CONTRACTOR AND BUILDER

PHILIP HAMMOND
METAL ROOFER

...ALL KINDS OF...
*TIN, COPPER AND SHEET IRON ROOFING
GALVANIZED IRON GUTTERS AND CHIMNEY TOPS*

ROOFS REPAIRED AND PAINTED

All Jobbing Promptly Attended To

318 LARKIN STREET   **SAN FRANCISCO**

RESIDENCE 2280 EDDY STREET

OAKLAND METAL WORKS

Manufacturers of

GALVANIZED IRON AND COPPER CORNICES, BAY WINDOWS
FINALS MOULDINGS AND GUTTERS

METAL SKYLIGHTS

SLATE AND METAL ROOFING IN ALL ITS BRANCHES

Office and Works, 858 WEBSTER ST., OAKLAND

PHILIP HAMMOND   — — —   **PROPRIETOR**

... Box 94, Builders Exchange ...

.. TELEPHONE 801 ..

Architectural Iron Works

O'CONNEL & LEWIS, Props.

Iron Founders and Manufacturers of

STRUCTURAL IRON WORK FOR BUILDINGS . . . .

Box at Builders Exchange
New Montgomery and Mission Sts.

S. W. Cor. Kearny and Francisco Sts.
SAN FRANCISCO, CAL.

Oscar Lewis, President

BOX 112   TEL. MAIN 5110

O. E. BRADY
Mason and Builder
...BRICK AND STONE...

Office: Builders' Exchange, New Montgomery and Mission Sts.
Residence: S. E. Cor. San Jose Ave. and Twenty-Fourth St.

Residence, 1616 Hayes St.   Telephone Main 5110

M. McGOWAN
Mason = and = Builder
...BUILDERS' EXCHANGE...

Box 17   New Montgomery and Mission, San Francisco

Fine
Wines
Liquors and
Cigars

JESSE MOORE
WHISKIES

The Exchange

THOS. J. WALSH   630 MISSION ST.
    PROPRIETOR   SAN FRANCISCO, CAL.

PHOTO BY Bouhney

O. E. BRADY,
Vice-President.

BOX 221.

JAMES A. WILSON

MASON AND BUILDER

ESTIMATES GIVEN ON BRICKWORK, ETC.

Builder's Exchange, New Montgomery and Mission Streets

BOX 104, BUILDER'S EXCHANGE   TELEPHONE, MAIN 5110

NEW MONTGOMERY AND MISSION STREETS

FRED. HARRISON....

MASON AND BUILDER

SAN FRANCISCO, CAL.

J. W. MILLER   ADAM BECK
Residence: 234 Eighteenth Street   Residence: 2018 Mission Street
Box 208   Box 11

MILLER & BECK

...MASONS, BUILDERS AND CONTRACTORS...

BUILDER'S EXCHANGE

NEW MONTGOMERY AND MISSION STREETS

Telephone, Main 5110   San Francisco

J. H. HANAVAN

✻ MASON AND BUILDER ✻

2412 SEVENTEENTH STREET

COR. FLORIDA STREET   SAN FRANCISCO, CAL.

BOX 198, BUILDER'S EXCHANGE....

....NEW MONTGOMERY and MISSION STS.

Particular attention paid to setting boilers, ovens and ranges

JOBBING PROMPTLY ATTENDED TO

JAS. A. WILSON,
Secretary.

L. B. Sibley

Contractor For Grading of Every Description

STABLES, CAROLINE STREET, Between Ninth and Tenth, Howard and Folsom

Lime, Cement, Common, Pressed & Fancy Brick

— HAULING A SPECIALTY —

OFFICE, BUILDERS' EXCHANGE, NEW MONTGOMERY & MISSION STS.

RESIDENCE, 1305 HOWARD STREET

BOX 151   TELEPHONE SOUTH 372

Member Builders' Exchange.   TELEPHONE—SOUTH 527

E. L. SNELL

MANUFACTURERS AGENT

Cienega Lime & Alpine Plaster ✳

— ALSO DEALER IN —

≋ NEPHI PLASTER ≋

Lath, Hair, Nails, Cement, Etc.

OFFICE, 16 HAYES ST.

Alpine Wall Plaster Co., Of Los Angeles, Cal.

S. W. HOLSINGER, President

Natural Product of California. No Chemicals. No Staining of Walls

✳ —— FIRE AND WATER PROOF —— ✳

One Thousand Tons Used in Parrott Building for Fire-proof Partitions.

E. L. SNELL ————

Sole Agent for San Francisco, Alameda, San Mateo, Santa Clara and Santa Cruz Counties.

OFFICE, 16 HAYES STREET, S. F.

SEE CIRCULAR . . .

L. B. SIBLEY
Treasurer.

RESIDENCE, No. 511 SANCHEZ ST.

THOMAS ELAM
CARPENTER AND BUILDER

OFFICE AND STORE FITTING A SPECIALTY

Jobbing Promptly Attended To

OFFICE, BUILDERS' EXCHANGE

BOX 202   TELEPHONE—MAIN 5110

BOX 84   BUILDERS' EXCHANGE
                               New Montgomery and Mission Sts.

W. J. GRANT

.. CONTRACTOR AND BUILDER ..

648 MISSION STREET, San Francisco

TELEPHONE—MAIN 5110   BOX 267

HENRY JACKS
CONTRACTOR AND BUILDER

BUILDERS' EXCHANGE

CORNER NEW MONTGOMERY AND MISSION STS., SAN FRANCISCO

RESIDENCE, 313 TWENTY-FIRST STREET

BOX 150

WILLIAM KNOWLES
CONTRACTOR AND BUILDER

BUILDERS' EXCHANGE

NEW MONTGOMERY AND MISSION STREETS, SAN FRANCISCO

TELEPHONE—MAIN 5110

THOS. ELAM,
Director.

TELEPHONE MAIN 5110   BOX No. 112

James McInerny

CONTRACTOR AND BUILDER

Office Builders' Exchange

New Montgomery and Mission Streets, San Francisco

RESIDENCE   152 HANCOCK STREET

BOX 152   TELEPHONE MAIN 5110

BUILDERS' EXCHANGE
NEW MONTGOMERY AND MISSION STREETS

JOHN FURNESS

CONTRACTOR AND BUILDER

JOBBING ATTENDED TO

No. 8 Steiner Street   San Francisco

WM. PATTERSON   WM. N. ACKERSON
  Residence, 2353 Mission St.   Residence, 740 Oak St.

Ackerson & Patterson

CONTRACTORS AND BUILDERS

OFFICE, ROOM 88 FLOOD BUILDING, 5th Floor

OFFICE HOURS, 12 to 1   SAN FRANCISCO, CAL.

T. M. McLACHLAN

.... Contractor and Builder ....

Office, Builders' Exchange, New Montgomery and Mission Sts.

BOX 91   RESIDENCE, 39 TWENTIETH ST., NEAR FOLSOM

Telephone 5110

JAS. McINERNY.
Director.

BOX 97   TEL. MAIN 5110

CHAS. DUNLOP

PLASTERER

BUILDERS' EXCHANGE   New Montgomery and Mission Sts.

J. BRENNAN   TELEPHONE—MAIN 5110   T. FRASER
221 Twenty-Fourth St.   BOX 138   123 Eddy Street

BRENNAN & FRASER

PLASTERERS

OFFICE   BUILDERS' EXCHANGE

New Montgomery and Mission Sts.   San Francisco

BOX 42   TEL. MAIN 5110

E. DAVIES

CONTRACTOR FOR

Plain and Ornamental Plastering

RESIDENCE   OFFICE
919 FOURTEENTH STREET   BUILDERS' EXCHANGE
Near Noe, San Francisco   New Montgomery and Mission Sts.

Orders by Mail Promptly Attended to

TELEPHONE MAIN 5110

J. J. MOREHOUSE

PLASTERER

PLAIN AND ORNAMENTAL

BUILDERS' EXCHANGE

Box 97   New Montgomery and Mission Sts.

CHAS. DUNLOP.
Director.

A. KENDALL, President   T. D. WHITMAN, Secretary
H. G. KENDALL, Vice-President   N. C. KENDALL, Treasurer

ESTABLISHED JULY ... INCORPORATED JULY 1, ...

..Pacific Coast Lumber and Mill Co...

SUCCESSOR TO A. KENDALL

Corner Second and Grove Streets, Oakland, Cal.

— WHOLESALE AND RETAIL DEALERS IN —

REDWOOD AND PINE LUMBER

MILL WORK OF ALL DESCRIPTIONS

TELEPHONE No. 88   COUNTRY ORDERS A SPECIALTY

UNION LUMBER CO.

WHOLESALE AND RETAIL DEALERS IN

LUMBER

    RAILROAD TIES

        TELEGRAPH POLES

            PINE AND

              REDWOOD PILES

                  SPARS, ETC.

YARD AND PLANING MILL - - CHANNEL STREET, COR. SIXTH

TELEPHONE SOUTH 82   SAN FRANCISCO

A. KENDALL,
Director.

THOS. W. BUTCHER
1428 20th Street

GEORGE PEACOCK
312 San Jose Ave.

PEACOCK & BUTCHER

MASONS
AND BUILDERS

Office, Builders' Exchange, New Montgomery and Mission Streets

BOX 22　　　　　　　　　　　　　　　　　　TELEPHONE 5110

Henry H. Larsen

Mason and Builder

OFFICE BUILDERS' EXCHANGE

New Montgomery and Mission Streets, San Francisco

OFFICE HOURS, 12 TO 1:30 P. M.　　　BOX 33. TELEPHONE--MAIN 5110

J. Ferdinand Wagner

Mason ✶ and ✶ Builder

Residence:　　　　　　　　　　　Office:
23 Clara Avenue　　　　　　　　Builders' Exchange
Between 17th and 18th Streets　　New Montgomery and Mission Streets
Box 181. Telephone 5110　　　　San Francisco

ESTIMATES GIVEN ON ALL KINDS OF WORK

JOHN G. LEIBERT　　TELEPHONE--MAIN　　VICTOR HOFFMAN

LEIBERT & HOFFMAN

Masons · and · Builders

OFFICE, BUILDERS' EXCHANGE

New Montgomery and Mission Streets

THOS. W. BUTCHER,
Director.

JOHN T. HAYES

CONTRACTOR AND BUILDER

2637 Mission Street, Bet. 22d and 23d

Box 167, Builders' Exchange
New Montgomery and Mission Sts.

Telephone 5110

JOHN TROTTER

 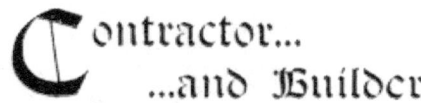

Contractor... ...and Builder

105 HOLLIS STREET, OAKLAND

San Francisco Address: Box 189, Builders' Exchange

FRUITVALE STATION TRACT   **TELEPHONE 715-3**
Lots for Sale and Houses Built on the Installment Plan

T. R. BASSETT & BROS.

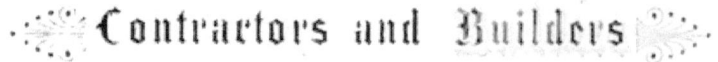

Contractors and Builders

Box 6, Builders' Exchange
New Montgomery and Mission Streets
San Francisco

Residence: Fruitvale Station, Alameda County

S. A. D. Schenck

BOOKKEEPER

WASHINGTON STREET PLANING MILL

Commercial Printing, Stationery and Office Supplies a Specialty

JOHN T. HAYES,
Director.

W. E. ANDERSON　　　　　　　　　　　　R. K. ANDERSON

ANDERSON BROS.
CARPENTERS ᙭ AND ᙭ BUILDERS

BOX 128, BUILDERS' EXCHANGE

NEW MONTGOMERY AND MISSION STREETS, SAN FRANCISCO

... TELEPHONE—MAIN 5110

TELEPHONE MAIN 5110

W. H. WICKERSHAM
Building Contractor

125 YORK STREET
San Francisco

Box 204, Builders' Exchange, New Montgomery and Mission Sts.

..., BOX 190

S. H. KENT
.. CONTRACTOR AND BUILDER ..

BUILDERS' EXCHANGE

Cor. New Montgomery and Mission Sts.　　　　SAN FRANCISCO

Residence, 64, Sutter St.　　　　BEST REFERENCES GIVEN

TEL. MAIN 5110　　　　　　　　　　　　　　　BOX 104

GEO. REICHLEY
CONTRACTOR AND BUILDER

Builders' Exchange

CORNER NEW MONTGOMERY AND MISSION STS., SAN FRANCISCO

RESIDENCE, 559 HERMANN STREET

W. B. ANDERSON,
Director.

TELEPHONE MAIN 1784

WILLIAM H. COBB
ATTORNEY AT LAW

137 MONTGOMERY STREET

Special Counsel for Builders' Exchange

Rooms 9, 10 and 11

SAN FRANCISCO, CAL.

Commercial Law and Mechanics' Liens a Specialty

References: Bancroft-Whitney Co., American Bank & Trust Co. and Columbia Banking Co.

CHAS. F. STRONG, Mgr. Printing Dept.

Methodist Book Concern

Cards, Letter Heads, Bill Heads, Contracts, Leases and Liens

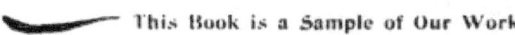 This Book is a Sample of Our Work

---

The Engravings in this Book were made by the

A. C. HUGILL, Manager

San Francisco Photo=Engraving Company

SAN FRANCISCO, CAL.

DESIGNING
HALF TONES
COPPER AND
ZINC ETCHING

PHONE MAIN 569

518-520 SACRAMENTO STREET

WM. H. COBB
Attorney.

GEORGE GOODMAN

Patentee and Manufacturer of

ARTIFICIAL STONE

In All Its Branches

Schillinger's Patent Sidewalk and Garden Walk a Specialty

Office: 307 Montgomery Street, Nevada Block, San Francisco

Particular attention given to concrete foundations

BOX 271   TELEPHONE MAIN 5119

THE S. GILETTI SYSTEM

Manufacturer of

ARTIFICIAL STONE

In any color of Natural Stone or Terra Cotta and Artificial Granite, suitable for Building Blocks, Copings, Steps, Columns, Caps, Buttresses, Cornices and Trimmings. Monuments and Ornamentations a Specialty. Artificial Marble or Scagliola Work, Roman and Venetian Mosaic Marble for Floors, Mantels, Fireplaces, Ceilings, Wainscoting, Mosaic Marble Tiles of any kind. Concrete Foundations. Prompt attention and Work Guaranteed.

Office: Builders' Exchange, New Montgomery and Mission Streets
Factory: 1121 and 1127 Folsom Street, San Francisco, Cal.

CARL GRIESE

Artificial Stone and Concrete Walks

PLAIN AND ORNAMENTAL CEMENT PLASTERING

And All Kinds of Cemetery Work

1318 Stanyan Street and
Box 231 Builders' Exchange, New Montgomery and Mission Streets
San Francisco, Cal.

BOX 310   TELEPHONE NO. MAIN 5110

W. F. Ambrose

Concrete and Artificial Stone

Sidewalks, Garden Walks, Basement Floors, Carriage Driveways, Curbing, Bulkheads, Copings, Steps, Foundations for Buildings, Ornamental Plastering, and All Kinds of Cement Work

Builders' Exchange, New Montgomery and Mission Streets
Residence: 508 Hayes Street   SAN FRANCISCO

S. D. NORTH,
Financial Secretary.

M. HANSEN   H. C. HANSEN

M. HANSEN & CO.
THE KING PLANING MILL
SCROLL SAWING, PLANING, SHAPING
MILL WORK OF ALL KINDS

Manufacturers of and Dealers in   **SASH, DOORS AND BLINDS**

ALL KINDS OF HOUSE FINISH ON HAND AND MADE TO ORDER.

231-251 King Street, Bet. 3d and 4th, SAN FRANCISCO, CAL.

Telephone No. 5836.   Box 187, Builders' Exchange, cor. New Montgomery and Mission Sts

---

EDWARD F. NIEHAUS & CO.
Successors to W. F. STRAUT and DIECKMANN & CO.

:—DEALERS IN—:

➤ HARDWOOD LUMBER ⭠

Cherry, Walnut, Spanish Cedar, Rosewood, Whitewood, Hickory, Oak, Ash, Oregon and Eastern Maple, Mahogany, Tea Primavera.

QUARTERED OAK AND WIDE STOCK A SPECIALTY

564-566 Brannan Street, Between Fourth and Fifth Streets.

Telephone No. 3316   **San Francisco, Cal.**

TELEPHONE South 399   MATT HARRIS   Formerly of Harris & Jones, MANAGER

Scott & Van Arsdale Lumber Co.
.... Successor to G. H. MORRISON ....

DEALERS   SUGAR AND YELLOW PINE

White Cedar, Curly Redwood, Burl Oregon Pine and Redwood Lumber

SASH, DOORS, ETC.

Office and Yards   **Agents for the**
Cor. FIFTH AND BRANNAN STS    **SISKIYOU MILL & LUMBER CO., SISSONS, CAL.**

BOX 4, BUILDERS' EXCHANGE   *TELEPHONE—SOUTH 399*

❦ R. HERRING ❦
MANUFACTURERS OF
Bank, Office and Store Fittings
HARDWOOD INTERIORS AND GENERAL MILL WORK

557 AND 559 BRANNAN STREET

Between Fourth and Fifth Streets   SAN FRANCISCO, CAL.

L. A. LARSEN,
Recording Secretary.

REMILLARD BRICK COMPANY

P. N. REMILLARD, PRESIDENT   P. H. LAMOUREUX, SECRETARY

MANUFACTURERS OF

PRESSED, STOCK AND COMMON

BRICK

ALSO DEALERS IN

FIRE BRICK, FIRE CLAY, LIME, PLASTER, CEMENT, ETC.

Principal Office	San Francisco Office
Oakland, Cor. Second and Clay Sts.	Berry, Near Fifth Street
Telephone No. 63	Telephone No. South 437

Box 209, Builders' Exchange

M. V. BRADY

Mason and Builder

OFFICE, BUILDERS' EXCHANGE

New Montgomery and Mission Streets

Box 71   San Francisco

BOX 192   **TELEPHONE MAIN 5110**

Thomas Butler

Mason... ...and Builder

BUILDERS' EXCHANGE

New Montgomery and Mission Streets

Residence: 1324 Hayes Street

PATENT BRICK COMPANY

Office, 240 Montgomery Street

Main Depot: Berry Street, bet. Fifth and Sixth Sts.

Main Office Telephone No. 093

Wharf Telephone South 620

PHILIP CADUC, President

GEO. P. KANE, Manager and Cashier

J. F. MEADDOWS.
Doorkeeper.

J. R. TOBIN,

BOX No. 173   TELEPHONE 5110

CONTRACTOR FOR

PLAIN & ORNAMENTAL PLASTERING.

INTERIOR DECORATIONS IN SOLID RELIEF

CEMENT WORK AND PATENT FIREPROOF PLASTERING

OFFICE:
BUILDERS' EXCHANGE
NEW MONTGOMERY STREET

SAN FRANCISCO.

TELEPHONE MAIN 5110   BOX 40

D. O'Sullivan

MASON CONTRACTOR

BUILDERS' EXCHANGE

New Montgomery and Mission Sts.   SAN FRANCISCO

DAVID DILLON
Teamster and Contractor

OFFICE—BUILDER'S EXCHANGE, Box 139

Residence, 3 Homer Street

Between 7th and 8th Streets   Harrison and Bryant, off Chesley

Telephone Main 5110

LIME, CEMENT, COMMON, PRESSED AND FANCY
BRICK HAULING A SPECIALTY

ARTICLES OF INCORPORATION
OF
The Builders' Exchange

KNOW ALL MEN BY THESE PRESENTS, That we, the undersigned, have this day associated ourselves together for the purpose of forming a corporation under the laws of the State of California, and we hereby certify:

I.

That the name of said corporation is and shall be "THE BUILDERS' EXCHANGE."

II.

That the purposes for which said corporation is formed are as follows, to wit: To join in one association all mechanics, manufacturers and dealers, of good repute, doing business in the City and County of San Francisco, whose vocation connects them wholly or generally with the industry of building, either as an employing contractor in any branch of the building business or as a manufacturer of, or dealer in, materials used and employed in the erection of buildings or other structures; to establish and maintain among the persons so associated a just and equitable system of dealing and a uniformity in commercial usages. To acquire, preserve and disseminate valuable information and statistics which may be of use to any or all of the several trades engaged in the building business. To procure and furnish, provide and regulate and maintain suitable rooms for the use of its members and for the meeting rooms of this corporation, and for offices and other purposes. To establish and enforce a system of arbitration for the settlement of disputes or misunderstandings which may arise between its members or be connected with the various trades in which its members are engaged; said system to be in accordance with the by-laws adopted by this corporation. To adjust differences and settle disputes between members or between members and others. To promote and secure the mutual improvement and advancement and welfare of all mechanical and industrial interests and all artisans and tradesmen in their several vocations; to the end that membership in this corporation may be an assurance to the public of skill, honorable reputation and probity. To collect from its members certain percentages of the business transacted by them, to hold the same in trust as security for the payment of all liabilities incurred by such members with the association or its members, and to invest and manage the same in accordance with the provisions of its by-laws. To take, purchase, hold and own a lot and tract of lots and tracts of land in the City and County of San Francisco, State of California, and elsewhere; to erect thereon, manage, supervise and control a structure and buildings, or structures and buildings for the meetings, use and occupation of "The Builders' Exchange," and other organizations, associations, persons and corporations and in connection therewith. To lease stores and offices and rooms in said building or buildings for said or other purposes. To engage in and carry on a general contracting business in all its branches and departments. To organize, conduct, carry on and control corporations and associations and to hold and deal in the shares and stock thereof. To purchase, take, own, hold mortgage, sell and convey such real and personal property as shall be necessary or convenient to carry out the object as aforesaid. And the said corporation shall have power to make all necessary rules, laws, regulations and by-laws for the use and government of "The Builders' Exchange" and for the members thereof. And generally to do and perform such acts as shall be necessary and proper to enable it to carry on, conduct, manage and supervise the business aforesaid.

III.

That the place where the principal business of said corporation is to be transacted is, and shall be the City and County of San Francisco, State of California.

IV.

That the term for which said corporation is to exist is, and shall be Fifty (50) Years, from and after the date of its incorporation.

V.

That the number of its Directors is and shall be Eleven, and the names and residences of those who are appointed for the first year are:

C. C. Terrill, who resides at the City and County of San Francisco, State of California.

William N. Miller, who resides at the City and County of San Francisco, State of California.

A. Hosmer, who resides at the City and County of San Francisco, State of California.

J. F. Riley, who resides at the City and County of San Francisco, State of California.

M. J. Donovan, who resides at the City and County of San Francisco, State of California.

C. C. Morehouse, who resides at the City and County of San Francisco, State of California.

William Cronan, who resides at the City and County of San Francisco, State of California.

A. W. Starbird, who resides at the City and County of San Francisco, State of California.

J. K. Firth, who resides at the City and County of San Francisco, State of California.

G. F. Duffey, who resides at the City and County of San Francisco, State of California.

J. R. Wilcox, who resides at the City and County of San Francisco, State of California.

VI.

That said corporation has no capital stock, it being a membership corporation only, and that therefore there being no capital stock, no stock has been subscribed.

VII.

We, William N. Miller, President, and C. C. Terrill, Secretary of the meeting of the members of "The Builders' Exchange," held for the purpose of electing Directors for said association, in order that the same may be incorporated under the laws of the State of California as a corporation, do hereby certify that on the 30th day of June, 1890, at No. 306 Pine street, in the City and County of San Francisco, State of California, at the hour of 1 o'clock P. M., a meeting of all of the members of said association was duly held for the purpose of electing Directors for said association, and that at said meeting so held as aforesaid a majority, to wit, all of the members of said association were present and voted at said election, and consented to the holding of said election at said time and place, and that at said election, and as a result of said vote eleven votes were cast for the following named persons: C. C. Terrill, William N. Miller, A. Hosmer, J. F. Riley, M. J. Donovan, C. C. Morehouse, William Cronan, A. W. Starbird, J. K. Firth, George F. Duffey, J. R. Wilcox, for Directors of said association, and that no votes were cast in opposition to said persons, or for any other person or Director, and that no other person was a candidate or was voted for for the office of Director of said association, and that as the result of said election the said C. C. Terrill, William N. Miller, A. Hosmer, J. F. Riley, M. J. Donovan, C. C. Morehouse, William Cronan, A. W. Starbird, J. K. Firth, George F. Duffey, J. R. Wilcox were duly elected Directors of the said "The Builders' Exchange," and that at said meeting and election the said William N. Miller acted as President; and the said C. C. Terrill acted as Secretary, and conducted the said election, and were the officers who conducted the election of Directors as aforesaid.

W. N. MILLER, President.
CHAS. C. TERRILL, Secretary.

STATE OF CALIFORNIA, } ss.
City and County of San Francisco. }

William N. Miller and C. C. Terrill, being duly sworn, each for himself, deposes and says, that he has read the foregoing certificate, and knows the contents thereof, and that the same is true of his own knowledge.

Subscribed and sworn to before me this 3rd day of July, 1890.

{ SEAL }

LEWIS B. HARRIS,
　　　Notary Public.
　　　　W. N. MILLER.
　　　　CHAS. C. TERRILL.

IN WITNESS WHEREOF, we have hereunto set our hands and seals this third day of July, 1890.

　　　　CHAS. C. TERRILL,　　　[Seal]
　　　　W. N. MILLER,　　　　　[Seal]
　　　　A. HOSMER,　　　　　　[Seal]
　　　　JNO. F. RILEY,　　　　　[Seal]
　　　　M. J. DONOVAN,　　　　[Seal]
　　　　C. C. MOREHOUSE,　　　[Seal]
　　　　WILLIAM CRONAN,　　　[Seal]
　　　　A. W. STARBIRD,　　　　[Seal]
　　　　J. K. FIRTH,　　　　　　[Seal]
　　　　G. F. DUFFEY,　　　　　[Seal]
　　　　J. R. WILCOX,　　　　　[Seal]

STATE OF CALIFORNIA, } ss.
City and County of San Francisco, }

On the 3rd day of July, A. D. 1890, before me Lewis B. Harris, a Notary Public in and for said City and County, residing therein, duly commissioned and sworn, personally appeared Charles C. Terrill, W. N. Miller, A. Hosmer, John F. Riley, M. J. Donovan, C. C. Morehouse, William Cronan, A. W. Starbird, J. K. Firth, G. F. Duffey and J. R. Wilcox, known to me to be the individuals described in, whose names are subscribed to, and who executed the within instrument, and the severally acknowledged to me that they executed the same.

IN WITNESS WHEREOF, I have hereunto set my hand and affixed my official seal, at my office in the City and County of San Francisco, the day and year last above written.

{ SEAL }

LEWIS B. HARRIS, Notary Public.
　　　　326 Pine street, San Francisco.

H. S. Bridge & Co.
— Merchant Tailors

622 MARKET STREET
SAN FRANCISCO. CAL.

Many Novelties in Imported Wear   Shirts to Order a Specialty

L. E. KNOWLES, PRES.
ABEL HOSMER, SEC.

Raymond Granite Company

INCORPORATED

Successors to L. E. KNOWLES & Co.

...Contractors for

OF EVERY DESCRIPTION
AND DEALERS IN DIMENSION STONE

Proprietors of **Raymond Granite Quarry**

RAYMOND, MADERA COUNTY, CAL.

※

Main Office and Yard
Tenth and Channel Sts.
SAN FRANCISCO
Telephone ... South

Branch Yard
S. W. Corner
Seventh and Castro Sts.
OAKLAND

Members Oakland and San Francisco Exchange

BY-LAWS
OF
THE BUILDERS' EXCHANGE
Adopted July 23, 1896.
[Amended and re-adopted August 4, 1899.]

ARTICLE I.
NAME AND LOCATION.

SECTION 1. The corporate name and title for this Association shall be "The Builders' Exchange."

SEC. 2. The location and place of business of this Association shall be in the City and County of San Francisco, State of California.

ARTICLE II.
OBJECTS.

SECTION 1. The objects of this Exchange shall be:

First.—To join in one association all mechanics, manufacturers and dealers of good repute, doing business in the city and county aforesaid, whose vocation connects them, wholly or generally, with the industry of building, either as an employing contractor in any branch of the building business, or as a manufacturer of or dealer in material used and employed in the erection of buildings or other structures.

Second.—To establish and maintain among the individuals so associated a just and equitable system of dealing, and a uniformity in commercial usages by rules and regulations; to acquire, preserve or disseminate valuable information regarding the business in which they are severally engaged.

Third.—To procure (either by lease or purchase) furnish and maintain suitable rooms for the use of its members for meeting rooms, offices and other purposes.

Fourth.—To establish and enforce a system of arbitration for the settlement of all disputes or controversies which may arise between its members or between its members and their employees and other persons.

Fifth.—To join or otherwise act in concert with other organizations of Employers of Labor, for the purpose of arbitrating all questions of dispute which may arise between said organization and the members thereof or any of them or between any of them and their employees. To the end that all matters of difference between the Employers of Labor and their employees may be amicably settled and adjusted without resort to strikes or lockouts.

ARTICLE III.
TERM OF EXISTENCE AND PROPERTY.

SECTION 1. The term of existence of this Exchange shall be Fifty years from and after the filing of the certificate of incorporation.

SEC. 2. No shares of Stock or individual right in the property of this Exchange shall exist or be acquired during its existence.

But the property belonging to and in the name of "The Builders' Exchange" shall be held in trust by the Directors for this Exchange, and shall not be diverted from the purposes and intentions for which it was organized.

ARTICLE IV.
ADMINISTRATION, ETC.

SECTION 1. The affairs of this Exchange shall be administered by a ⸺d of Eleven Directors, who shall be members thereof in good standing, residents of the State of California.

SEC. 2.
Jos. R. WILCOX, C. C. MOREHOUSE,
J. F. RILEY, A. HOSMER,
CHAS. C. TERRILL, WM. CRONAN,
WM. N. MILLER, A. W. STARBIRD,
J. K. FIRTH, GEO. F. DUFFY, and
M. J. DONOVAN,

shall constitute the first Board of Directors, and shall serve until the third Monday of April, 1891.

SEC. 3. At the annual meeting of members, to be held on the third Monday of March in each year, there shall be elected from among the members in good standing Eleven Directors, to serve for one year, from the third Monday of April following, and until their successors have been elected and qualified.

SEC. 4. Nominations for Directors may be made at the semi-annual meeting in September, or at a special meeting called for that purpose, or they may be made at the time of the election by a two-thirds vote of the members present.

SEC. 5. On or before the third Monday in April, after their election, the Directors shall organize as a Board by electing from among their number a President, a Vice President, and a Treasurer, who shall hold office for one year.

They shall also elect a Recording and a Financial Secretary, an Attorney and a Doorkeeper, who shall hold office during the pleasure of the Board, and who need not be members of the Exchange.

SEC. 6. The Board shall elect or appoint such other officers or employees as may be authorized by the laws of the Exchange, or as may be required by the business thereof. At least six votes shall be necessary to elect any officer.

SEC. 7. The Board shall provide a seal, to be hereafter devised and adopted by this Exchange.

SEC. 8. The Board of Directors shall have and is hereby vested with powers—

First.—To adopt By-Laws, Rules and Regulations for the management of the affairs of the Exchange, not in conflict with the laws of the State, and amend or repeal the same, or these By-Laws, subject to the approval of the Exchange by a majority vote of the members present at the next regular meeting of the members thereafter, or at a special meeting duly called for that purpose, except as hereinafter provided in Section 9 of this Article.

Second.—To fill all vacancies which may occur in its own body, until the next election.

Third.—To have and exercise a supervisory care over the affairs of the Exchange and its members, to designate the bank in which the funds of the Exchange shall be deposited, and require the Treasurer to keep them deposited there, and to change the same when in their judgment the interest of the Exchange requires it.

Fourth.—They shall hear, examine into, and if possible settle all disputes between members when they can do so to the satisfaction of the parties concerned; otherwise direct the parties to submit the matter in controversy to arbitration in the usual manner, or as may hereafter be provided in the By-Laws.

Fifth.—To hear and determine all charges brought against any member for a violation of the Laws, Rules and Agreements, for unbusinesslike conduct or for any other cause, or to cause the same to be heard and determined by a committee, to be appointed by the President from among the members of the Exchange, subject, however, to revision by the Exchange as a body at the next or a subsequent meeting. And the said Board shall, when any charges are preferred by one member against another, proceed to hear and determine the same without delay, or appoint a committee for that purpose, which committee shall have the powers provided for in these By-Laws.

Sixth.—To receive, hold in trust and invest such funds of individual members as may under the provisions of the By-Laws be placed in their hands for that purpose, and in the manner and form and subject to all the conditions therein prescribed.

Seventh.—To obtain by lease or purchase, and to hold in trust for and in the name of "The Builders' Exchange," any real or personal property necessary for the use of or benefit of the Exchange, and to mortgage, sell, lease or otherwise dispose of the same whenever in their judgment it may be necessary to do so; and they are hereby vested with full power to appropriate the funds and manage the affairs of "The Builders' Exchange," subject to the laws of this State and the By-Laws and Rules of this Exchange.

SEC. 9. Neither the Board of Directors nor the members of the Exchange shall have power to pass any By-Law or Rule abridging the right of any member to conduct or transact his business in such a manner as he shall deem just and proper, unless such law or rule shall have received the affirmative consent of at least three-fourths of all the members of this Exchange.

Due notice of the passage of any such By-Law or Rule shall be given to each member in writing (or be mailed to him at his address as given to the Secretary) at least two weeks before the same shall be in force, and a minute to that effect made in the records.

SEC. 10. Any member of the Exchange may propose an amendment to the By-Laws, and the same shall be acted on at the next regular meeting of the Board, after having been posted in the rooms of the Exchange for one week; or any member may propose an amendment at a meeting of members, and the same having been first posted in the rooms of the Exchange for one month previous to the meeting shall be acted upon; and if it receives a two-thirds vote of the members present it shall become a law, except as provided in Section 9 of this Article.

SEC. 11. The removal from the State of any officers or Director, or the voluntary absence from three successive meetings without leave from the Board, of any Director or officer required to be present at such meetings, shall be sufficient cause for their removal from office; and they may so be removed in accordance with the provisions of the law of this State, either by the Board of Directors or by the members.

SEC. 12. Any agreement entered into by and between the members of this Exchange relating to the manner of transacting their business as Builders, either in estimating upon, bidding or contracting for any kind of work or regarding the form of contracts to be used or signed by them, shall when the same shall have received the affirmative consent of three-fourths of all the members of this Exchange, be and become the rule and law of the Exchange and shall have the full force and effect of a By-Law thereof.

SEC. 13. Any agreement made and entered into in accordance with the provisions of Section 12 of this Article, shall be filed by the Secretary and a copy thereof furnished each member by delivering it to the member or his representative personally, or by placing the same in the letter box of said member in the rooms of the Exchange. Before any such agreement shall be put in force or become a law of this Exchange, the Secretary or his assistant shall file with the Board of Directors a certificate to the effect that the provisions of this section have been fully complied with, which certificate shall be entered in full on the minutes of the Board.

ARTICLE V.

SECTION 1. Any person creditably and practically engaged as an employing contractor in any trade connected with the business of building or in manufacturing, or dealing generally in building material, shall be eligible to membership in this Exchange, and may be admitted as hereinafter provided.

SEC. 2. A copartnership or corporation may become a member of this Exchange as one person in the manner hereinafter provided for the election and admission of members, and subject to all the laws herein or hereinafter provided.

Such copartnership may be represented by any member thereof; but a corporation shall be represented only by some officer duly authorized to act for them. Neither a copartnership nor a corporation shall be entitled to but one vote on any question.

SEC. 3. Applications for membership must be made in writing, upon forms provided by this Exchange, and must state the full name, residence, place of business and trade or vocation of the applicant, and must be duly signed by him.

If the applicant be a copartnership, the application must be signed by one of its members in the firm's name.

If a corporation, the application must be signed by some one legally authorized to sign the same. Provided that if an applicant be following an occupation or business that has a trade organization, said person shall first apply to said organization before being eligible to membership in the Exchange, and if refused admission in his trade organization he shall not be eligible to membership in this Exchange.

SEC. 4. All applications must be signed by some member of this Exchange recommending the applicant for membership, and contain the names of two or more persons as references.

It must also be accompanied by the admission fee, as provided by the By-Laws.

SEC. 5. All applications, after being read by the Secretary, shall be referred to a standing committee of three Directors for investigation.

This committee shall make a careful examination as to the character and business standing of the applicant, and report the result thereof to the Board of Directors at the next regular meeting, unless further time be granted them, when a vote shall be taken on the admission of the applicant; and, if no more than two members vote against the same, he shall be admitted.

If more than two, he shall be rejected.

SEC. 6. The name, place of business and trade or vocation of all applicants for membership, with the name of the member recommending them, the name and residence or place of business of their references, shall be kept posted in the rooms of the Exchange from the date of its presentation until the final disposition of the same.

SEC. 7. When elected, the member shall sign a book containing the By-Laws, Rules and Agreements entered into by and between the members, among which shall be an Agreement to conform to and abide by the By-Laws, Rules and Agreements then in force, or that may thereafter be adopted, in the manner provided therein; and no person shall become a member of, or be entitled to any of the rights or privileges of this Exchange as a member until their names have been subscribed in said book.

SEC. 8. Any member can resign his membership in this Exchange by filing with the Secretary a notice to that effect in writing and paying in full all demands that may be against him; provided, however, that if there are any charges pending against him, or any matter of dispute existing between him and any other member which is being investigated by the Exchange, or a committee thereof, his resignation cannot be accepted until the same shall have been finally disposed of.

Upon the acceptance of the resignation of a member, all his interest in the property of the Exchange shall be vested absolutely in the Exchange.

SEC. 9. A member who fails to pay his dues or the fines imposed upon him, as provided by the By-Laws or Rules, for the period of six months, after the same shall have become due and payable, having first been duly notified of his delinquency by the Secretary, shall be suspended from membership, and from all the rights, privileges and benefits appertaining thereto.

SEC. 10. Any member guilty of a willful violation of any agreement made with any other member or members, or with this Exchange, either at the time of his admission or afterward, or a willful violation of the laws or rules of the Exchange, or of a willful destruction of the property thereof, or of unbusinesslike or ungentlemanly conduct in his dealings with the Exchange or with any member or members thereof, first having been duly tried by a proper committee, as provided by the By-Laws or Rules, and duly convicted by their report and a vote of the Exchange, shall be fined, suspended or expelled, as provided by the laws of the Exchange, or in case no penalty shall have been provided, as shall be adjudged by a two-thirds vote of the Directors present at a regular meeting.

Upon the suspension or expulsion of a member, all his interest in the Exchange, or in the property belonging thereto, shall be forfeited, and the same vested absolutely in the Exchange, except that portion of such property as may be held in trust for him under the provisions of clause 6, Section 1, Article IV, of these By-Laws, as may remain after deducting therefrom all demands against him on the books of the Exchange.

SEC. 11. Any member of the Exchange who fails to discharge all his honest obligations, or to pay in full all just debts legally contracted, unless such failure is caused by, or is the result of some loss or accident, against which he could not reasonably have provided, and which is not the result of carelessness in or inability to properly estimate the value of work he has contracted to do, shall, after due trial and conviction, be expelled from this Exchange.

The fact as to whether or not the cause or causes assigned by any member for his failure to discharge the obligations or to pay the debts contracted by him as aforesaid, is sufficient to justify his exemption from the penalty imposed in this section shall be determined by the committee appointed to try the case, subject to appeal to the Exchange at any regular meeting, or a special meeting called for that purpose.

SEC. 12. Any member of this Exchange who shall settle his account with any other member for less than the full amount legally and justly due him from such member, or who participates in any way in what is known as a *pro rata* settlement thereof with any one and who fails to report the same, together with the facts and circumstances connected therewith, to the President and Board of Directors of the Exchange within four weeks thereafter, shall be deemed and held to be guilty of conduct unbecoming a member of this Exchange, and on conviction thereof by a committee duly appointed to try the case, shall be punished by a fine to be imposed by a majority vote of the Board of Directors of not less than Twenty-five ($25) Dollars, nor more than One Hundred ($100) Dollars for the first offense and shall stand suspended until such fine is paid. For the second offense he shall be in the same manner suspended for not less than six months nor more than a year; and for the third offense he shall be expelled.

SEC. 13. Any Architect who permits any member, whether a person, firm or corporation who has been expelled from this Exchange for cause, after due trial and conviction, to figure in his office, or to contract to do work therefrom, after due notice has been given him of such Expulsion shall be deprived of all the rights and privileges accorded to him as an Architect by this Exchange.

Any member who shall, after notice duly given him of the violation of this section by any Architect, figure in the office of, bid upon or contract to do work for such Architect, shall be expelled as provided in section 12.

SEC. 14. Any member suspended in accordance with the provisions of Section 9 of this Article may be reinstated at any time thereafter by a vote of the majority of the Directors present at a regular meeting upon the payment of such sum as the said Board may require which shall in no case be less than six months' dues.

Any member suspended for cause, as provided in Section 10 of this Article, may be reinstated upon the removal of the cause, or at the expiration of the time during which he was declared to be suspended, without action on the part of the Directors, upon the payment of all arrearages due by him.

Any member expelled for cause, as provided in Section 10, must make application for reinstatement in like manner as candidates for admission in the first instance, except that they must state the fact that they were expelled, and the reasons therefor.

Such application shall be treated in all respects as other applications for membership.

ARTICLE VI.

GENERAL MEETINGS AND QUORUM.

SECTION 1. The annual meetings of the members of the Exchange shall be held on the third Monday of March in each year for the election

THE
California Sandstone & Contracting Co.

J. C. MOFFAT, Manager.

Location of Quarries:
REDDING,
SHASTA COUNTY
CAL.

San Francisco Address:
BUILDERS' EXCHANGE
N. Montgomery and Mission Sts.
Box 230.   Tel. Main, 5110

J. W. RYLAND, Pres.   J. W. WALTHALL, Manager.   M. VERGIN, Sec'y.
B. D. MURPHY, Vice Pres.   T. O'NEIL, Supt.

Western Granite and Marble Co.

Capital Stock, Paid Up, $—

370 to 378 NORTH FIRST STREET, SAN JOSE, CAL.

P. O. Box 375, San Jose ... Telephone No. 73.

MAUSOLEUMS, VAULTS, MONUMENTS, HEADSTONES, COPINGS, CURBINGS, and all kinds of BUILDING WORK in GRANITE, SANDSTONE or MARBLE

ESTIMATES FURNISHED ON APPLICATION

San Francisco Office: Box 280, Builders' Exchange, New Montgomery and Mission

---

Telephone Main ---

M. J. HEALY
...Contractor for STONE WORK
OF ALL KINDS

Penryston Stone and Street Curbing For Sale

QUARRIES, LOOMIS, PLACER CO., CAL.
OFFICE, BUILDERS' EXCHANGE

Box 75   Residence, Loomis, Cal.

Diggins Bros....
→STREET CONTRACTORS←

PROPRIETORS OF THE FLINT TRACT QUARRY

CONCRETE STONE FURNISHED
RESIDENCE, 2416 AND 2420 SUTTER STREET

Telephone W. 862   OFFICE, BUILDERS' EXCHANGE

of Directors and the transaction of any other business. A semi-annual meeting for the transaction of the general business of the Exchange shall be held on the third Monday of September of each year.

SEC. 2. Special meetings may be called by the Board of Directors, when in their judgment it may be necessary, and shall be called by the President of the Board of Directors, when requested in writing to do so by any ten members in good standing.

Said request shall state the business which the said meeting is to be called to consider, and the same shall be stated in the call for the meeting, and no other business shall be transacted thereat.

SEC. 3. At all meetings of the members, until the membership shall reach fifty, eight members shall constitute a quorum; after that time, fifteen members shall be necessary to form a quorum for the transaction of business and the election of officers.

SEC. 4. Notices of special meetings shall be published at least three times in each of two or more of the daily papers of the city of San Francisco, having a general circulation, and be posted in the rooms of the Exchange; and at least five days shall elapse between the first publication and the date of the meeting.

ARTICLE VII.

MEETINGS OF THE BOARD OF DIRECTORS AND QUORUM.

SECTION 1. The regular meeting of the Board of Directors of the "Builders' Exchange" shall be held at least once in each month, upon such days and at such hours as the Board of Directors shall from time to time determine, and also at such other times as the Board of Directors shall from time to time prescribe.

No notice shall be required to be given of any regular meeting.

SEC. 2. Special meetings of the Board of Directors may be called by the President, or, in his absence or inability to act, by the Vice President, and shall be so called at the request in writing of six members of the Board of Directors, stating the business for which the call was made.

Notice of all special meetings shall be given to the Directors personally at least 24 hours before the time of holding the same, or by leaving a written or printed notice of the time and place of holding said meeting, at the last known place of business or residence of each Director, or by mailing said written or printed notice to the last known place of business or residence of each Director at least 24 hours before said meeting.

Such service of notice shall be entered upon the minutes of said corporation and shall, upon being read and approved at a subsequent regular meeting of the Board of Directors, be conclusive upon the question of service and notice.

Notice of a special meeting shall contain a statement of the business to be transacted, and no other business shall be transacted at such meeting except that stated in the notice, unless all of the Directors are present.

Any notice issued in accordance with the provisions of this section shall be deemed sufficient to give full and legal notice of all meetings of the Board of Directors, or of the members of this corporation.

SEC. 3. Six Directors shall form a quorum for the transaction of business, but it shall require the affirmative vote of six Directors on a call of the roll, and to be recorded in the minutes, to pass any By-Law or to make any appropriation of money, except to pay the necessary general expenses of the Exchange, including rent, salaries and the payment of bills already contracted for by order of the Board.

ARTICLE VIII.

FEES, DUES, FINES, ETC.

SECTION 1. The fee for admission to this Exchange shall be *Twenty-five Dollars* ($25), until the membership herein reaches three hundred and fifty.

The fee shall then be *Fifty Dollars* ($50), until the membership reaches four hundred, after which time it shall be One Hundred Dollars ($100).

SEC. 2. The dues to be paid by each member shall be two dollars ($2) per month, payable monthly in advance, and no member shall be entitled to vote at any meeting of members who owes more than three months' dues.

SEC. 3. Fines may be imposed upon the members or Directors by the presiding officer when in the chair, or by a vote of the Board of Directors, or of the members of the Exchange, for a violation of the rules of order or decorum; and shall be imposed as provided by the By-Laws, Rules or Agreements, for a violation of the same.

All fines imposed for a violation of the rules of order or decorum shall be added to and considered as dues, and shall be paid at the same time and subject to the same penalties.

All fines imposed for the violation of the rules or agreements shall be paid within one month after being imposed, or the member will stand suspended until the same has been paid.

ARTICLE IX.
DUTIES OF OFFICERS.

SECTION 1. The President (or in case of his absence or inability to act, the Vice President) shall preside at all meetings of the members or Directors; preserve order, enforce the laws and rules, sign drafts duly passed by the Board of Directors and appoint committees not already provided for.

He shall have and exercise a supervisory care over the property and business of the Exchange, and report to the Board of Directors any failure of the employees to do their duty. He may suspend any employee not a member of the Board of Directors, and appoint some one in their place until the next meeting of the Board, when he shall report his action, with the reason therefor, to the Board for *its* action.

He shall not speak upon any question except one of order, at any meeting while in the chair, and shall vote only upon applications for membership, or upon questions requiring a two-thirds or three-fourths vote, except to give the casting vote when the members of the Board are equally divided.

He shall appoint, at the commencement of his term, a finance committee of three members of the Board of Directors, not having the care or control of the funds of the Exchange.

He shall also appoint the following committees of three members each, to wit, on Rooms, on Membership and on Arbitration.

He shall perform such other duties as the By-Laws or Rules prescribe.

SEC. 2. The Vice President shall, during the absence or inability of the President to act, perform all the duties of that officer.

He shall preside, when called upon to do so by the President, and shall perform such other duties as may be prescribed by the By-Laws.

SEC. 3. The Recording Secretary shall correctly keep a record of the minutes of all meetings of the Exchange and Board of Directors; keep and use the seal when ordered to do so by the laws or the Board of Directors: attest with his hand and seal all drafts for money voted by the Board; and perform all other duties usually devolving upon a Secretary, or which may be imposed by the By-Laws or Rules.

His compensation shall be fixed by the Board of Directors.

SEC. 4. The Financial Secretary shall keep correctly the accounts between the Exchange and its members and other persons, in books provided and properly kept.

He shall collect and receipt for all money due from any source, and pay the same to the Treasurer, as may be required by the laws or rules of the Board of Directors, taking his receipt therefor.

He shall report at least once each month the amount and source of all money received, and the amount paid out and for what paid.

He shall keep his books so posted that the financial affairs of the Exchange and the accounts of each member can be ascertained at any time.

shall assist the Finance Committee with the examination of the books and affairs of the Exchange, and perform any other duties imposed by the By-Laws or Rules.

He shall give such bonds and receive such compensation as shall be fixed by the Board of Directors.

The Board may require the duties of the Recording and Financial Secretary to be performed by one person.

SEC. 5. The Treasurer shall receive and receipt for all money paid to him by the Financial Secretary, or any other person on behalf of the Exchange, and deposit the same in some bank to be designated by the Board of Directors, in the name of "The Builders' Exchange," with the understanding that the same shall be drawn only upon drafts or checks signed by the President; attested by the Secretary, with the seal of the Exchange, and countersigned by the Treasurer.

The Treasurer shall keep a correct account of the money received, deposited and paid out, and render a report thereof to the Board of Directors at least once each month, and also an annual report to the members at the meeting held on the third Monday of March of each year.

At the expiration of his term of office, or upon retiring therefrom, he shall deliver to his successor, or some person designated by the Board of Directors, the books, papers, money and property in his hands or under his control belonging to the Exchange.

He shall give such bonds as the Board of Directors may require.

SEC. 6. The attorney shall be the legal adviser of the Board and its officers. He shall be present at all meetings when required by the Board, and shall receive such compensation for his services as may be fixed by the Board of Directors.

SEC. 7. The Doorkeeper shall have general charge of the rooms and offices of the Exchange. He shall keep the same clean and in order.

See that no one enters or uses the same, except those authorized by the rules adopted for the government of the Exchange rooms to do so, and see that perfect order and decorum are preserved therein.

He shall perform such further duties and receive such compensation as shall be fixed from time to time by the Board of Directors.

SEC. 8. The Committee on Rooms shall have under the Board of Directors the charge of the rooms and offices of the Exchange.

See that all necessaries are provided and properly appointed, and the rooms kept clean and in order.

See that the Doorkeeper attends to his duties and preserves order therein.

They shall formulate and present to the Board for adoption such rules for the government of the Exchange, its members and visitors, as they may deem for the best interest thereof, and when adopted keep the same posted in the rooms, and see that they are properly enforced.

SEC. 9. The Committee on Membership shall meet once each week to receive and consider objections to applicants for membership.

They shall treat all such objections as confidential when requested to do so, and shall report their findings and recommendations to the Board at its next meeting.

SEC. 10. The Finance Committe shall examine and report on all bills presented to the Exchange for payment, examine and audit all the books and accounts of the officers or committees having charge of the funds of the Exchange.

They shall have the right to examine the books and accounts of any officer or committee at any time, and report at each annual meeting and whenever required by the Board or the Rules.

SEC. 11. The Arbitration Committee shall hear and determine any matter in dispute, or differences arising among its members, or between members and others, when referred to them for settlement.

The Recording Secretary shall act as Clerk of the Arbitration Committee.

Before proceeding with any examination they shall require all parties interested to sign an agreement to submit their case to the Committee and to be bound by their decision.

When such agreement has been filed, the Committee shall proceed as soon as possible to hear and decide upon the matter in controversy. After such hearing shall have commenced, each party shall be required to diligently attend to and present his side of the case; and if he neglects or refuses to do so the Committee shall report the matter to the Board of Directors, who shall notify the party so in default to proceed at once with his case, or show cause for not doing so, on pain of expulsion from the Exchange; and in case of his refusal to comply with the orders of the Board they shall expel him from the Exchange.

Any member so expelled may appeal to the members of the Exchange from the action of the Board.

SEC. 12. Any member or person interested in any controversy who has objections to any one or more members of the Arbitration Committee may apply to the Board of Directors to appoint a special Committee from among the members of the Exchange to arbitrate any cause in which they are interested; or both or all parties interested may select a Committee for themselves from among the members, or each party may select one or more members, and the ones thus selected shall choose an umpire if they cannot agree among themselves, and the decision of the majority of those thus selected shall be final and binding upon all parties.

Provided, that if either party to said dispute is not a member of this Exchange said party may select an arbitrator or arbitrators to represent them who are not members of this Exchange; and the umpire, if any be chosen in such a case, need not be a member of this Exchange.

But all members of this Exchange must agree to submit all controversies arising between them and all other members when requested to do so by the other members to said controversy, in some one of the manners herein provided, or be liable to expulsion from the Exchange for not doing so, after the trial and conviction as provided by the By-Laws.

SEC. 13. Each member of an Arbitration Committee and the Secretary, when acting as Secretary thereof, shall receive such compensation for their services as may be fixed from time to time by the Board of Directors, to be paid as may be agreed upon by the parties to the dispute, or, in case of their failure to agree, as may be decided by the committee engaged in the arbitration of the case.

SEC. 14. Any committee appointed by the Board of Directors to hear and determine charges preferred by one member against another shall take and keep a record of the statement of each party, also a record of the evidence of the witnesses produced by each party, and shall require the party making the statement and the witness giving evidence to sign their statement or evidence, after reading the same or having it read to them.

They shall also note any exception taken by either party to any ruling or action of the Committee, or of the opposite party, and shall report the evidence, statements and their findings and determinations to the Board of Directors, to be by them laid before the Exchange at the next or a subsequent meeting, for revision and confirmation and the enforcement of the decision.

Box 322   Builders' Exchange

SACRAMENTO TRANSPORTATION COMPANY

MANUFACTURERS OF

FRESH WATER PATENT KILN BRICK
—— AND ——
STOCK BRICK

OFFICE AND DEPOT—THIRD AND BERRY STREETS

Telephone 1925   **CHAS. E. LIPP, Agent**

BUILDING AND FIRE ORDINANCE

OF THE

City and County of San Francisco.

Order No.—— defining the fire limits of the City and County of San Francisco, and making regulations concerning the erection and use of buildings in said city and county.

The people of the City and County of San Francisco do ordain as follows:

[FIRE LIMITS.]

SECTION 1. The fire limits shall be bounded by a line commencing at the intersection of the shore line of the bay of San Francisco with the easterly end of Greenwich street; running thence westerly along the center line of said Greenwich street to its intersection with the center line of Sansome street; thence southerly along the center line of Sansome street to its intersection with the center line of Broadway street; thence westerly along the center line of Broadway street to the center of the crossing of Broadway and Powell streets; thence southerly along the center line of Powell street to the center of the crossing of Powell and Sacramento streets; thence easterly along the center line of Sacramento street to the center of the crossing of Sacramento and Stockton streets; thence southerly along the center line of Stockton street to the center of the crossing of Stockton and Sutter streets; thence westerly along the center line of Sutter street to a point in said center line of Sutter street distant 206 feet westerly from Powell street; thence at right angles southerly parallel with Powell street and 206 feet westerly therefrom to the center line of O'Farrel street; thence westerly along the center line of O'Farrell street to the center of the crossing of O'Farrell and Mason streets; thence southerly along the center line of Mason street to the center of the crossing of Mason and Ellis streets; thence westerly along the center line of Ellis street to the center of the crossing of Ellis and Taylor streets; thence southerly along the center line of Taylor street to the center of the crossing of Taylor and Eddy streets; thence westerly along the center line of Eddy street to the center of the crossing of Eddy and Jones streets; thence southerly along the center line of Jones street to the center of the crossing of Jones and Turk streets; thence westerly along the center line of Turk street to the center of the crossing of Turk and Leavenworth streets; thence southerly along the center line of Leavenworth street to the center of the crossing of Leavenworth street and Golden Gate avenue; thence westerly along the center line of Golden Gate avenue to a point distant one hundred and thirty-seven and a half (137½) feet east of the easterly line of Larkin street; thence at right angles northerly parallel with and one hundred and thirty-seven and a half (137½) feet from the easterly line of Larkin street to Sutter street; thence westerly along the center line of Sutter street to a point distant one hundred and thirty-seven and a half (137½) feet west of the westerly line of Larkin street; thence at right angles southerly parallel with and one hundred and thirty-seven and a half (137½) feet from the westerly line of Larkin street to McAllister street; thence westerly along the center line of McAllister street to the center of the crossing of McAllister and Polk streets; thence southerly along the center line of Polk street to the center of the crossing of Polk and Hayes streets; thence westerly along the center line of Hayes street to the center of the crossing of Hayes street and Van Ness avenue; thence southerly along the center line of Van Ness avenue to the center of the crossing of Van Ness avenue and Fell street; thence westerly along the center line of Fell street to the center of the crossing of Fell and Franklin streets; thence southerly along the center line of Franklin street to the center of the cross-

Bass Hueter Paint Co.

Paints Oils Varnishes

Hueter's Interior and Exterior
DURABLE WOOD FINISH —— A Varnish that is not easily scratched or marred, will not crack or blister, and will retain its brilliancy for a long period. . . .

18-20-22 ELLIS ST., SAN FRANCISCO

L. J. DWYER

PAINTER

1320 UTAH ST.,
Between
Sonoma and Yolo Streets
SAN FRANCISCO, CAL.

Box 197, AND ——
Telephone No. 5110,
Builders' Exchange,
New Montgomery and Mission.

BOX 286   BUILDERS' EXCHANGE

G. & R. GILLOGLEY

TEAMSTERS

AT S. F. LUMBER CO.

Stand, South Side Channel Street, Between 4th and 5th

Residence, 1304 Folsom St.
San Francisco.

Telephone, 3631

ing of Franklin and Page streets; thence westerly along the center line of Page street to the center of the crossing of Page and Gough streets; thence southerly along the center line of Gough street to its intersection with the center line of Market street; thence southerly and westerly along the center line of Market street to Valencia street; thence southerly along the center line of Valencia street to the center line of the crossing of Valencia and Hermann streets; thence easterly along the center line of Hermann street to the center of the crossing of Hermann and West Mission streets; thence in a northerly and easterly direction along the center line of West Mission street and Mission street to the center of the crossing of Mission and Ninth streets; thence in a southerly and easterly direction along the center line of Ninth street to the center of the crossing of Ninth and Minna streets; thence in a northerly and easterly direction along the center line of Minna street to Sixth street; thence in a southerly and easterly direction along the center line of Sixth street to the center of the crossing of Sixth and Howard streets; thence in a northerly and easterly direction along the center line of Howard street to the center of the crossing of Howard and First streets; thence in a southerly and easterly direction along the center line of First street to the center of the crossing of First and Folsom streets; thence in a northerly and easterly direction along the center line of Folsom street to the center of the crossing of Folsom and Steuart streets; thence in a northerly and westerly direction along the center line of Steuart street to the center of the crossing of Steuart and Howard streets; thence in a northerly and easterly direction along the center line of Howard street to the bay of San Francisco; thence in a northerly and westerly direction following the line of the water front to the point of commencement.

[REGISTER OF FIRE LIMIT BLOCKS.]

SECTION 2. It shall be the duty of the Clerk of the Board of Supervisors to register every block or portion of block declared to be within the fire limits, and to notify the Chief Engineer of the Fire Department and the Fire Marshall in writing.

[HOUSES OF LEGISLATION.]

SECTION 3. Whenever in this Order the term or words "Board of Supervisors," "Committee," or "Committees" are used they shall be deemed to have reference to any Board or Boards, committee or committees of Supervisors, or houses of legislation that may constitute the municipal Legislature of the City and County of San Francisco, which are now or may hereafter be provided for by any charter of said city and county.

[BUILDINGS HEREAFTER ERECTED, ALTERED, ENLARGED OR BUILT UPON.]

SECTION 4. Sub. 1. Every building hereafter erected, altered, enlarged or built upon in the City and County of San Francisco shall be erected, altered, enlarged and built upon in accordance with the requirements of such sections of this Order as are applicable thereto.

Provided, that nothing in this Order shall effect or apply to the height of buildings to be erected, when the plans and specifications have been prepared and actual work has been commenced under a contract in the preparation and excavation, of the site for the foundation of the proposed building, prior to the passage of this Order.

[TIME FOR COMMENCING WORK ON BUILDING.]

Sub. 2. In granting permits to erect, enlarge, build upon, alter or change any building or buildings within the fire limits, the permit shall be void if the work is not commenced within thirty days after said permit becomes a law, and finished within a reasonable time thereafter, and no such permit shall be transferable to a second party. All such permits shall bear the date of issuance.

[BUILDINGS ENLARGED, RAISED, ALTERED, OR BUILT UPON WITHIN THE FIRE LIMITS.]

Sub. 3. No building already erected or hereafter built within the fire limits of said city and county shall be enlarged, raised, altered or built upon in such a manner that were the said building wholly built or constructed after the passage of this Order it would be a violation of any of the essential provisions of this Order.

And before any building within the fire limits of said city and county shall be enlarged, raised, altered or built upon, or any addition built or made in or to the interior or exterior thereof, the owner, lessee, agent or person having the control of the same shall petition the Board of Supervisors in writing for permission to make the desired alterations, at the same time submitting complete plans and specifications for the same, and if the building is in a good, safe condition to be enlarged, raised, altered or built upon, the Board of Supervisors shall then be authorized to grant the same, such permit to be approved by the Mayor of said city and county, a copy of which shall be filed by the grantee within two days after the granting of the same in the office of the Chief Engineer of the Fire Department.

Sub. 4. No wooden building within the fire limits shall be enlarged or built upon.

And no wooden building within the fire limits shall be repaired without first obtaining a permit to do so from the Board of Supervisors, approved by the Mayor.

[BUILDINGS TO BE ENLARGED, RAISED, ALTERED, OR BUILT UPON OUTSIDE OF THE FIRE LIMITS.]

Sub. 5. No building already erected or hereafter to be built outside of the fire limits of this city and county shall be enlarged, raised, altered or built upon in such a manner that were the said building wholly built or constructed after the passage of this Order it would be a violation of any of the essential provisions thereof. And before any such building shall be enlarged, raised, altered or built upon, as aforesaid, the owner, agent, lessee, or person having the control of the same shall petition the Board of Supervisors in writing for permission to make the desired alterations, at the same time submitting the complete plans and specifications for the same, and if the building is in a good, safe condition to be enlarged, raised, altered or built upon, the Board of Supervisors shall then be authorized to grant the same, such permit to be approved by the Mayor of said city and county, a copy of which shall be filed by the grantee within two days after the granting of the same in the office of the Chief Engineer of the Fire Department.

In this Order the following terms shall have the meanings respectfully assigned to them:

[MEANING OF TERMS.]

SECTION 5. "Alterations" mean any change or addition.

"Cellar" or "basement" means a lower story of which one-half or more of the height from the floor to the ceiling is below the level of the street adjoining or the general level of the ground.

"Foundation" means that portion of the wall below the level of the street curb, and where the wall is not on a street, that portion of the wall below the level of the highest ground next to the wall.

"Height of a building" means the perpendicular distance of the highest point of the main roof above the curb level at the center of the principal front. When the walls of a structure do not adjoin a street, then the average level for the ground adjoining the walls may be taken instead of the curb level for the height of such structure.

"Lodging-house" means a building in which persons are accommodated with sleeping apartments, and includes hotels and apartment houses in which cooking is not done in the several departments.

"Repairs" means the reconstruction or renewal of any existing part of a building or of its fixtures or appurtenances by which the strength or fire risk is not affected or modified.

"Tenement house" is a building which is or is intended to be occupied as a dwelling by more than two families above the second story, living independently of one another and doing their cooking in the premises.

"Party or division wall" means a wall that separates two or more buildings, and is used or is to be used jointly by said buildings.

"Partition wall" means any interior wall in a building.

"Bearing partition wall" means any wall supporting a floor, beam, or any portion of a floor.

"External wall" means every outer wall or vertical inclosure of a building other than a party wall.

"Thickness of a wall" means the minimum thickness of such wall.

"Height of wall" means the height from the mean grade of the sidewalk or adjoining ground to the highest point of the wall.

[DUTY OF FIRE WARDENS.]

SECTION 6. It shall be the duty of the Board of Fire Wardens of this city and county to enforce all ordinances relating to the erection, construction, alteration, repair, removal or the safety of buildings.

[CONSTRUCTION OF BUILDINGS WITHIN THE FIRE LIMITS.]

SECTION 7. All buildings hereafter erected within the fire limits of this city and county, excepting structures as provided for in Section 9, shall be one of two kinds, viz.:

"Class A," termed fireproof.

"Class B," termed non-fireproof.

The term "skeleton construction" shall apply to all buildings wherein all external and internal loads and strains are transmitted from the top of the building to the foundation by a skeleton or frame work, and the beams and girders thereof are riveted to each other at their respective junction points. If buildings are made fireproof entirely and have skeleton constructions so designed that their inclosing walls do not carry the weight of floors or roof, then their walls may be reduced in thickness one-third from the thickness of walls hereinafter provided for buildings of the different classes, excepting only that no wall shall be less than twelve inches in thickness, and provided, also, that such walls shall be thoroughly anchored to the iron skeleton, and provided, also, that wherever the weight of such walls rest upon beams or pillars, such beams or pillars must be made strong enough in each story to carry the weight of the wall resting upon them without reliance upon the walls below them.

Class A. (a) A building of class "A" shall be constructed of non-inflammable material throughout. In a building of this class all interior constructive metal work, with the exception of the framing for elevators and staircases, shall be protected from fire by brick or terra-cotta at least one and one-half inches thick, or by plastering three-fourths of an inch thick applied to metal lath, the face of the plastering to be one and one-half inches from the metal.

Wood may only be used for window and door-frames, sashes, standing finish, hand rails for stairs and for upper and under floors and their necessary sleepers, provided there is no air space between the tops of any floors, arches and the floor boarding.

Wood may also be used for isolated furring blocks, but this clause shall not permit the use of lath or furring of wood.

(b) A building of class "B" shall be constructed with all exterior, party and bearing walls or piers of masonry, or such walls may be constructed in part of masonry and iron or steel, provided all such bearing material (excepting in fronts) is protected by means of terra-cotta, brick, or plastering three-fourths of an inch thick applied to metal lath; the face of plastering to be one and one-half inches from the metal supports.

Wood may be used as allowed in buildings of class "A," and in addition the floor and ceiling joists, girders, posts, roof boards, partitions, furring and lathing may be of wood, provided the use of wood in such places does not violate the requirements of any other section or clause of this ordinance.

All outside finish, if not constructed of fire-proof material, excepting window frames and sashes, shall be inclosed with fireproof material.

The roof shall be covered with fireproof material, and if the same extends one hundred feet from the ground, the whole thereof shall be constructed of fireproof material.

L. B. Sibley,

CONTRACTOR FOR

Grading ✳ of ✳ Every ✳ Description

Stables, Caroline St., Bet. Ninth and Tenth, Howard and Folsom

LIME, CEMENT, COMMON, PRESSED & FANCY BRICK
HAULING A SPECIALTY

Office, Builders' Exchange, New Montgomery and Mission Streets

RESIDENCE, 1305 HOWARD STREET

Box 336   Telephone South 372

Central Lumber & Mill Co.

SAWING, PLANING AND GENERAL MILL WORK

LUMBER   MOULDINGS
LATHS   DOORS
SHINGLES   SASH
AND BLINDS

20 to 26 TENTH ST.   Tel. S 98

[HEIGHT OF BUILDINGS.]

No building shall hereafter be erected fronting on any street within the City and County of San Francisco of a height exceeding that herein provided for, to wit:

On all streets one hundred feet and more in width, no building shall be constructed exceeding one hundred and thirty feet in height.

On all streets less than one hundred feet in width, no building shall be constructed exceeding one hundred feet in height.

No building shall hereafter be erected of a height exceeding eighty feet, unless the same is constructed of fireproof material and in conformity with all the provisions of this Order relative thereto: The said buildings being embraced and classified in this Order as "Class A."

No building shall hereafter be erected of eighty feet or less in height within the fire limits unless the same is constructed in conformity with all the provisions of this Order relative thereto: The said buildings being embraced and classified in this Order as "Class B."

[STRENGTH OF MATERIALS.]

SECTION 8. The dimensions of each piece or combination of materials used in the construction of any building shall be ascertained by computation, according to the rules given by Trautwine's "Engineer's Pocket-Book," F. E. Kidder's "Architects' and Engineers' Pocket-Book," or Haswell's "Mechanics' and Engineers' Pocket-Book," except as may be otherwise provided in this section.

[WEIGHTS OF MATERIALS.]

In computing the weights of walls, floors and materials, a cubic foot of material shall be deemed to weigh as given in the tables of the above-mentioned handbooks.

[FACTORS OF SAFETY.]

The factors of safety shall not be less than one is to four for wood, wrought iron and steel, and as one is to six for all cast metals, and as one is to eight for all mason-work.

[SUSTAINING POWER OF SOIL.]

Good, solid, natural earth, or confined dry sand, shall be deemed to safely sustain a load of four tons to the superficial foot.

[QUALITY OF MATERIALS.]

All materials are to be of good quality and shall conform to legal, trade and manufacturers' standards, and shall be subject to the approval of the Board of Fire Wardens.

[MORTAR.]

Mortar shall be made with such proportion of sand as will insure a proper degree of cohesion and tenacity.

The following rules shall be complied with:

Mortar below level of water shall be no poorer than one part good Portland cement and three parts sand.

Mortar for buildings of class "A" and "B" shall be no poorer than one part good Portland cement and eight parts of lime mortar, made with A No. 1 fresh slacked lime, with the proper proportion of sand.

The best lime mortar shall be used for all other purposes.

[WOODEN BUILDINGS USED FOR MANUFACTURING PURPOSES ALLOWED WITHIN CERTAIN LIMITS.]

SECTION 9. In that portion of the city and county bounded by a line drawn at right angles from Howard to Folsom, 137 6-12 feet northeasterly from and parallel with First street; the northerly line of Folsom street; the southerly line of Howard street and the waters of the bay; frame buildings may be erected for manufacturing purposes.

The frame of said buildings to be constructed of heavy timbers and to be covered with corrugated or sheet iron or cement plaster, the work to be done under the supervision and to the entire satisfaction of the Chief Engineer of the Fire Department and the Committee on Fire Department.

Any person or persons desiring to erect a building for manufacturing purposes in the district above described shall file the plans and specifications, accompanied with a statement that the building proposed is to be used for manufacturing purposes, in the office of the Chief Engineer of the Fire Department, and upon the approval of the said plans and specifications by said Chief Engineer, the person or persons so applying shall have the right to erect such a building. The plans and specifications or a copy thereof shall be filed and kept for reference and public inspection in the office of said Chief Engineer.

[EXEMPTIONS IN FIRE LIMITS.]

The following buildings and structures are exempt from the provisions of this ordinance, viz.:

Sheds, built on wharves, the extreme height of which do not exceed fifteen feet.

Temporary sheds of the same height to facilitate the erection of authorized buildings.

[PRIVIES OR WATER-CLOSETS OF WOOD, CONSTRUCTED IN FIRE LIMITS.]

Privies or water-closets of wood constructed within the fire limits shall not exceed eight feet in height in the clear of the surface of the floor and ceiling line. For a hotel and lodging-house, they shall not have more than fifty superficial feet of floor room, and for all other buildings they shall not have more than twenty-five superficial feet of floor room. The roof and the frame work shall be covered with fireproof material, and they shall not be placed higher than the fourth story of any building, nor project over the line of any street, lane, alley, or place, and they shall not be used for any other purpose.

[SHEDS.]

Sheds erected in this city and county shall not exceed twelve feet in height to the highest point of the roof. They shall be understood to be open structures, inclosed only on one side and end, and erected on the ground. No wooden shed shall be erected or maintained within the fire limits.

[FOOTINGS AND FOUNDATION.]

SECTION 10. Every masonry wall or pier shall have a footing or base course, which shall be of stone, concrete or brick, resting upon good, solid bottom.

The footings under every wall shall be of sufficient widths to reduce the load on the soil less than four tons per square foot.

The footings under every pier shall be sufficient to reduce the maximum load on the soil to less than four tons per square foot.

[OFFSETS.]

When the footings are formed of brick, the steps or offsets laid in single courses, shall not exceed 1¼ inches, or if laid in double courses, then each shall not exceed 2½ inches.

When footings are of stone the thickness of each course shall not be less than 12 inches, and shall not project more than six inches.

When footings are of concrete they may be formed in courses similar to those of stone, or they may be battered at any angle not less than sixty degrees to the horizontal. The bottom of all footings in all buildings within the fire limits must be at least four feet below the curb line unless resting on solid rock.

[FOUNDATIONS.]

SECTION 11. The foundation or basement walls of every brick or stone building must be built of stone, concrete or brick. Those under the inclosing or party walls of masonry must be at least four inches thicker than the walls immediately above them to a depth of sixteen feet below the curb level, and shall be increased four inches in thickness for every additional four feet in depth below said sixteen feet.

Concrete walls for buildings shall not extend above the basement story.

[PILES AND TIMBER FOUNDATIONS.]

When the nature of the ground requires it, all buildings shall be supported on foundation piles not more than three feet apart on centers in the direction of the wall, and the number, diameter and bearing of such piles shall be sufficient to support the superstructure proposed.

Buildings over seventy feet in height shall rest, where the nature of the ground permits, upon at least three rows of piles, or an equivalent number of piles, ranged in not less than three rows.

All piles shall be capped with block granite or timber levelers, each leveler having a firm bearing on the pile or piles it covers, or the piles may be capped with good Portland cement concrete extending at least four inches below the tops of the piles, and at least twenty inches above them. In case piles are not used, the footings must be spread sufficiently to reduce the weight per square foot of bearing on the ground to what such ground will bear with safety without yielding or settling.

[VAULTS UNDER SIDEWALKS.]

SECTION 12. In buildings where the space under the sidewalk is utilized concrete, stone or brick walls shall be built to retain the roadway of the street, and the side, end or party walls of such buildings shall extend in proper thickness under the sidewalk to such wall.

[EMBANKMENT, AREA, RETAINING AND BULKHEAD WALLS.]

In general, all such walls, area walls, embankment, retaining and bulkhead walls, shall not be less than twelve inches in thickness for a height not to exceed four feet and shall be increased four inches in thickness for every four feet or part thereof in height additional, but said walls shall be increased to a greater thickness if, in the opinion of the Fire Wardens, walls constructed according to the above requirements would not be of sufficient strength.

Embankment or retainining walls which do not have sidewalks or buildings to support them, must be of such thickness as good engineering practice requires.

[FIRE-PROOF SIDEWALKS.]

All vaults and all work supporting the sidewalk shall rest upon and be of fireproof material

[OPENINGS IN VAULTS.]

Openings in the roofs of vaults for the admission of coal or light, shall be covered with lens lights in iron or cement frames, or with iron covers having a rough surface and rabbeted flush with the sidewalk.

No plane surface of glass or iron more than four inches in diameter shall be placed in any sidewalk.

[DRAINAGE.]

Proper provisions must be made for the drainage of the areas. Open areas shall be properly protected by suitable railings, and shall not encroach on the sidewalks more than one-fifth of the official width of the sidewalks where they occur.

[WALLS IN PART OF MASONRY AND IRON.]

SECTION 13. In every building erected within the fire limits, either of class A or B, all the external and party walls shall be built of masonry and of such thickness as is provided for in table 1, except dwelling houses, provided that:

(a) Such walls may be built in part of masonry or terra cotta, iron or steel, in which case the walls may be built of one-third less thickness than is required for solid masonry walls, provided such walls meet the requirements of this Act as to strength, and provided all such weight-bearing or constructional metal is protected from fire by brick or terra cotta.

[TRUSSES OVER FIFTY FEET LONG ON WALLS.]

(b) When trusses over fifty feet span are used in any building the walls upon which they rest shall be built at least four inches thicker than is re-

SMITH & YOUNG

BOX 374, BUILDERS' EXCHANGE

Building Supplies

723 Market St., San Francisco   Tel. Main 1370
230 South Spring St., Los Angeles Tel. 1370

→ː OUR SPECIALTIES ːϵ—

Asbestos Sheathing Paper, S. & Y.
Ten square feet to one pound. Heavy or light grade furnished on orders.

Asphalt
Paving Cement, Rock Asphalt and Liquid Asphalt Flux (crude and refined). Reservoir Linings, Pipe Dip and Roofing Cement.

Blue Print Paper
Coated and Uncoated.

Blue Prints
Made from tracings on paper and linen and copies on muslin for shop work.

Brick Wash
For washing down common brick walls.

Brick Preservative
For water-proofing both brick and stone. Does not change color of brick or stone. Also furnished with coloring pigment to get even color to pressed brick.

Casing Blocks
Corner, Head, Center and Base Blocks. Turned and Pressed Centers.

Carvings
In stock and made to order details.

Ceiling
Steel Ceilings.

Cement—S. & Y. ELASTIC ROOFING CEMENT
For repairing leaks about chimneys, skylights, copings and old tin and shingle roofs, etc.

Cement ASBESTOS FURNACE CEMENT
Instructions for fittings, furnaces and stoves furnished free where the cement is to be used. Asbestos.

Cement—IRON STOVE CEMENT
Fresh made, does not crumble, has quality and tenacity, sticks to castings — slightly porous.

Chimney Hood CLAUSON'S PAT.
Prevents smoky fireplaces and nuisances.

Deadening Felt S. & Y. BRANDS
No. 1 two pounds, No. 1½, 1½ pounds, No. 2 2 pounds per square yard.

Infusorial Earth
Fire proof, Will toughen asphaltum and bituminous rocks. Also good for boiler and pipe covering and making fire proof materials generally.

Lath
Bostwick Steel Lath, Painted and Unpainted.

Lath
G. & B. System of fire-proofing with wire lath.

Marble
Serpentine — Fire and electric proof.

Mineral Wool
For fire-proofing and deadening.

Mortar Stain PECORA
For coloring mortar and cement in the wall finish.

Mouldings
Turned, Carved, Pressed.

Ornaments—PRESSED WOOD

Paints
Mixed, Roofing and House Paints.

Paper S. & Y. BRANDS SHEATHING PAPERS
Nos. 1, 2, 3, 4, 5, 6, 7, 8, 9 and 14.

Roofing
Mastic, Steel and Slate Roofing.

Shingle Stains
Dexter Bros. English Shingle Stains.

Slate
For Blackboards and Roofing.

Soapstone
Crude, Ground and Bolted.

Tablet Gum
For printers and book binders.

Turnings
Spindles, Balls and Dowels.

Universal System of Couplings and Valves for Plumbing
Takes the place of soldered joints for lead and screw joints for brass pipe.

Wall Ties MORSE'S PATENT

quired by the several paragraphs and table of this section for every addition of twenty-five feet or part thereof to the length of the trusses over fifty feet, or shall have buttresses or pilasters under such trusses at least two feet on the face and of the thickness required for the wall.

[ASHLAR.]

(c) When a wall is faced with ashlar or facing the thickness of the wall must be calculated exclusively of the same, unless said ashlar is eight or more inches thick, in which case the excess over four inches may be calculated as part of the wall, provided it is laid in alternate courses of different thicknesses, in such a manner as to bond to the backing at least four inches every two feet in height.

[PARTITION AND DIVISION WALLS.]

(d) Bearing partition or division walls may be four inches less in thickness than is required in this Act for external and party walls of the same height, but must in no case be less than twelve inches thick, unless such walls are not more than twelve feet high, in which case they may be nine inches thick.

(e) Partitions supporting floors or roofs in buildings of class A and B shall rest upon girders, trusses or walls, and no brick or stone work or constructional iron-work of any kind shall rest upon wooden supports, and no stone or iron steps shall rest upon wooden carriages.

[RECESSES AND CHASES.]

Recesses, flues and chases may be made in walls, provided that in party and external walls the backs of said recesses, flues and chases shall not be less than eight inches in thickness, and in addition or partition walls not less than four inches in thickness.

No vertical recess other than flues in stacks shall be nearer than seven feet to any other recess, unless by special permission of the Board of Supervisors.

(f) All roof and floor timbers entering the same party wall from opposite sides shall have at least four inches of solid brickwork between the ends of such timbers.

(g) The height of every wall referred to in this section shall be measured from the top of said wall, exclusive of the firewall; the firewall being that portion of the wall extending above the roof boarding.

[WALLS BUILT WITH BUTTRESSES.]

SECTION 13. (Continued) (h). Any building in which all the weight is concentrated on certain points, walls may be built of less thickness than is required by paragraphs "a" "e," and table 1 of this section, provided such points are re-enforced by buttresses and pilasters, which shall not be more than fourteen feet from centers and provided the sectional area of such wall, taken at any point, shall not be less than that of a wall of similar height taken at the same distance from the ground built according to paragraphs a, b, c, g, and table 1.

The walls between the buttresses shall at no point be less than twelve inches in thickness.

(i) If any story exceeds in height sixteen times the thickness prescribed for the walls of such story in the tables, the thickness of each external and party wall throughout such story shall be increased four inches for every five feet or fraction thereof in excess of the tabulated height.

[OUTER WALLS OF BRICK OR STONE BUILDINGS.]

(j) The outer walls of brick or stone buildings shall be the front, rear and side walls, and such walls shall extend from the foundation to the top of such buildings, and they shall be securely tied or locked at all angles formed thereby.

TABLE NO. 1.
Class "A" and "B" erected within the Fire Limits.

STORIES	Basement	1st story 17 feet	2d story 34 feet	3d story 46 feet	4th story 57 feet	5th story 68 feet	6th story 79 feet	7th story 90 feet	8th story 100 feet
1	17 in	13 in							
2	17 in	17 in	13 in						
3	21 in	17 in	17 in	13 in					
4	21 in	17 in	17 in	17 in	13 in				
5	25 in	21 in	17 in	17 in	17 in	13 in			
6	25 in	21 in	21 in	17 in	17 in	17 in	13 in		
7	29 in	25 in	21 in	17 in	17 in	17 in	17 in	13 in	
8	33 in	29 in	25 in	21 in	17 in	17 in	17 in	17 in	13 in

(k) No building shall have more stories in the given height than provided for in the above table.

[OPENINGS IN PARTY OR DIVISION WALLS.]

(l) Party or division walls shall be understood to be either of solid brick or stone. Should openings be required in said walls, such openings shall not exceed six feet in width and shall have an iron lintel or a solid brick arch formed with three rollocks, with wooden doors on each side of such opening not less than two inches in thickness and enveloped in tin, and not more than two openings shall be allowed in said walls for each story.

[THICKNESS OF WALLS IN CERTAIN BUILDINGS.]

(m) The outer walls of churches, theatres, foundries, machine shops, schoolhouses and other buildings of a public character shall in no case be less than as specified in class A and B of this Order for warehouses and stores, and shall have in addition thereto such piers or buttresses as may be in the judgment of the Board of Fire Wardens necessary to make a substantial building. In all walls that are built hollow, the same amount of material shall be used in their construction as if they were solid, and no hollow wall shall be built unless the two walls are connected by proper ties, either of brick or galvanized iron straps, placed not over twenty inches apart and of proper stiffness. Such walls shall be securely anchored with iron anchors to each tier of beams every six feet by tie anchors made of $1\frac{1}{2}$ inches by $\frac{3}{8}$ of an inch wrought iron. Said anchors shall be built into the full thickness of the walls and shall have flat heads not less than eight inches in diameter on the outside of said walls.

If one or both of the solid parts of the walls are less than eight inches in thickness, such walls shall not be used for supports for any part of the structure of such building, but if both the solid parts of such hollow walls are eight inches or more in thickness, such walls may be used as bearing walls, and in all cases where the load is imposed upon such hollow walls or any part thereof, there shall be bond stones or iron bond plates covering the whole of the solid parts of such walls and so proportioned as not to strain either the material of the wall or of such bond stones or bond plates.

[FIREWALLS IN FLAT-ROOFED BUILDINGS.]

SECTION 14. All flat-roofed brick buildings in this city and county more than two stories in height shall have the party or division, side and rear walls carried up at least twenty-six inches above the roof line, forming firewalls, which within the fire limits shall be not less than twelve inches in thickness, and outside of the fire limits not less than nine inches in thickness.

[COPING.]

All firewalls shall either be coped with incombustible material or the tops of such walls shall be cemented.

[PIERS.]

SECTION 15. Brick piers shall be built of good, hard, well-burned brick of uniform size, laid in cement and lime mortar, as per Section 8, with uniform joints throughout, not more than ⅜ of an inch in thickness. They shall be of sufficient size to carry safely the load which they are intended to carry, and shall never be more than eight times higher than the smallest width at the base and shall be thoroughly bonded.

The tops of all piers, either of brick or concrete, shall be leveled off to receive a cap or bond plate, which shall either be of granite not less than ten inches in thickness, of iron or steel of equal strength. In the case of an external brick pier the plate may be reduced sufficiently in size to allow four inches of brickwork to intervene between the edge of the plate and the face of the pier exposed to the weather.

[SWELLED, REFUSE AND BADLY BURNED BRICK NOT ALLOWED.]

SECTION 16. No swelled, refuse or badly burned brick shall be allowed in the construction of any wall or pier.

All brick and stone and similar material must be well laid and bedded with well-filled joints in mortar, as provided in Section 8, well flushed up at every course with mortar.

[BOND.]

Every eighth course at least of a brick wall there shall be a heading or bonding course, excepting where walls are faced with face brick, in which case every eighth course shall be bonded with Flemish headers or by cutting the corners off the face brick and putting in diagonal headers behind the same.

[STRENGTH OF COLUMNS AND POSTS.]

SECTION 17. All columns and posts shall be made of sufficient strength to bear safely the weight which they are intended to support in addition to the weight of the material employed in their construction, and shall rest upon a cap or plate of sufficient dimensions to properly distribute the load; ten tons to a square foot to be the maximum load placed on brick work.

[TIERS OF COLUMNS.]

When one column is set upon another, it shall be properly connected to the lower one.

All bearing parts of columns or plates shall be turned or planed to a true surface.

In all buildings hereafter erected or altered, where any iron or steel column or columns are used to support a wall or part thereof, whether the same be an exterior or an interior wall, excepting a wall fronting on a street, and columns located below the level of the sidewalk which are used to support exterior walls, girders of iron or wood, or arches over vaults, the said column or columns shall be constructed double, that is, an outer and an inner column, the inner column to be of sufficient strength alone, and so protected, as to be wholly secured against fire; where the column or columns is or are protected by means of terra cotta, brick or plastering, three-quarters of an inch in thickness applied to metal laths, with face of plastering one and one half inches from the metal supports, then, and in that case the outer column may be omitted.

[GIRDERS, BEAMS AND LINTELS.]

SECTION 18. Girders, beams and lintels employed in the construction of any building, shall be so proportioned as to sustain the load placed upon them with the factors of safety called for in Section 8. When they rest upon brick walls or piers, they shall rest upon granite blocks at least ten inches in thickness, and of proper size to distribute the load, so that the maximum load on the brick work shall not exceed ten tons per square foot, or upon iron or steel plates of equal strength of the same width and length; and in all cases where the girder carries a wall and rests upon brick piers, the bearing shall be sufficient to carry the weight above with safety. And where the beams are supported by girders, the ends of the beams resting on the girders shall be

Pacific Refining and Roofing Company

Manufacturers of

> BUILDING PAPERS
> ROOFING FELTS
> ROOFING PITCH
> ROOF PAINTS
> ASPHALT PAINTS
> and VARNISHES

Contractors for

Felt, Pitch and Gravel Roofing

Roofs as put on by us are the Standard Roof for all best buildings in Chicago, St. Louis and other progressive cities. Thirty years experience, and an extensive establishment for the manufacture of our own materials, enable us to do the best of work.

SAN FRANCISCO

Office, 153 Crocker Building   Works at Potrero

TEL. MAIN 5982

strapped with wrought-iron straps of the same size, and at the same distance apart, and in the same beams as the wall anchors.

Cast-iron or stone lintels, spanning openings exceeding eight feet in width, shall not be permitted.

[STRENGTH OF FLOORS AND ROOFS.]

SECTION 19. In every building used as a tenement, dwelling, apartment house or hotel, each floor shall be of sufficient strength in all its parts to bear safely at least seventy pounds upon each superficial foot of its surface, in addition to the weight of the materials of which the floor is composed; and if used as an office building, not less than one hundred pounds; and if used as a place of public assembly, not less than one hundred and twenty pounds; and if used as a store, factory, warehouse or for any other manufacturing or commercial purpose, two hundred and fifty pounds and upwards.

[ROOFS.]

The roofs of all buildings shall be proportioned to bear safely forty pounds upon every superficial foot of their surface, in addition to the weight of the materials composing the same.

[COLUMNS AND POSTS.]

Every column, post or other vertical support, shall be of sufficient strength to bear safely the weight of the portion of each and every floor depending on it for support, in addition to the weight required as before stated to be supported safely upon said portions of said floors.

[ROOF COVERING.]

SECTION. 20. Sub. 1. The roofs of all buildings hereafter erected within the fire limits, and the roofs of all brick or stone buildings within the City and County of San Francisco, shall be covered with either metal, slate, tiles, terra cotta or asphaltum; (provided the asphaltum be covered with at least ¼ of an inch of fine gravel) so as to protect the said building from fire.

Sub. 2. Whenever the roof or roofs of any building or buildings within the fire limits shall, (in the judgment of the Board or Fire Wardens) be, or become damaged to the extent of 40 per cent of the value of said roof or roofs then said roof or roofs shall be covered as provided in Subdivision 1 of this section.

Sub. 3. The supports, rafters and all parts of roofs within the fire limits rising at any point to a height of more than twenty feet from the top of the masonry walls, or one hundred feet above the ground, shall be constructed entirely of fireproof material.

Sub. 4. All mansard roofs, or mansard stories within the fire limits, shall be constructed of fireproof materials.

Sub. 5. Appendages within the fire limits, such as skylights, dormer windows, cornices, gutters, moldings, eaves, parapets, balconies, bay windows, towers, spires, ventilators, erections over elevators, turrets, lantern lights, or other erections on roofs, if not wholly fireproof, shall be enveloped with fireproof material, in which case the sheathing underneath is to be covered with the best fireproof paint.

Sub. 6. No staging of any kind, nor stand for observation purposes of wood, shall be constructed upon the roof of any building within the fire limits.

[ATTICS TO BE DIVIDED INTO COMPARTMENTS.]

SECTION 21. The attic or the unfinished space between the ceiling and roof rafters of every building shall be divided into compartments or rooms, in order to prevent the rapid progress of fire. No such compartments shall have a floor area of more than 2,500 square feet, provided this section shall not apply to buildings of Class "A."

[CORNICES, BELTS, ETC.]

SECTION 22. All exterior cornices, belts, gutters, etc., on buildings within the fire limits shall be constructed of or covered entirely with fireproof material.

T. W. PETERSEN
SAN JOSE

ED. KARTSCHOKE
SAN FRANCISCO

PETERSEN BRICK CO,

Manufacturers of

PRESSED and COMMON BRICK

RED PRESSED BRICK A SPECIALTY

GUS KARTSCHOKE, General Agent
—SAN FRANCISCO, CAL.

Office
SAN JOSE
P. O. Box 1187
San Jose, Cal.

Our RED PRESSED BRICK
[illegible list of buildings]

Office at
Builders' Exchange
New Montgomery and Mission Sts.
Box 68, Phone, M. 5110

GEO M DYER — R W DYER

GOLDEN WEST IRON WORKS

DYER BROS

BANK AND OFFICE RAILINGS, CRESTINGS, GRILLES, BANK VAULTS, IRON DOORS, SAFES, SHUTTERS, FIRE-ESCAPES, ETC.

ELEVATOR ENCLOSURES AND CAGES

TELEPHONE, 979

No. 110 MAIN STREET. SAN FRANCISCO, CAL.

ORDERS FROM THE COUNTRY SOLICITED AND PROMPTLY ATTENTED TO

F. W. MULLER, President. C. HORTON, Secretary.

SAN JOAQUIN BRICK COMPANY

Manufacturers of

FRESH WATER KILN BRICK

YARD: BERRY ST., BET. 6TH AND 7TH.
BOX 327 BUILDERS' EXCHANGE.

TELEPHONE, Main 5110
San Francisco, Cal.

If of metal all shall be riveted and well secured to iron brackets not over two feet apart and properly built into the wall.

If stone, brick or other masonry, the entire cornice shall be properly supported on, and well secured to the wall, and the greatest weight of material of such cornices shall be on the inside of the face of the wall.

All wooden cornices and gutters on buildings within the fire limits hereafter repaired, altered, changed or replaced, shall be constructed of or covered with fireproof material.

[ELEVATOR SHAFTS AND HATCHWAYS.]

SECTION 23. Open elevators or elevators without fireproof inclosures may be used in buildings of Class "A"; they may also be used in buildings of Class "B," provided they are located and operated in well-holes of fireproof staircases, which staircases must be surrounded by walls either entirely of fireproof material or of studding covered on both sides with wire or metal lath and plastering.

Open elevators may be used in all buildings, provided they do not pass the ceiling of the first story.

[ELEVATORS, ETC., TO BE ENCLOSED.]

Elevators, hoists, dumb-waiters and lifts, and all openings or shafts passing through the floor or floors, in all other buildings and under all other conditions, shall be entirely inclosed by walls of non-combustible material, or of studding covered on both sides with iron, or with metal lath and plastering, not less than $\frac{1}{4}$ of an inch in thickness.

[TOPS OF SHAFTS.]

If the shafts of said elevators, hoists, dumb-waiters, and lifts pass the upper floor of any building, they shall be carried through, and at least eighteen inches above the roof, and be covered with a skylight; if they do not pass the upper floor, their tops shall be covered with some non-combustible material.

[WINDOWS AND DOORS IN ELEVATOR SHAFTS.]

The inside faces of all doors opening into elevator shafts shall be covered with metal. Windows shall not exceed one for each floor, nor shall any window have an area greater than eighteen square feet. The frames and sashes shall be covered with metal. Sashes shall be glazed with glass three-sixteenths of an inch in thickness.

[ROPES AND GEARING.]

SECTION 24. The strength of the ropes, gearing and all other portions of the mechanism of passenger elevators shall be calculated with a factor of safety of twenty.

For other elevators ten is to be used as the factor of safety.

[SAFETY APPLIANCES.]

Every elevator shall be provided with approved device for preventing the car from falling in case of accident.

[OPENINGS IN SHAFTS.]

Every opening in a shaft or hoist well within two and one-half feet above the floor shall be protected by a rail, gate, door or drop-door.

Doors opening into passenger elevator shafts shall be entirely under the control of the operator, and shall be so arranged that they can only be opened from the inside.

[WIRE SCREENS.]

Elevator cabs shall be so covered by wire screens as to protect them from falling machinery. Every part of the elevator not inclosed in a shaft shall be protected by a wire grill.

[SCUTTLES AND SKYLIGHTS.]

SECTION 25. All buildings over twenty feet high shall have prominent means of access to the roof from the inside. The opening in the roof shall not be less than 18 by 30 inches.

ENAMELLED BRICK

GLADDING McBEAN & CO.
MANUFACTURERS
ARCHITECTURAL TERRA COTTA
HOLLOW TILE FIRE PROOFING
SEWER AND CHIMNEY PIPE.
PRESSED BRICK, DRAIN TILE, ETC.
1358 & 1360 MARKET STREET, S. F.
MANUFACTORY AT LINCOLN, CAL.

TELEPHONE, SOUTH 41

Architect

CROCKER BUILDING
Room 227

San Francisco

TELEPHONE MAIN 5110　　　　　　　　　　　　　BOX NO. 178

F. A. Williams

Contractor and Builder

OFFICE:
BUILDERS' EXCHANGE
New Montgomery St.

SAN FRANCISCO

HENRY A. SCHULZE　　　　　　　A. C. LUTGENS

Architect　　　　　　### Architect

　　　　　　　　　　　　　　PHELAN BUILDING
　　　　　　　　　　　　　　Rooms 125 & 127

Flood Building.　San Francisco　　　　San Francisco

B. ALLEN BROWN

Architect

Market and Taylor Sts　　　　　　San Francisco

[SKYLIGHTS.]

All skylights on roofs projecting at an angle less than 22½ degrees, not inclosed by a substantial railing at least three feet high, shall be protected by screens of No. 10 wire, with meshes not more than 1½ inches square. The screens are to be secured to the sash and are to be kept at least four inches above the glass.

All skylights placed in brick buildings shall be made of metal and shall be glazed with three-sixteenths of an inch glass.

Wire-rolled glass may be used, in which case the wire netting may be omitted.

[SHAFTS.]

SECTION 26. The walls of all shafts passing from one floor to another shall be constructed of or covered on both sides with non-combustible material.

All openings in light shafts shall have metal or metal-covered frames and sashes.

Sashes shall be glazed with wire-rolled glass or glass not less than 3-16 of an inch in thickness.

All openings in floors, excepting those necessary to admit stairways, shall have walls and ceilings within ten feet of such openings, made fireproof with metal lathing and plastering of ¾ of an inch in thickness, or of fireproof construction. Wooden facings on such openings shall not be allowed.

[FIRE ESCAPES AND STAND PIPES.]

SECTION 27. Every building in the City and County of San Francisco that is occupied or so constructed as to be occupied by two or more families on the third story, not having proper exits or facilities for escape in case of fire, and every building of four or more stories in height, and every building used or occupied or so constructed as to be used or occupied as a theatre, hospital, asylum, seminary, hotel, rooming-house, tenement or lodging house, or for a factory, mill or manufactory, or for offices or workshop, or place of or for public entertainments or assemblages, above the second story, and every school building more than two stories in height, shall be provided with metallic fire escapes, combined with suitable metallic balconies and railings at each floor, firmly secured to the outer walls, and in such proximity to one or more windows of each story as to render access to the same from each such story easy and safe. Said fire escapes shall be of such construction, location and numbers as the Board of Fire Wardens of this city and county may determine, and erected and built in accordance with the specifications hereinafter mentioned in Section 28 of this Order.

Said fire escapes shall at all times be kept in good order and free from all obstructions.

Every building of four or more stories in height, in this city and county, shall be provided with one or more metallic stand pipes outside of the walls, extending from four feet above the line of the sidewalk to the roof, resting on the fire-wall, and at each story there shall be proper branches with gate valves.

Buildings of four stories in height shall have a two way siamese inlet attached to said stand pipe four feet above the line of the sidewalk, and an outlet at the end of the same over the roof consisting of a three inch gate valve with proper reducers.

Buildings of five or more stories in height shall have a three-way siamese inlet with proper valves attached to said stand pipes, four feet above the line of the sidewalk, and an outlet at the end of the same over the roof, consisting of a two-way siamese with proper gate valves; all of which shall be of proper dimensions to connect with the couplings attached to the hose used by the Fire Department.

Said stand pipes to be of such location and numbers, and of such material and construction as the Board of Fire Wardens of this city and county may determine; the same to be at all times kept in good order and free from all obstructions.

This section, however, shall not apply to buildings of Class "A," or to buildings of Class "B" of this Order, whose stairs and stairways, halls, lobbies and corridors are constructed according to the requirements of Class "A"; provided, that buildings of Class A and Class B shall have a 4-inch stand pipe either on the exterior or interior of their front walls, with a three-way siamese inlet four feet above the sidewalk and a two-way siamese outlet on the roof.

After the Board of Fire Wardens shall have determined as to the number, location and construction of the metallic ladders or stair fire escapes and stand pipes to be erected and placed on such buildings as heretofore mentioned in this Section, the said Board shall notify the owner, agent, lessee, or person or persons having the control of such building or buildings, or either of them in writing of such determination, and commanding them or either of them to comply therewith within thirty days after the service of the same. The said notice may be served by delivering to and leaving with such owner, agent, lessee, or person or persons having the control of such building or buildings, or either of them, personally a copy of such notice, or by leaving the same at his, or her, or their residence or place of business and the person or persons so notified as aforesaid shall within thirty days thereafter comply with all the requirements thereof; and it shall be unlawful to use or continue the use of such buildings if said notice of said Board of Fire Wardens is not complied with.

All buildings already erected that come within the designation of buildings heretofore mentioned in this Section, that are not provided with fire escapes and stand pipes, which are hereafter enlarged, raised, altered or built upon, shall be subject to all the provisions and requirements of this Section, and shall be provided with fire escapes and stand pipes in accordance therewith.

All buildings that may hereafter be enlarged, raised, altered or built upon in such a manner as to come within the designation of buildings heretofore mentioned in this Section, shall be subject to all the provisions and requirements thereof, and shall be provided with fire escapes and stand pipes in accordance therewith.

The location of all fire escapes shall be plainly indicated by a sign in bold letters not less than three inches high, in a conspicuous place in every hall where the building is occupied by persons at night, and a red light shall be there placed, and kept burning from sunset to sunrise; that the said sign may be readily seen.

[INSPECTION OF FIRE ESCAPES AND STAND PIPES.]

For the purpose of examining, inspecting, and otherwise attending to the condition of fire escapes and stand pipes erected on buildings in this city and county, the Fire Wardens, acting Assistant Engineers and Hydrantmen of the Fire Department shall have access thereto through any building equipped therewith, during the daytime; and it shall be unlawful for any person or persons to obstruct them or either of them in the performance of such duties.

[SPECIFICATIONS FOR THE ERECTION AND CONSTRUCTION OF FIRE ESCAPES.]

SECTION 28. Where a verticle metallic ladder is required, it shall be constructed according to the following requirements:

Size of metal for ladders...2 x $\frac{3}{8}$ in.
Size of rungs for ladders... $\frac{3}{4}$ in. diameter
Size of grating bars for balconies......................................1$\frac{1}{2}$ x 5-16 in.
Size of cross-bearing bars carrying gratings.....................1$\frac{1}{2}$ x $\frac{3}{8}$ in.

The outside frames of all fire escapes carrying the gratings shall be of two-inch angle iron, and to extend all around the platform, and bolted to the building.

The size of the bearing metal carrying platforms shall not be less than two-inch channel iron, and the braces carrying the same shall be 1$\frac{1}{2}$ x $\frac{1}{2}$ in., bolted through the building.

The top rail for balconies of eight feet or less shall be 1$\frac{1}{2}$ x $\frac{3}{8}$ in.

Balconies over eight feet in length shall have one extra rail in center, of the same size as the top rail.

The trimmings for finishing outside rails shall be $\frac{3}{4}$ x $\frac{1}{4}$ in.

Height of balconies shall not be less than two feet, six inches, and the width not less than three feet.

All rails and bearing beams shall extend through the wall or studding with washers and nuts on the same.

Where the verticle ladders join, they shall be connected and bolted with not less than four bolts on each side.

No screws or lag screws shall be used in the construction of fire escapes.

Piping of 1¼ in. may be used for rails.

All balconies shall be constructed with circular corners.

All nuts to show on the outside of building.

Openings in balconies shall not be less than two feet square.

Brackets carrying platforms shall not be more than five feet apart.

Perpendicular ladders shall be at least eight inches from the building.

Finishing on balconies shall not extend outside the rail.

Gratings of platforms may be placed on edge, and the grating bars of all platforms shall not be more than one inch apart, and in all cases shall be made of iron and steel.

All brackets carrying balconies shall be bolted through the entire walls or studding, and bolts shall not be less than ⅝ in. with nuts and washers.

In frame buildings where the studding does not correspond with the measurements for balconies and ladders, extra headers shall be inserted between the studding, and shall be of the same thickness of the studding and securely spiked.

Where metallic stair fire escapes are required, they shall be constructed according to the following requirements:

All balconies shall be placed upon buildings as the Board of Fire Wardens may direct.

Where the brackets support the stairs on stair fire escapes the brackets shall be constructed of three-inch channel iron.

The platforms of balconies shall be the same as required for vertical ladders, and shall be placed on the line of the top of the flooring boards of each story. Said platforms shall be supported upon iron brackets, not more than five feet apart, and shall in all cases be built into, and anchored to the walls of masonry, during the construction of the walls, and shall go through the entire thickness of said walls, and securely fastened on the inside of the building.

The width of all balconies from the face of the wall out, shall not be less than three feet six inches; and the length of all balconies shall be regulated by the Board of Fire Wardens.

There shall be an opening in the floor or platform of all balconies not less than two feet wide, and three feet six inches long inclosed and protected on three sides.

The railings and balconies shall be constructed as required for ladders. There shall be a communication from balcony to balcony by means of inclined stairs, and no ladder will be allowed below the line of the flooring of the upper story of any building.

Said stairs shall have an inclination from the perpendicular of not less than four inches to every twelve inches of rise. Said stairs shall be made of side stringers of not less than 4x½ in. steel; threads to be turned down on ends and riveted well into each stringer at a distance apart of sixteen inches for said inclination. All said stairs to be provided with substantial railings of 1¼ in. pipe; the sides well supported by suitable standards of 1¼ in. pipe at proper distances apart, viz: four standards to each run of steps and thoroughly bolted to the stringers.

The ladders extending from the upper balconies to the roof may be perpendicular but well braced with iron brackets.

[IRON SHUTTERS AND GRATINGS IN FRONT OF OPENINGS.]

SECTION 29. All brick or stone buildings, excepting those of Class "A," used as stores, store-houses, mills or manufactories hereafter erected in this city and county, which are more than two stories, or more than twenty-five feet in height above the curb level, shall have doors, blinds or shutters made of either fireproof material or of two thicknesses of wood, aggregating 1½ inches, and covered with tin on every window, and opening where the same do not open on a street, which is above and within thirty feet of the roof of another building; or within thirty feet of any opposite or diagonally exposed building. Such shutters shall be hung upon iron eyes or frames independent of any woodwork, and those above the first floor shall be so arranged that they can be readily opened and closed from the outside.

Those on the first floor shall be hung on hinges, and the locks shall be so arranged as to admit of easy destruction by the Fire Department or Fire Patrol.

No gratings or bars of iron, wood, brass, or other material shall be either temporarily or permanently placed, fixed, built or maintained in the walls or frame work of any brick, stone or wooden building in this city and county, in the basement, or in any story or portion of any story of any building, or in the openings made for affording access or exit to or from any building, or in any space or opening for affording light or air or in any opening made in any building for doors, windows or any other purpose, without permission of the Board of Supervisors.

[ANCHORS AND TIES.]

SECTION 30. In all brick or stone buildings, beams and joists shall be tied to the walls or to themselves, so as to form a continuous tie across the building, every eight feet.

All anchors shall be of ⅜ x 1½ inch band iron or heavier, or if formed of round iron, they shall be of equal strength. They shall be at least three feet long, with washers of iron at least 6 x 6 inches secured to them at the outer ends. The other ends shall be turned down two inches, and shall be securely tied to the beam or joist, either at the side or bottom, and in such a way that the anchor is self-releasing.

Self-releasing box anchors, provided they act satisfactorily as a tie, and answer the above requirements as to strength, may be used.

When walls run parallel or nearly parallel with floor beams, they shall be properly tied by iron straps and anchors to said floor beams every ten feet.

All walls of brick meeting at an angle, if not carried up together, shall be united every ten feet of their height by anchors made of 2½x½ inch wrought iron bands securely built into the side or partition walls not less than 36 inches, and into the front and rear walls at least one-half the thickness of such walls. In case a new wall is built against, and at an angle to an old wall, the anchors must be inserted every five feet of their height, and of the size above specified. The stone facing of any building, except when such facing is built with alternate headers and stretchers, shall be strongly and securely anchored to the wall with iron anchors laid into the stone at least one inch.

[CHIMNEYS AND FLUES.]

SECTION 31. No chimney except patent chimney as hereinafter provided shall be built with inclosing and division walls, less than four inches thick; chimneys having four-inch walls shall have safe guards against the spread of fire to adjacent woodwork as follows: If the interior of the flue is lined throughout the entire length with terra cotta flue liners, no further protection shall be required; if, however, there are no flue liners, then the inside of such chimney shall be plastered with mortar, and the outside covered with metallic or wire lath and plastered. All unlined flues shall be laid up with struck joints, or they shall be pargetted on the inside. No smoke flue of brick shall be less than 8x8 inches in the clear, and such flue shall have but one inlet; for a two-story building with two inlets the flue shall be 8x12 inches in the clear, and for a three-story building the flue shall be 8x16 inches in the clear. Flues in buildings of greater height shall be increased in size proportionately. Flues larger than 200 square inches and less than 500 square inches must be surrounded by walls of not less than 8 inches in thickness; flues larger than 500 and less than 1000 square inches must be surrounded by walls of not less than 12 inches in thickness up to a height of 15 feet above the inlet, and 8 inches in thickness the remaining height; flues larger than 1000 square inches shall be proportionately increased in size and shall be lined with fire brick for at least twenty feet above the opening.

For bakeries the oven flues shall be not less than 12x12 inches in the clear, and such flues shall have the sides, back and front of brickwork not less than eight inches in thickness.

[TOPS OF CHIMNEYS.]

No chimney top shall be carried to a height of less than four feet above flat roofs, and two feet above the ridge of pitched roofs. Tops of chimneys larger than 200 and less than 500 square inches, shall be carried up to a height of eight feet above the roof immediately surrounding or five feet above the highest part of the roof within a radius of fifty feet of said chimney.

Tops of chimneys larger than 500 and less than 1000 square inches shall be carried up to a height of ten feet above the roofs immediately surrounding or seven feet above the highest part of the roof within a radius of fifty feet of said chimney.

[ANCHORS AND THIMBLES.]

Every chimney extending to a height above the roof equal to more than six times its thickness, shall be properly anchored and secured.

When a smoke pipe enters a brick chimney, a thimble shall be used. All thimbles used shall be made of fire-clay not less than ½ an inch in thickness. Such thimbles shall have the casing of galvanized iron ½ an inch larger than the thimble, with the intervening space filled with cement.

Chimneys built outside of frame structures shall be well anchored at intervals, not over ten feet apart to the stud walls.

[CONSTRUCTION.]

Chimneys forming part of a wall shall not be corbelled out beyond the face of the wall to a distance more than ⅔ of the thickness of the wall, nor shall they be corbelled out from any wall less than twelve inches thick, nor shall they rest upon any woodwork.

[FOUNDATION OF CHIMNEYS.]

Every chimney and fireplace excepting as hereinafter provided for under patent flues, shall rest upon the ground or on other sufficient fireproof foundation well protected from heat.

[OFFSETS.]

Offsets for reducing the size of chimneys shall not be greater than one inch to each course. All chimneys isolated from brick walls shall be so built as not to increase in size from the foundation up.

[FRAMING AROUND CHIMNEYS.]

All floor and ceiling joists, furring timbers, rafters and all other woodwork, must be kept 1½ inches from every chimney.

In no building shall any wooden beam or timber be placed within six inches of the inside of any flue.

Flues of ranges, boilers and stoves in hotels, restaurants and boarding-houses shall not be furred with wood, but shall be plastered directly on the brick or on metal lath in the story where the fires are located.

[FIRE OPENINGS.]

SECTION 32. Open fireplaces shall have arched heads which shall, wherever possible, extend to the back of the tile or marble facing. Said arch and head shall be supported by a permanent wrought iron arch bar, not less than three inches wide and ¼ inch thick. If the arch head is not extended to the tile or marble facing, or if there is an open joint between the brickwork facing of the mantel, then a solid iron casting of the full width of the opening shall be inserted, which shall effectively cover the joint, thereby preventing the passage of fire, heat and smoke through the joint between the facing of the mantel and the fireplace.

[HEARTHS.]

Hearths of open fireplaces shall be of brick or stone, or of some other incombustible material, and shall rest upon brick trimmer arches or other fireproof material.

Such trimmer arches shall not be less than twelve inches on each side of the fire opening, and no woodwork of any kind shall be placed under any fireplace or hearthstone.

STEVENS' PATENT CHIMNEY

Telephone South 10

This Chimney is Recommended by all the Leading Architects . . . and Builders . . .

AND HAS BEEN APPROVED BY THE

FIRE WARDENS AND BOARD OF UNDERWRITERS

This chimney consists of a smoke flue of fire clay earthen pipe, one inch thick and two feet in length, and is put together with heavy, galvanized iron bands; each joint being thoroughly cemented and cleaned. The bands have three one-inch projections riveted to them, which hold in place a galvanized iron pipe (also two feet in length) and therefore forms an inch air space around the earthen pipe. The galvanized iron pipe is perforated with ventilating holes, thereby forming a continuous circulation of air from top to bottom of the chimney, which prevents any possibility of the earthen pipe cracking or overheating, which is so prevalent in the common run of patent chimneys.

The chimney is made fast with rings to the studding or side of the building, and is topped out with a fancy terra cotta chimney-top, making altogether the lightest, best and most durable patent chimney in the world.

The Immense Quantity of these Chimneys being used at present is a Sufficient Guarantee that it is

THE ONLY SAFE CHIMNEY IN USE

· · · ALSO DEALER IN · · ·

Terra Cotta Pipe, Sewer Pipe, Chimney Tops and Flower Pots

Office, N. E. Cor. Larkin and Market Sts.

F. M. STEVENS, Proprietor

[FIRES IN OPEN TINS, CANS, ETC.]

No person shall kindle or maintain any fire of charcoal, coal, wood or other combustible material in or upon any open tin, metal can or any earthen vessel or vessel whatsoever, in or upon any building or premises in this city and county, or in any furnace or stove of any kind, unless the same be connected by means of a good sheet-iron flue or pipe with a brick or earthen pipe chimney to conduct the smoke and fire into said brick or earthen pipe chimney.

Provided, however, that the foregoing provisions of this Order shall not be deemed to apply to portable stoves, furnaces or lamps used by artisans in the prosecution of their regular and lawful business, or to properly constructed and authorized kerosene, gasoline or gas stoves used for cooking purposes or for the heating of chambers.

[GAS LOGS.]

No gas grate or gas log shall be placed in any building except the same be set in a fireproof fireplace; said fireplace to have at least four inches of brickwork outside of the metal or tile facings, and shall have a vent pipe of at least 12 inches area made of terra-cotta or of No. 24 galvanized iron wrapped with asbestos ⅛ of an inch thick. The vent pipes to extend at least ten feet above the gas log and have free discharge to the open air, and such vent pipe must not come within one inch of any woodwork.

[PATENT FLUES.]

SECTION 33. Flues for which United States patents have been issued, stamped with the name of the manufacturer, may be used in lieu of the brick chimneys, provided they answer the following requirements, to-wit:

They shall in no case be suspended to any timber or beam, but shall be built from the floor up. They shall rest on an iron plate ¼ of an inch thick, well secured to the floor timbers, sunk at least four inches below the top of the finished floor; the intervening space must be filled up flush with the floor with cement, brick or tiling. The strength of the floor must not be impaired by the cutting out for the chimney. All space between the floor joists or partitions shall be filled with brick, concrete or cement. No patent flue shall have more than one inlet.

[OPENING AND COVER.]

There must be an opening near the bottom of the chimney for cleaning, which is to be provided with a smoke and spark-proof cover.

[JOINTS.]

All joints must be cemented, and when bands are used they must be filled with cement or plaster of Paris, to make them smoke and spark-proof. If of galvanized iron, the bands must be five inches wide and of No. 24 iron, closely riveted together. No patent chimney shall be placed less than 1½ inches from any woodwork. Where a patent chimney passes through a roof the opening around the same must be covered with a plate of cast iron or of some other fireproof material. Patent flues shall be braced every four feet of their height.

[INSIDE DIMENSIONS OF PATENT CHIMNEYS.]

For fireplace flues, 18-inch openings, 6 inch.
For fireplace flues, 21-inch openings, 7 inch.
For fireplace flues, 24-inch openings, 8 inch.
For ordinary stove flues, 6 inch.
For French range flues, 8 inch.
For steel range flues, 8 inch.
For furnace flues, 8 or 10 inch.

All pipe used for patent chimneys shall be composed of pure calcine fire clay, not less than one inch in thickness, and shall have the name of the manufacturer stamped on each piece of pipe.

[PATENT FIREPLACES.]

Fireplaces with patent chimneys shall be placed on ½ inch boiler plate, and shall extend the full size of the opening of such fireplace, and sunk 4 inches below the top of the finished floor; this space shall then be filled in with cement or tiling, stone or brick set in cement. The strength of the floor must not be impaired by cutting out for the fireplace.

[SMOKE PIPES.]

SECTION 34. No smoke pipe shall project through any external wall or window of any building; and no smoke flue shall pass through any wooden partition of any building unless there is a ventilated air space of at least 4 inches around the pipe. Any smoke pipe passing through the floor or floors of any building shall be protected by a metal casing extending from the ceiling to at least one foot above the floor, and there shall be a ventilated air space of at least 4 inches around the said pipe.

[SPARK CATCHERS.]

SECTION 35. Spark catchers shall be placed upon all chimneys, cupolas and smokestacks used for conveying off smoke, whenever in the judgment of the Board of Fire Wardens the same is deemed necessary for the safety of the surrounding property.

[HEATING FURNACE.]

SECTION 36. The top of all heating furnaces, set in brick, shall be covered with brick supported by iron bars so constructed as to be perfectly tight; said covering shall be in addition to and not less than six inches from the ordinary covering of the hot air chamber. Smoke pipes and furnaces not set in brick shall be kept at least six inches from any woodwork. If said smoke pipes and furnaces are less than two feet from any woodwork, said woodwork must be protected by sheets of tin plate in such a manner that an air space of at least two inches is formed between the wood work and the tin plate; such tin plate to extend one foot beyond the furnace on all sides.

[FIREPROOF ROOM FOR HEATERS.]

Every steam boiler or furnace in any building used either for offices, mechanical or manufacturing purposes, or in hotels, lodging or tenement houses, theatres or assembly halls, or places of public entertainment, shall be enclosed in a fireproof room of brick, terra cotta, iron or other incombustible materials. All doors leading to such rooms shall be covered on both sides with metal, and shall be hung to rabbeted iron frames or iron hinges set in brick.

[HOT-AIR BOXES.]

All hot air boxes hereafter placed in the floors or partitions of buildings, except when such are of entirely incombustible material, shall be made of double pipes of tin plate, such pipes to be not less than ½ inch apart and shall be set in soapstone or equally fireproof borders not less than two inches in width, to which the pipes shall be tightly joined by inserting the same into a groove, or the pipes and boxes shall be covered with asbestos ⅛ of an inch in thickness cemented thereon.

Hot-air boxes or pipes less than 10x12 inches in size shall be kept at least ½ inch from any wood work; those of greater size shall be kept at least one inch from any woodwork. No woodwork shall be placed within one inch of any metal pipe intended to convey steam or heated air, unless such pipe is protected by a casing of metal, soapstone or earthen ring.

[ERECTION OF FURNACES, BOILERS, ETC.]

No boiler used for generating steam for heating or motive power, or any furnace, shall be placed on any floor above the cellar of any building, unless the same is set on noncombustible beams and arches, and such beams shall be built into the walls. All steam boilers shall be provided with a tank or other receptacle of sufficient capacity to at least hold a sufficient supply of water to last six hours.

Whenever steam boilers, ovens, coffee roasters or other structures in which fires are maintained, are set or kept in buildings with wooden floors, such floors shall be protected by a covering of brick or concrete not less than five inches in thickness, set in mortar upon a continuous sheet metal-bearing plate not less than 3-16 of an inch in thickness, all the joints of the same to be securely riveted and the edges turned up five inches all around, and shall extend eight feet in front and three feet on the other three sides.

This section shall apply to all buildings in the City and County of San Francisco.

[BAY WINDOWS.]

SECTION 37. No person shall build or cause to be built any bay or oriel window within the City and County of San Francisco, which shall project more than three feet over the line of any street, nor shall the width of any projection from a building exceed ten feet.

Said measurements when applied to base, etc., framed in wood, are to be taken on the outside of the studding, and when applied to base or masonry, are to be taken from the outside of the main wall lines.

The bottom of any bay or oriel window projecting over the line of any street, shall not be less than ten feet above the sidewalk.

No bay or oriel window shall project over the line of any street or alley less than .35 feet in width.

All bay or oriel windows within the fire limits shall either be constructed of or covered with fireproof material.

Piers between bay or oriel windows in brick or stone buildings shall not be less than four feet for a two-story building, and shall be increased in width at least one foot for each additional story.

The openings for bay or oriel windows in brick walls shall have iron beams of proper strength to support the floors and load; these beams to extend at least eight inches into the walls on both sides of openings, and be well anchored; such beams to be protected with fireproof material.

The brick wall shall be carried over the upper bay window on beams or arches.

[BAY OR ORIEL WINDOWS CONSTRUCTED IN FRAME BUILDINGS.]

SECTION 38. Bay or oriel windows constructed in frame buildings shall have piers or spaces of not less than five feet in width between them. Provided, that buildings built on lots having a frontage of twenty-five feet or less the space between said bay or oriel windows may be decreased, provided, the studding in said space or piers shall be increased in thickness so as to contain the same amount of lumber as would be contained in the studding of piers or spaces of five feet.

[FRAMING.]

SECTION 39. All joints and beams entering brick walls shall have the ends thereof so beveled that in case of fire, they shall fall without doing any injury to the walls. All joists and beams shall have a bearing upon their supports of at least four inches. All girders and trusses shall have sufficient bearing on their supports to insure stability—eight inches being the minimum. Timbers in party walls shall be separated from each other by solid masonry not less than four inches thick.

Bridging shall be placed in rows between the joists; in no case shall these rows be more than ten feet apart. Solid bridging not less than two inches thick shall be placed between joists over all beams and girders.

Cutting for piping or other purposes shall not be done so as to reduce the strength of the supporting parts below, that are required by the provisions of this Order.

All wood partitions shall have solid caps and sills, and at least one row of bridging not less than two inches thick, and of the full width of the standing studding to effectually prevent the passage of fire or smoke.

Double studs shall be used on both sides of all openings with heads and truss braces cut in and secured.

Furring against brick walls in buildings of Class "A" and Class "B" within the fire limits, shall not exceed one inch in thickness, and no wedges

F. W. WRIGHT

IMPORTER AND DEALER IN

BUILDERS' HARDWARE

Mechanics' Tools, Etc.

Fine Artistic Bronze Hardware

Building Papers, Sash Weights,
Nails, Etc.,

WHOLESALE AND RETAIL

727 Market St., Opposite "Examiner" Office

Chas. M. Sorensen

422 Post Street
Bet. Powell and Mason Sts.

San Francisco

of wood or iron shall be driven into any wall within eight inches of any flue or fireplace. When a wall is furred or lathed with wood, the space between the lathing and the wall shall be filled with plaster at the top and bottom sides of the floor beams and joists of each story and of the roof so as to prevent the passage of fire.

[STIRRUPS AND HANGERS.]

Every header or trimmer over six feet long in floors constructed to carry more than seventy-five pounds per foot of service shall at connections with other beams be hung in stirrup irons; such stirrups shall not be less than 2½ inches wide.

[AWNINGS, SHADES AND BALCONIES]

SECTION 40. All awnings, shades or balconies shall be securely supported only on wrought-iron brackets built into the walls, and shall be not less than ten feet above the line of the curb level of the sidewalk, and a gutter shall thereon be formed to carry off the water to the line of the building and to the street gutter. No gutters shall be required on cloth or canvas awnings or shades. The height of all movable canvas or cloth awnings or shades shall not be less than seven and one-half feet above said curb level. Said awnings, shades and balconies shall not extend beyond the line of the curb and the same shall not be inclosed to a greater height than three feet, six inches; provided, however, that no awning, shade or balcony shall be erected on any building facing on any street, lane, alley or place which is twenty feet or less in width; and no awning, shade or balcony shall be constructed on the sides or rear of any building within the fire limits unless there is a clear space of not less than thirty feet between the adjacent building, and in such case the same shall be constructed of fire-proof material.

[SIGNS.]

No person owning, possessing, occupying, or having the control of any building in this city and county, shall put, place, construct, erect, build, maintain, or suffer to be or remain thereon any sign, or advertisement, or framework, boards or materials on which any sign, advertisement, picture, bill or notice is painted, printed, or made, or fastened, which exceeds three feet in height, and where the same is constructed in parts, such parts together shall not exceed said height. And where more than one sign, advertisement, etc., heretofore enumerated, shall be placed on a building the same shall be placed at least ten feet apart from the top of one to the bottom of the other.

No sign, or advertisement, or framework, boards or materials on which any sign, advertisement, picture, bill or notice is painted, printed, made or fastened, shall be placed or maintained higher than the blocking-course or firewall of any building; and no framework covered with inflammable material for signs, advertisements, or any other purpose, shall be placed or maintained above such blocking-course or firewall.

All signs must be securely bolted or fastened to the building upon which they are placed.

[SIGNS, ETC., ERECTED ON REAL PROPERTY.]

It shall be unlawful for any person owning, possessing, occupying or having the control of any premises, or any real property, or for any person, to put, place, construct, erect, build, maintain or suffer to be or remain thereon, or thereover, or on or over any premises, or any real property, any sign, or advertisement, or fence, or framework, boards or materials on which any sign, advertisement, bill or notice is painted, printed or made, or fastened, and which sign, advertisement, fence, framework, boards or materials is more than ten feet in height, or more than ten feet above the ground, or more than ten feet above the level of the street adjoining said premises, or said real property, or shall suspend, or suffer the same to be so suspended thereon, or thereover, more than ten feet above the ground or the level of said street.

[TANK TOWERS.]

SECTION 41. Tank towers erected within the fire limits shall be constructed entirely of non-combustible materials.

Money Loaned on Real Estate

BUILDERS, ARCHITECTS AND CONTRACTORS

Should know that the CALIFORNIA TITLE INSURANCE & TRUST COMPANY
Loans Money on Real Estate.

It makes its own searches, and is able to accommodate its patrons at short notice. All loans made at lowest current rates of interest.
Call at the office of the Company in the Mills Building, and ask for particulars. Title Insurance effected at lowest rates. Paid Up Capital $250,000. Cash Reserve $50,000.

L. R. ELLERT, Manager, Mills Building

P. N. KUSS

Painter, Decorator and Wood Finisher

DEALER IN

PAINTS AND GLASS

422 Sutter Street, San Francisco . . . . . . Telephone Main 1882
409 Thirteenth Street, Oakland

TELEPHONE EAST 677

⇌ WM. R. JACK ⇌

Carpenter and Builder

RESIDENCE, 1210 TURK ST.   OFFICE, 913 ELLIS ST., S. F.

TELEPHONE No. 5369   BOX 175 BUILDERS' EXCHANGE

RALSTON ✥ IRON ✥ WORKS

H. RALSTON, Prop'r. Manufacturer of all Kinds

Agricultural and Ornamental Iron Work, Vaults, Fire Escapes, Crestings, Doors, Shutters, House and Cemetery Railing

222 & 224 HOWARD ST.   NEAR BEAL

SAN FRANCISCO, CAL.

[WATER TANKS.]

SECTION 42. All water tanks erected on brick buildings shall rest directly upon supports of masonry or upon metal beams resting upon walls of masonry. Said walls and beams shall be of sufficient strength to support the weights of tank and water that may be placed upon them.

[TANK TOWERS ON BUILDINGS.]

No tank tower or frame shall be constructed on any building unless said tower or frame is constructed entirely independent of the roof and floors of the building.

[SMOKEHOUSES.]

SECTION 43. All smokehouses or dryhouses in this city and county shall be built of brick or stone, or hollow fire-clay tiles, and the doors and roofs thereof shall be constructed of some non-combustible material.

[REMOVAL OF BUILDINGS.]

SECTION 44. No building within the fire limit blocks shall be removed without the written permission of the Superintendent of Public Streets and Highways and the Chairman of the Committee on Fire Department of the Board of Supervisors, and such permission shall not be given except to remove a building or buildings to any portion of the same lot on which it or they may stand to make room for more permanent improvements, (the meaning of the words, "for permanent improvements,' means brick or stone), or for the removal of wooden buildings from within the fire limits to any part of the city outside of said limits, in which latter case the party or parties making application for such privilege shall give security to the satisfaction of the Superintendent of Public Streets, Highways, and Squares, that they will leave the street or streets over which said building or buildings shall be moved in as good order as they were before such removal, and that they will make such removal continuous, day by day, until completed, with the least possible obstruction to the thoroughfares then occupied, and that they will keep a watchman in or around each building from sundown to sunrise continuously during the time of such removal, and the said removal shall be subject to the control and direction of the Superintendent of Public Streets, Highways and Squares, who may prescribe the mode and routine of such removal, and notice of such removal shall be left at the office of said Superintendent and the Chief Engineer of the Fire Department; provided, that no frame building shall be moved from its present location unless said building is worth at least fifty (50) per cent of what it would cost to construct such building of new material; and that in case of dispute as to valuation between the owner and the Fire Wardens, said dispute shall be determined by arbitration of competent mechanics, the owner to select one arbitrator, the Fire Wardens the other, and in case the arbitrators cannot agree, they shall call in the third, and their decision shall be final; all expenses of arbitration to be paid by owner.

[THEATRES AND ASSEMBLY HALLS.]

SECTION 45. Every building in the City and County of San Francisco hereafter so built or altered as to contain an audience or assembly hall capable of holding 800 persons or more, excepting churches used solely for worship, and every theatre (that is, every building used for theatrical or operatic purposes, or any public entertainments of any kind in which stage scenery and apparatus are employed), regardless of its capacity, shall be built according to the requirements of Sections 46-60, inclusive, provided that in the said sections or parts of said sections in which reference is made to theatres, such sections or parts of sections shall only apply to theatres—as above defined—but all other sections or parts of sections in which no specific mention is made of any particular class, or kind of public hall, shall apply to all places of public assembly capable of holding 800 or more, except churches used solely as places of worship.

SECTION 46. No portion of any building hereafter erected, altered or used for theatrical or operatic purposes, or for public entertainments of any kind, in which stage scenery and apparatus are employed, shall be occupied or used as a hotel, boarding, lodging-house, or factory, or for storage purposes, unless the same is completely isolated by brick walls, which shall extend through and at least 4 feet above the roof.

In all theatres hereafter built, the level of the stage above the street level shall not exceed five feet.

[FRONTAGE.]

SECTION 47. Every building hereafter so built or altered as to contain an audience or assembly hall capable of holding 800 persons or more, shall have at least one frontage on a public highway or street, and in such there shall be such means of entrance and exit for the audience as hereafter required.

[EXITS.]

SECTION 48. Plans of all exits shall be printed on every programme.

The word "Exit" shall be painted over exit; the letters to be not less than eight inches high.

The audience hall and each apartment, division and gallery of every such building shall respectively have at least two exits as far apart as may be.

Every such exit shall have a width at least 20 inches for every 100 persons which the hall, apartment, division or gallery from which it leads, is capable of holding.

Two or more exits of the same aggregate width may be substituted for either of the two exits above required, but no exit shall be less than five feet wide.

[LOBBIES.]

SECTION 49. Every division of the auditorium shall have adjoining lobbies sufficiently large to furnish standing room for all persons that such a division may at any one time contain.

Said lobbies shall be separated from the auditorium by brick or terra cota walls, or walls lathed on both sides with iron lath, and plastered with three coats of mortar, and pierced only by such openings as are required for exits by this section.

[DOORS.]

SECTION 50. All doors shall open outward, and shall not be so placed as to reduce the width of the passage above required.

No such doors shall be closed or locked during any representation, or when the building is open to the public.

Every doorway communicating between the aisles and passageways in the auditorium, and any lobby or corridor, shall have a square opening of not less than the full width of the aisles and passageways leading to such doorways.

[STAIRWAYS.]

SECTION 51. (a) All stairways and walls surrounding them shall be constructed of fireproof material throughout, provided that outside of the fire limits the walls surrounding stairways may be stud partitions covered with iron lath and plaster, three coats.

(b) The rise of the stairways shall not exceed $7\frac{1}{2}$ inches, and the tread shall not be less than $10\frac{1}{2}$ inches.

There shall be no flights of more than 15, nor less than 3 steps between landings, and every landing shall be at least four feet wide from step to step.

Stairs and landings of all buildings of this class shall have proper handrails on both sides, firmly secured to the walls, or to strong posts and balusters.

Stairways serving for the exit of 50 people must be at least 4 feet wide; for every 50 additional people, width must be increased 6 inches. Stairways shall have no winders.

[AUDITORIUM.]

SECTION 52. The ceilings of the auditorium and of the lobbies, halls and staircases, dressing-rooms and boxes, shall be lathed with iron lath and finished with three good coats of mortar, or in lieu of the iron lath fire-clay furring tile may be used, plastered with two coats of mortar.

In every theatre a firewall of brick shall separate the auditorium from the stage, and the same shall extend at least four feet above the roof.

There shall be but two openings in this wall in addition to the curtain opening. The former openings shall not be located above the level of the stage, and shall not exceed 21 superficial feet each. They shall be provided with self-closing iron or wooden doors, tinned on both sides, with the tin turned over the edges. These doors shall be hung to rabbeted iron or frames or rabbeted in the brickwork, and so arranged that they can be opened from both sides at all times.

Direct access shall be provided to these doors from both sides of the same and shall always be left free from incumbrance.

Above the proscenium opening there shall be an iron girder, covered with fireproof material, over which there shall be constructed a relieving arch; the space between the girder and the arch being filled with hard-burned brick of the full thickness of the proscenium wall.

[FINISH AROUND CURTAIN OPENING.]

SECTION 53. All finish and ornamental work around the curtain opening shall be of fireproof material, secured to the masonry with iron.

[SCENERY.]

All stage scenery or decorations made of combustible material, and all woodwork about the stage, shall be saturated with some incombustible preparation or material, or otherwise rendered safe against fire, to the satisfaction of the Board of Fire Wardens.

[CURTAIN.]

The proscenium curtain shall be placed at least three feet from all footlights. In every theatre the proscenium opening shall be provided with a fireproof curtain which shall be made to lower from the top, in such a manner as to stop at a height of seven feet above the stage floor; the remaining opening to be closed by a curtain of some such fire resisting fabric as shall hereinafter be described.

In lieu of the metal curtain, one of asbestos or of similar fireproof material, reinforced by wire netting may be used. All such curtains shall be raised at the beginning and lowered at the end of each and every performance.

[SEATS.]

SECTION 54. All seats in the auditorium, except those in the boxes, shall be firmly secured to the floor, and no seat in the auditorium shall have more than six seats intervening between it and the aisles.

[AISLES.]

No aisle or passageway shall be less than three feet six inches wide at the narrowest point, and shall be increased in width to the point of exit at least one inch for every five running feet or part thereof; and no aisle or passageway shall have a gradient within the auditorium of more than two inches in ten inches or without more than one inch in ten inches. All aisles, passageways and stairways in such buildings shall be of even increasing widths toward the exits, and shall be at least seven feet high without obstruction.

[AISLES, ETC., NOT TO BE OBSTRUCTED.]

All aisles and passageways in said buildings shall be kept free from camp stools, chairs, sofas and other obstructions, and no person shall be allowed to stand in or occupy any of said aisles and passageways during any performance, service, exhibition, lecture, concert, ball, or any public assemblage, nor shall there be any chairs, settees or camp-stools in such aisles, passageways or corridors at such times or occasions.

[WORK SHOPS.]

SECTION 55. No boiler, furnace, engine or heating apparatus, excepting steam or hot air pipes or radiators, and no work shops, storage or general property room, shall be allowed above or below the auditorium, stage or any of the fly-galleries, or any passageway or stairway of any exit.

R. F. OSBORN & CO.

ESTABLISHED
1863

THE SAME OLD PLACE

751-753 Market St., Bet. 3d and 4th, Opp. Phelan Bldg.

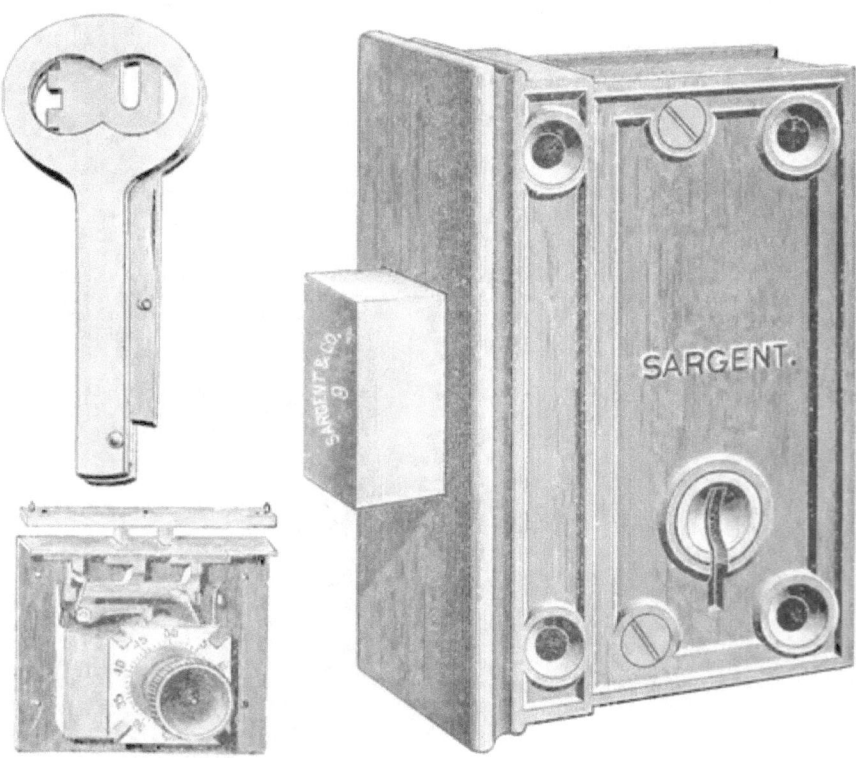

BUILDING HARDWARE
CABINET HARDWARE
MECHANICS' TOOLS

Tools of All Description Made to Order and Repaired

ESTIMATES GIVEN ON ALL MECHANICAL WORK

Locks Repaired, Keys Fitted Etc.   Razors and Scissors Sharpened

All work shops, scenery docks, storage or general property rooms shall be separated from the stage, dressing rooms and auditorium, by solid brick walls or fireproof partitions. All openings shall have iron or tinned wood self-closing doors hung to rabbets in the brickwork.

[VENTILATION.]

SECTION 56. All ventilator shafts from the ceiling line shall be of fireproof material, and shall pass at least four feet above the roof.

The roof over the stage of every theatre shall have skylights equal in area to one-quarter of said roof, and the whole shall be so arranged as to open instantly on the cutting or burning of a hempen cord, which shall be arranged to hold said skylight closed; or some other device may be used if equally simple in the judgment of the Fire Wardens.

[LIGHTS.]

SECTION 57. Gas and electric lights shall have independent connections for the auditorium, passages, stairways and the stage.

Provision shall be made for shutting off light from the outside. All stage gas lights shall have strong metal guards of sufficient fineness to protect any combustible material from contact with the flame.

Every portion of the building devoted to the use or accommodation of the public, also all outlets leading to the highway or street, shall be well and properly lighted during every performance, and the same shall be kept lighted until the audience shall have departed from the premises.

[FIRE PROTECTION.]

SECTION 58. Stand pipes shall be provided with proper hose attachment on every floor and gallery, as follows, viz.: One on each side of the auditorium and one on each side of the stage, and one in the property room, and they shall be kept full of water with a pressure direct from the street main; at least 50 feet of rubber hose, such as is used by the Fire Department, with proper nozzles, shall be provided and set at each hose connection, and shall be kept in full view, ready for immediate use and free from obstructions at all times.

There shall be kept upon the stage on each side thereof, in full view, not less than 12 buckets, always to be full of water, and the words "Fire Buckets" plainly painted thereon, and they shall not be used for any other purpose. There shall be kept in readiness for immediate use on the stage, buckets of water, hand pumps or other portable fire extinguishing apparatus.

Axes and fire hooks shall also be placed on every floor; and all of the stand pipes are not to be less than four inches in diameter; the hose, pumps, buckets, fire extinguishers, gas pipes, footlights and all other apparatus herein provided shall be in charge of the Fire Department, and the Fire Wardens are hereby directed to see that the arrangements in respect thereto are carried out and enforced.

[WATER CURTAIN.]

The proscenium opening of every theatre shall be provided with two-and-one-half inch perforated pipe, or with equivalent equipment of automatic or open sprinklers, which shall form when in operation a complete water curtain for the entire proscenium opening.

Similar sprinklers shall be placed over the stage at such intervals as to protect every square foot of stage surface, when said sprinklers are in use.

[DOORWAYS AND EXITS.]

SECTION 59. Every theatre, concert hall, or building seating one thousand persons or over, used for dramatic, operatic or other entertainments or public assemblages, involving the use of a stage with movable scenery, curtains or machinery, shall for the public safety have on three sides of the auditorium a clear space for the use of the audience in leaving the building; the space on each side from the side walls to the seats shall not be less than six feet wide; provided that in every building used as aforesaid seating less than one thousand persons the space on such sides shall not be less than five feet wide; the side facing the stage and in the rear of the auditorium shall be at least ten feet wide from the seats to the wall.

All doorways, in buildings used as aforesaid, in whole or in part, shall have the doors for the ingress and egress of the public constructed so as to swing inwardly and outwardly.

In no case shall the main entrance to such buildings or places heretofore mentioned be less than 16 feet in width, and they shall be kept free from all obstructions of any kind whatsoever at all times.

SECTION 60. Sections 48, 50, 51B and 57 shall apply to every building in the City and County of San Francisco hereafter so built or altered as to contain an audience or assembly hall capable of holding more than 300 persons and less than 800, excepting churches used solely for worship.

[PLANING MILLS, ETC.]

SECTION 61. In buildings of Class B within the fire limits used as planing mills, wagon or carriage manufactories, furniture manufactories, or any other wood-working factories, all joists and studding bearing weight shall be covered with metal lath and plaster, and the floors shall be double, with the top floor over $\frac{3}{4}$ inch of mortar, or two thicknesses of asbestos paper—unless such a building is constructed on what is known as the slow-burning or mill construction.

All buildings of this class (slow-burning) the weight shall be concentrated on piers and buttresses, with a thin wall containing the windows therein.

Such piers shall not be more than 9 feet centers, and upon them shall est the beams or girders.

The floors shall be double; the under floor, extending from one beam to another, shall be not less than 3 inches thick, and the upper floor running at right angles or diagonally across them, shall be $1\frac{1}{4}$ inches thick.

All planks shall be laid to the end of the timbers. The brick walls and piers shall be of the size required by Section No. 13.

All rooms in which special danger exists, such as hot drying, shall be protected over-head with metal lath and plaster, following the line of the ceiling or timber, so as to avoid any cavity in the ceiling.

[BRICK BUILDINGS]

SECTION 62. All the requirements of Section 11 shall apply to buildings of this class.

[BRICK WALLS.]

(a) Every external, party and interior weight-bearing wall of every brick building outside the fire limits, any point of which exceeds 60 feet in height above the foundation wall, shall be built of such thickness and in such manner as is required for the walls of buildings of Class A and B within the fire limits. (See Section 13 and Table 1.) All other walls shall be built throughout the different stories of the thickness shown in Table 2.

(b) When a wall is only 50 feet long, or when it is interrupted by cross walls at intervals of 50 feet or less, said cross walls being the same height as the outside walls and of the same thickness, said walls shall be constructed according to the dimensions given in the columns "A" of Table 2, but if said walls are more than 50 feet long and are not interrupted by cross walls at intervals of 50 feet, then said walls shall be constructed according to the dimensions given in columns "B" of Table 2.

(c) No wall shall be built less than 9 inches thick.

(d) In all brick or stone buildings in this city and county over 25 feet in width, if there are no brick partition walls or girders supported on iron or wooden columns, or piers of masonry, the partition walls or girders shall be so placed as not to exceed 25 feet apart; and in case iron or wooden girders are substituted for partition walls, the building shall not exceed 100 feet between the brick walls.

In all buildings hereafter erected in this city and county, on a street corner, the bearing wall—that is, the outside wall upon which the beam rests (if there are openings in it)—shall in all cases be four inches thicker than is otherwise provided for in this Order; and where the joists or timbers rest upon a front or rear wall, the said wall shall be four inches thicker than is provided for in this Order.

(e) The material used in the extra four inches above-mentioned may be concentrated in piers or buttresses.

(f) When walls are hollow the same amount of material must be used, and ties inserted every twenty inches.

(g) If any story exceeds in height sixteen times the thickness prescribed for the walls of such story in the tables, the thickness of each external and party wall throughout such story shall be increased four inches for every five feet or fraction thereof in excess of the tabulated height.

TABLE No. 2.

BUILDINGS OUTSIDE FIRE LIMITS AND DWELLING-HOUSES WITHIN THE FIRE LIMITS.

(Thickness of External, Party and Bearing Partition Walls.)

Height up to.....	15 feet.		26 feet.		36 feet.		48 feet.		60 feet.	
Length of walls up to..........	50 feet.		50 feet.		50 feet.		50 feet.		50 feet.	
	A.	B.	A.	B.	A.	B.	A.	B.	A.	B.
Foundat'n	13 in.	13 in.	13 in.	17 in.	17 in.	17 in.	17 in.	21 in.	21 in.	21 in.
1st Story..	9 in.	13 in.	13 in.	13 in.	13 in.	13 in.	13 in.	17 in.	17 in.	17 in.
2d Story...			9 in.	13 in.	13 in.	13 in.	13 in.	13 in.	17 in.	17 in.
3d Story...					9 in.	13 in.	13 in.	13 in.	13 in.	17 in.
4th Story..							9 in.	13 in.	13 in.	13 in.
5th Story..									13 in.	13 in.

The height of all walls referred to in this section shall be measured from the top of the foundation to the extreme top of said walls, exclusive of the firewall; the firewall being that portion of the wall extending above the roof boarding.

No building shall have more stories in the given height than provided for in the foregoing table.

[HEIGHT OF FRAME BUILDINGS.]

SECTION 63. No frame building, excepting churches, shall be built more than fifty-five feet high from the line of the sidewalk or ground upon which it is to be erected. Churches may be built to a greater height, provided the roofs and appendages thereof more than fifty-five feet above the ground are covered with fireproof material; the height shall be measured from the sidewalk line, through the center of the facade of the building, and shall include attics, mansards and cornices.

[WALLS.]

The walls of frame buildings shall be constructed with studding, covered with weather boarding on the outside. In no case shall uncovered studding be allowed against the weather boarding of an adjoining building. The outer walls of frame buildings over one story in height, veneered with brick, shall be at least eight inches in thickness.

[SIZE OF STUDDING FOR OUTER WALLS.]

For a building of two stories or less in height, except factories, the studding of the outside walls and bearing partitions shall not be less than 2 x 4 inches; for buildings of three stories in height the studding shall be not less than 2 x 6 inches to the bottom of the upper floor joists, and 2 x 4 inches for the remaining height, provided that where a lot is 25 feet or less frontage the studding may be 3 x 4 inches; for buildings more than three stories the studding of the first and second stories shall be 3 x 6 inches, and the studding of the third story 2 x 6 inches, and for the fourth story 2 x 4 inches. Studding on the outer walls of buildings shall not be placed more than 16 inches from centers.

M. BLUMENTHAL & CO.

Wine and Liquor Merchants

Whiskey in Bond or Tax Paid Shipped from Distillery or Warehouse

DISTILLERS AND MANUFACTURERS OF
SYRUPS, CORDIALS, BITTERS, EXTRACTS

EXTRA FINE COLORING A SPECIALTY

FAMILY TRADE SOLICITED

658 and 660 Mission St.
Bet. Second and Third

TELEPHONE MAIN 966

SAN FRANCISCO, CAL.

TELEPHONE SOUTH 732

FRESH CUT FLOWERS ALWAYS ON HAND AT REASONABLE PRICES

Fredrick K. Weiss

Wedding Decorations
Funeral Designs
...A Specialty

9 Eddy Street
Near Market

ORDERS PROMPTLY ATTENDED TO

Builders' Cafe and Oyster House

641 MISSION STREET

CHOICE STEAKS AND CHOPS SERVED AT ALL HOURS

Finest Brands of Cigars Constantly on Hand   Oyster Loaves a Specialty

A. E. BARBICH, PROPRIETOR

TELEPHONE 711 RED

GIVE ME A TRIAL

[DIVIDING PARTITIONS.]

All dividing partitions between buildings shall be close boarded from the lower floors to the ground, and from the upper ceilings close to the under side of the roof boarding; the same shall be done with redwood so as to effectually check all connection from one building to another. Where a large building is divided into tenements the boarding shall be applied on each dividing partition. The distance apart of each dividing partition shall not exceed 25 feet.

[THICKNESS OF FOUNDATION WALLS FOR FRAME BUILDINGS.]

Brick foundations for frame buildings used as dwellings, one and two stories in height, must not be less than 8 inches thick, and not over 4 feet high. When the foundations are more than 4 feet high they must not be less than 12 inches thick.

All foundations for three-story frame buildings shall not be less than 12 inches thick, and for buildings over three stories the foundation shall not be less than 16 inches thick.

Where the foundation walls are used for embankment or retaining walls they shall be increased 4 inches in thickness for every 4 feet or part thereof in height; said walls, however, shall be increased to a greater thickness if in the judgment of the Board of Fire Wardens the same is necessary for the safety thereof.

[FRAMING.]

No floor joist except attic is to rest on a ribbon; every story is to be framed separately and every tier of joists is to have top and bottom plates. Said ribbon shall have a solid row of bridging at the ceiling line.

[BRIDGING.]

All stud walls or petitions hereafter built, altered or repaired, shall have not less than one row of bridging for every 14 feet in height, or fraction thereof. Said bridging is in all cases to extend to the lathing or sheeting, so as to prevent the passage of fire and smoke, and shall be the same thickness as the studding.

[UNDERPINNING.]

Underpinning shall never be less than 3 inches in thickness by the full width of the studding above.

SECTION 64. Section 39 shall apply to buildings outside the fire limits, excepting that the thickness of the furring against brick walls is not limited to one inch in thickness, but when a chimney breast is furred out the space between the chimney and the breast shall be so bridged or intercepted that the passage of fire and smoke is intercepted.

[STOVEPIPES AND CHIMNEYS—DUTY OF FIRE WARDENS.]

SECTION 65. It shall be the duty of the Chief Engineer of the Fire Department, the Assistant Chief Engineer, the Assistant Engineers and the Fire Marshals, in their official capacities to cause every stovepipe and chimney to be carried up at least four feet above the extreme height of the building to which such pipe or chimney is attached; and should they deem them unsafe to the building or buildings adjoining they shall order the same to be carried up at least four feet above the extreme height of the building to which such pipe or chimney is attached, and should they deem them unsafe to the building or buildings adjoining they shall order the same to be carried four feet above the extreme top of said building or adjoining buildings; and if, in the opinion of a majority of the Board of Fire Wardens, a sheet-iron pipe is not sufficient for the safety of the building or buildings, they shall inform the owner or owners, or the person having control thereof, and order a brick or earthen chimney, as provided in this order, which order shall be complied with within ten days, or such less number of days as may be prescribed by such Board of Fire Wardens; provided, that hotels and restaurants shall in all cases provide brick chimneys to be used instead of stovepipes.

[FACTORIES AND WAREHOUSES.]

SECTION 66. No frame building now used as a dwelling shall hereafter be used as a factory, warehouse, or for any other purpose, excepting the same be altered to conform to the provisions of this order.

[FRAME FACTORIES NOT OVER TWO STORIES HIGH.]

The exterior and bearing walls of frame buildings used as factories, two stories high or less (height of buildings limited to 30 feet), shall be built of 2x6 inch studs, 16 inches from centers; foundation thereof, if of brick, stone or concrete, shall be not less than 12 inches in thickness.

[FACTORIES OVER TWO STORIES HIGH.]

All frame buildings more than two stories high, hereafter erected or enlarged, to be used as factories, shall be constructed as follows: (a) The weights of all the floors shall be concentrated at certain points, and no support shall rest directly upon a stud wall, but all beams, girders, etc., supporting floors, shall rest directly on posts.

[FLOORS.]

(b) Said beams, girders, etc., supporting floors, shall be not more than 9 feet apart; upon these shall rest a double floor. The under floor shall extend from one girder or beam to another and shall not be less than 3 inches thick. The upper floor shall be not less than 1½ inches thick. A layer of mortar ¾ inches thick shall be placed between the two floors.

All planks shall be laid to the ends of the timbers.

[ROOF.]

The roof shall be covered with incombustible materials.

[STUDS.]

The filling in between posts and walls shall be built of not less than 2x4-inch studs.

SECTION 67. The following sections, classified under heading of "Buildings Within Fire Limits," shall also apply verbatim with the limitations indicated in said sections, to all other buildings erected anywhere within the City and County of San Francisco, to wit:

Section 8—Strength of Materials.
Section 10—Footings.
Section 11—Foundations.
Section 12—Vaults Under Sidewalks.
Section 14—Fire Walls.
Section 15—Brick Piers.
Section 16—Brick Work.
Section 17—Columns and Posts.
Section 18—Girders.
Section 19—Floors and Roofs (Carrying Capacity.)
Section 21—Attic (Dividing into Compartments.)
Sections 23 and 24—Elevators.
Section 25—Skylights.
Section 26—Shafts.
Sections 27 and 28—Fire Escapes and Stand Pipes.
Section 29—Shutters.
Section 30—Anchors and Ties.
Section 35—Spark Catchers.
Section 36—Heating Furnaces and Registers.
Section 37—Brick Buildings—Bay Windows.
Section 38—Frame Buildings—Bay Windows.
Section 40—Awnings.
Section 43—Smokehouses.

[RAISING OR LOWERING FRAME BUILDINGS TO GRADE.]

SECTION 68. Frame buildings within the fire limits may be raised or lowered to the official grade of the street by permission in writing of the Board of Supervisors, provided that in case said building is to be raised, a brick basement or foundation shall be built under it up to the line of the curb level, of such dimensions as is required by Section 63.

[PERMIT TO KINDLE FIRES.]

SECTION 69. No person shall kindle or light, or cause to be kindled or lighted, any bonfire without first having obtained a written permit from the Mayor.

[PERMIT TO KINDLE FIRE ON STREETS.]

(Fire used in laying roofs or pavements and engines on wharves, etc.)

SECTION 70. No person shall kindle or use, or cause to be kindled or used, any fire upon a public street or highway, or anywhere in open air, in that portion of the city and county lying east of Larkin street and northeast of Ninth street, without first having obtained a written permit so to do, signed by the Mayor and approved by a majority of the Committee of the Board of Supervisors on Fire Department.

But this section shall not include fire in furnaces necessarily used in laying roofs or pavement, nor the fire used upon the wharves in the discharge of vessels, nor to fire in the open air upon private property, necessarily used in setting tires upon the wheels of vehicles, or in heating tar or pitch in the construction or repair of boats or vessels.

[PORTABLE LIGHTS: PROTECTION COMBUSTIBLE MATERIALS.]

SECTION 71. No person shall use any portable light in any building or place where combustible materials are kept, unless such light be securely inclosed in a lantern; and no person shall use a light in any place where combustible materials shall be suspended above it, without so protecting it as to prevent such materials from falling upon leads or coming in contact with it.

[PROHIBITING THE MANUFACTURING OF MATCHES.]

SECTION 72. No person shall manufacture matches, erect or cause to be erected, any apparatus, machinery or building for the manufacture of matches within that portion of the City and County of San Francisco lying east of Ninth and Larkin streets.

[OBSTRUCTIONS ON STAIRS.]

SECTION 73. No stairs or stairway, passing from one floor to another in any building shall be covered with a permanent flooring, but may be inclosed with a board partition, running from the floor to the ceiling, to be provided with a door; said door to be kept free from all obstructions at all times, so as to give easy access to the Fire Department and Fire Patrol from one floor to another, provided this section shall not apply to buildings used for public assemblages.

No goods or obstructions of any kind shall be placed on the stairs of any building.

No explosive or inflammable compound or combustible material shall be stored or placed under any stairway of any building, or used in any such place or manner as to obstruct or render hazardous in case of fire.

[STORAGE OF CRUDE PETROLEUM.]

SECTION 74. It shall be unlawful, without the permission of the Board of Supervisors, for any person or persons, firm or corporation, to store, permit the storage of, or keep for sale within the corporate limits of the City and County of San Francisco, in a larger quantity than 100 gallons, to be always kept in metal cans in any one building or premises, or upon any street, any crude petroleum, unless the same be stored in building or warehouse.

Said building or warehouse must be of brick or stone, not exceeding one story in height, licensed for, used for and devoted exclusively to the storage of crude petroleum and its products, excepting such products from petroleum, the storage of which shall be hereafter provided for in Section 75.

MARTIN FENNELL & SON

Masons and Builders

OFFICE, BUILDERS' EXCHANGE

New Montgomery and Mission Sts.

Telephone Main 5110
Box 58

San Francisco

J. H. WILSON

MASON AND BUILDER

OFFICE, BUILDERS' EXCHANGE

New Montgomery and Mission Sts.

BOX 114   SAN FRANCISCO

For the BEST VALUE in

HATS
or
CAPS

... GO TO

C. HERRMANN & CO.

The <u>ONLY</u> Manufacturing Hatters

328 KEARNY ST., <u>NEAR PINE</u>

Everything in the Line of Hats or Caps Made to Order

[STORAGE OF GASOLINE.]

SECTION 75. It shall not be lawful for any person or persons, firm or corporation to store or permit the storage of, or keep for sale within the City and County of San Francisco, in a larger quantity than 50 gallons, always kept in metal cans, in any one building, upon any premises or street, any gasoline, or any product of petroleum or hydrocarbon liquid which shall flash or emit an inflammable vapor at a temperature below 110 degrees Fahrenheit, unless the same be kept in iron tanks and stored in a building or warehouse as provided in Section 76 of this Order.

[STORAGE AND USE OF GASOLINE, ETC.]

SECTION 76. Subdivision 1. It shall be unlawful for any person or persons, firm or corporation, to keep, store or permit the storage of, within the limits of the City and County of San Francisco, any gasoline, benzine or naphtha in greater quantities than fifty (50) gallons, to be always kept in metal cans or iron tanks, in any one building, or upon any premises or street, except in that portion of said city and county bounded and described as follows, to wit:

Commencing at the intersection of the shore line of the bay of San Francisco with the northerly and easterly end of King street; running thence in a southwesterly and westerly direction along the center line of King street to its intersection with the center line of Channel street; thence along the center line of Channel street to the center line of Potrero avenue; thence in a southerly direction along the center line of Potrero avenue to its intersection with the center line of Army street; thence in an easterly direction along the center line of Army street to its intersection with the center line of San Bruno road; thence in a southerly direction along the center line of San Bruno road to its intersection with the center line of Monongahela street; thence in a southwesterly direction along the center line of Monongahela street to its intersection with the center line of Temple street; thence in a southerly direction along the center line of Temple street to the county line of San Francisco; thence in an easterly direction following the county line of San Francisco to the shore line of the bay of San Francisco; thence in a northerly and northwesterly direction following the line of the water front to the point of commencement.

Subdivision 2. All buildings to be used for the storage of any of the articles named in Subdivision 1 of this section, and within that portion of the City and County of San Francisco which is particularly described in Subdivision 1 hereof, shall be constructed of brick or stone, not to exceed one story in height, and the walls of said buildings shall be not less than sixteen (16) inches in thickness, and must in all respects be fireproof and devoted exclusively to the storage of said articles.

[USE OF GASOLINE, ETC.]

Subdivision 3. No person or persons, firm or corporation, shall use for burning, heating or illuminating purposes any gasoline, benzine or naphtha within the the limits of the City and County of San Francisco, without a printed permit signed by the Chief Engineer of the Fire Department and the Fire Marshal of the City and County of San Francisco.

Applications for permits must be made in writing to either of the above-named officers, and must give the name of the applicant, the location of the premises, where it is proposed to use the above-named liquid and the manner in which it is proposed to use it.

Said permits will be granted by said officers in all cases except where, in their judgment, the use by the applicant in the manner provided by him would endanger the safety of life and property.

No charge whatever will be made for the issuance of said permits, and the Fire Marshal shall keep a record of all permits so issued.

[STORAGE OF KEROSENE OR COAL OIL IN CERTAIN LIMITS.]

Subdivision 4. It shall be unlawful for any person or persons, firm or corporation to keep, store or permit the storage of, within the limits of the

City and County of San Francisco, any kerosene or coal oil, in any one building or upon any premises or street, in larger quantities than five hundred (500) gallons, to be always kept in metal cans or iron tanks, except in that portion of said city and county which is particularly bounded and described in Subdivision 1 of this section, and all buildings to be used for the storage of the articles herein named shall be constructed as provided in Subdivision 2 of this section.

[CRUDE PETROLEUM, GASOLINE, ETC., NOT TO BE KEPT ON STREETS, ETC.]

SECTION 77. No crude petroleum, gasoline, naphtha, benzine, carbon oil, camphene, spirit gas, burning fluid or spirits of turpentine, shall be kept or stored in front of any building, or on any street, alley, wharf, lot or sidewalk, for a longer time than is sufficient to receive in store or in delivering the same; provided, such time shall not exceed six hours.

[ADULTERATION OF OILS PROHIBITED.]

SECTION 78. It shall be unlawful for any person or persons, firm or corporation, to mix, adulterate, or offer for sale any oils used for illuminating purposes, with benzine, naphtha, gasoline or any other substance; and all oils or fluids manufactured from petroleum or its products to be used for illuminating purposes, shall be required to stand a fire test of 110 degrees Fahrenheit, or better, before it shall flash or emit an inflammable vapor.

[CASES AND PACKAGES OF ILLUMINATING OILS TO BE STAMPED.]

SECTION 79. Any person or persons manufacturing or selling illuminating oils or fluids made of petroleum or its products shall be required to have stamped upon the case or package where easily seen, and in plain letters at least one-half an inch in length, the name of the manufacturer, where manufactured, the seller thereof and his place of business, together with the words, "Warranted to stand a fire test of 110 degrees Fahrenheit or better, before it will flash or emit an inflammable vapor," and any seller disposing of 5 gallons, more or less in metal cans or otherwise, shall furnish a certificate of the test as above whenever ordered by the Chief Engineer of the Fire Department and Fire Marshal, or either of them.

[QUALITY AND TEST OF OILS.]

SECTION 80. Any question arising under the provisions of this Order, as to the character of the oils herein mentioned, the same shall be tested by or in the presence of the Chief Engineer of the Fire Department and Fire Marshal, or either of them, and they or either of them shall decide the test of such oils, and the decision of either or both of them shall be final.

[THE INSTRUMENT TO BE USED IN TESTING OILS, AND THE DUTY OF THE FIRE WARDENS.]

SECTION 81. The said oils shall be tested and their quality determined by the Chief Engineer and the Fire Marshal, or either of those persons using Tagliabue's open tester; or Saybolt's electric spark tester; and it shall be the duty of the Fire Wardens, or either of them, to carry out the provisions of this Order in regard to all products of petroleum, and they or either of them may enter on any premises or place where such oils are manufactured, stored, kept or sold, for the purpose of examining such oils and its products, and no person shall hinder or obstruct such officer or officers in carrying out the foregoing provisions of the section.

[MANUFACTURE OF EXPLOSIVE OR COMBUSTIBLE CHEMICALS PROHIBITED WITHIN CERTAIN LIMITS.]

SECTION 82. Subdivision 1. No person shall manufacture acids or boil or refine oils, or maintain or erect, or cause to be erected, any works for manufacturing acids or for boiling or refining oils, within that portion of the city and county bounded by Steiner, Market, Castro and Twenty-sixth streets; San Bruno road, Brannan, Sixth and Channel streets, and the waters of the bay.

Subdivision 2. No person shall manufacture, or cause to be manufactured, or bring or cause to be brought into, or receive, or keep, or store, or suffer to remain in that portion of the city and county bounded by the dividing line between the City and County of San Francisco and San Mateo County, and by said line projected westerly a distance of ½ a mile into the Pacific Ocean; thence by a line northerly and easterly drawn ½ a mile uniformly distant from the shore line of said Pacific Ocean to the bay of San Francisco; thence by a line drawn easterly and southerly ½ a mile distant from the shore line and water front line of said bay of San Francisco to a point opposite to and ½ a mile easterly from a point where the southerly line of Islais creek channel intersects the waters of the bay; thence to the southerly line of Islais creek; thence by said southerly line of Islais creek channel to Kentucky street; thence by Kentucky street, Railroad avenue and San Bruno road to county line, except at the Government Reservation at the Presidio and Fort Mason (Black Point), for the purpose of the Government, or within 500 feet of any dwelling house or place of business, any blasting powder, or nitro-glycerine or daulin or dynamite or other explosive material or compound having an explosive power greater than that of ordinary gunpowder.

[PROHIBITING THE TRANSPORTATION OF NITRO-GLYCERINE.]

SECTION 83. No person shall convey or cause to be conveyed or assist in conveying from one place to another in this city and county, any liquid nitro-glycerine; and no person shall manufacture, or cause to be manufactured, or assist in manufacturing any liquid nitro-glycerine in this city and county; and no liquid nitro-glycerine shall be kept or stored in, about or on any premises in this city and county.

[PROHIBITING STORAGE OF PERCUSSION CAPS IN PREMISES WHERE GUN-POWDER, ETC., IS KEPT.]

SECTION 84. No person shall keep or store, or aid or assist any person in keeping or storing any package containing percussion or detonating caps in or about any building or premises where Hercules powder or dynamite or Giant powder or any other explosive powder greater than that of ordinary gunpowder is kept or stored.

[PROHIBITING THE CONVEYANCE OF GUNPOWDER, ETC., IN VEHICLES TRANSPORTING HERCULES, DYNAMITE OR GIANT POWDER.]

SECTION 85. No person shall receive or convey, or cause to be received or conveyed, or assist in receiving or conveying or transporting percussion or detonating caps, or gunpowder, or other blasting powder, or any other explosive substance, in or upon any vehicle, the same time in which Hercules, dynamite or giant powder or any other explosive material or compound having an explosive power greater than that of ordinary gunpowder, is being transported, carried or conveyed outside of that portion of the city and county described in Subdivision 2 of Section 82 of this Order; and this section shall not be construed to authorize any person to violate any of the provisions of said subdivision.

[PROHIBITING THE STORAGE OF HERCULES, DYNAMITE AND GIANT POWDER, ETC.—PROVISO.]

SECTION 86. No person shall keep or store, or caused to be kept or stored, or aid or assist any person in keeping or storing, Hercules, dynamite or giant powder into or upon any building or premises except in duly licensed magazines, or any vessels, railroad cars or vehicles receiving or keeping the same in the course of and for the purpose of transportation; provided this section shall not be construed to authorize any person to violate any of the provisions of Subdivision 2 of Section 82 of this Order.

SECTION 87. No person shall receive, keep or store, or cause to be received, kept or stored, or aid or assist any person in receiving, keeping or storing gunpowder in a larger quantity than 10 pounds, into or in any building or upon any premises except duly licensed powder magazines, unless the persons receiving, keeping or storing the same shall be authorized and licensed to sell gunpowder, or shall be in the daily use thereof in excavating rock.

No person shall receive, keep or store, or have at any one time in any one place, except duly licensed powder magazines, more than 50 pounds of gunpowder.

[MANUFACTURE OR STORAGE OF POWDER OR FIREWORKS PROHIBITED WITHIN CERTAIN LIMITS.]

SECTION 88. No person shall receive, keep or store, or have in any one place, more than 50 pounds of powder, or shall erect or maintain any building for the storage or keeping of powder, or for the manufacture and storage of fireworks, except within that portion of the city and county bounded on the westerly side by Kentucky street, Railroad avenue and San Bruno road, on the south by the county line, on the east by the water front of said city and county, and on the north by Islais creek.

It shall be unlawful for any person to sell, or to offer to sell, or to keep in his or her possession for sale, or to fire or discharge any fireworks commonly known or called bombs, or double-headers, or any rocket commonly known or called "Chinese sky rocket," or any sky rocket so made that when the same is fired off or the powder therein is burned, the material that is fastened to or may have been fastened to the stick retains or carries fire or still burns after the same is fired off or the powder is burned.

No person or persons, firm or corporation shall use, keep, sell or offer for sale any fireworks consisting of crackers, rockets, blue lights, candles, colored pots, lancewheels and other works of brilliant-colored fires, or any other kind of fireworks in any wooden building in that portion of the said city and county known and designated as the fire limits of said city and county.

No person or persons, firm or corporation shall keep, store, sell or offer for sale fireworks of any description within the City and County of San Francisco without a written or printed permit signed by the Chief Engineer of the Fire Department and the Fire Marshal of the City and County of San Francisco, and a license issued thereon by the Collector of Licenses. The said permits shall be issued only under the following regulations, viz.:

[SALES AT RETAIL.]

First—Permits for the sale of fireworks at retail, consisting of crackers, rockets, blue lights, candles, colored pots, lancewheels and other works of brilliant-colored fire, will be issued under the following regulations, viz:

Applications for permits must be made in writing to the Chief Engineer of the Fire Department and the Fire Marshal of the said city and county. Such application must give the name of the person or persons by whom the permit is desired, the location of the premises at which the goods are to be kept or sold, the nature of the business in which such person or persons are engaged at said premises, and the quantity and description of fireworks intended to be kept and offered for sale.

No permit will be issued for such sales to be made at any public building or premises where either of the following kinds of business is conducted or carried on: Where cigars or tobacco are kept for sale; where paints, oils or varnish are manufactured or kept, either for use or sale; where dry goods of any kind, toys (unless the toys are entirely removed from the premises during the period of the sale of fireworks), or other light material of a combustible nature are kept for sale; neither shall such sales be made in any carpenter shop, drug store, any building or premises where coal oil or kerosene oil or other products of petroleum are offered for sale or kept, or any building in which gunpowder, nitro-glycerine, camphene, burning fluid or other products or compounds containing any of said substances, matches, tar, pitch, resin or turpentine, hay, cotton or hemp are manufactured, stored or kept for sale.

All premises for which such permits are issued must be lighted with gas or electricity, and all lights must be protected with glass or wire coverings, or globes.

The person or persons to whom such permit is issued must sign an agreement not to permit smoking, nor the making or keeping of any fire in the room where said fireworks are kept, nor the use of any substance for illuminating purposes, except gas and electricity, upon or about the premises for which such permit is issued, nor to expose any of such fireworks for sale outside the walls of said building, nor in any door or window.

The entire amount of said fireworks shall not be in excess of the aggregate market value of two hundred dollars. Any person, firm or corporation violating any of the aforesaid regulations shall forfeit the permit and the license issued thereunder, and be guilty of a misdemeanor. All permits shall recite that the same are of no force or effect unless the person having such permit shall also have a license to sell, which license shall be issued by the Collector of Licenses on presentation of said permit and the payment of the license, which is hereby fixed at the sum of ten dollars per annum.

[STORAGE AND SALE AT WHOLESALE.]

Second—Permits for the storage and sale at wholesale of fireworks, consisting of crackers, rockets, blue lights, candles, colored pots, lancewheels and other works of brilliant-colored fires will be issued under the following regulations:

Applications must be made in writing to the Chief Engineer of the Fire Department and the Fire Marshal of the city and county in the form required by retail permits.

No permit will be issued for such storage or sales at wholesale in that portion of the city and county known and designated as the fire limits of said city and county in other than brick or stone buildings. No permit shall be issued for the storage or sale at wholesale of any of said articles in any building in which the sale of fireworks at retail would not be authorized under the rules governing the granting of permits for retail sales. Nor will the storage or sale at wholesale of any of said articles be permitted in any building, any part for which is used for dwelling or sleeping purposes.

Smoking of tobacco or opium must not be permitted in any building for which such permit has been issued. Any permit issued pursuant to the foregoing regulations may be revoked by the Chief Engineer of the Fire Department and the Fire Marshal at any time when in their opinion the public interest so require, which revocation shall operate as a forfeiture of the license.

Nothing in these regulations contained shall be deemed to authorize the storage and sale of tableau or colored fires containing sulphur or sulphate in any form.

All permits shall recite that the same are of no force or effect unless the person having such permit shall also have a license to sell, which license shall be issued by the Collector of License on presentation of said permit and the payment of the license fee, which is hereby fixed at the sum of fifty dollars per annum.

Third—The Collector of Licenses shall collect the licenses imposed by this Section and pay the same into the General Fund.

Fourth—The Auditor is hereby required to prepare, furnish and charge to the Collector of Licenses, the license blanks required by this section in the same manner as other license blanks are issued.

[GUNPOWDER, HOW KEPT.]

SECTION 89. Any person keeping, storing, or having more than 10 pounds of gunpowder in any one place, except duly licensed powder magazines, shall keep the same in an air-tight metallic vessel, which vessel shall be marked with the word "Gunpowder" in plain Roman letters, painted in white on a dark ground, not less than 3 inches in height, and of proportionate width, and shall be kept at all times conspicuously in view near the entrance of the premises where kept, and convenient for removal therefrom.

[GUNPOWDER, CONVEYANCE OF.]

SECTION 90. No person shall convey, or cause to be conveyed or assist in conveying, in any vehicle, any gunpowder, unless the same shall be securely tacked in close packages, nor unless such packages shall be securely covered while in the vehicle.

[GUNPOWDER—SHIPPING, DISCHARGING AND HAVING IT ON BOARD—
WHEN LANDED TO BE IMMEDIATELY FORWARDED.]

SECTION 91. No person shall discharge gunpowder from any vessel except from ships' side or tackles, and before the vessel shall have been hauled up to the wharf.

No vessel shall be permitted to remain at the wharf more than twenty-four (24) hours after receiving gunpowder on board; and if the vessel shall lie at the wharf over night, a watchman shall be kept on duty on board all night.

SECTION 92. All gunpowder deposited on the wharf for shipment shall be immediately passed on board the vessel which is to receive the same. All gunpowder landed or placed on any sidewalk, street or public way for forwarding or shipment, shall be forwarded or shipped immediately after it shall have been so landed or placed.

[VESSELS HAVING POWDER ABOARD TO BE AFLOAT AT LOW TIDE.]

SECTION 93. It shall be unlawful for any vessel to lie at any wharf, pier or bulkhead, with powder on board, unless such vessel will be afloat at low tide.

[VOID PERMITS.]

SECTION 94. No permit shall be considered valid unless all the requirements of this Order applying to the granting of permits shall have been complied with.

[FALSE ALARMS—REWARDS.]

SECTION 95. It shall be unlawful for any person to give false alarm of fire by means of fire-alarm boxes. A reward of one hundred dollars ($100) will be paid by the Board of Supervisors for such information as will lead to the arrest and conviction of any person or persons for giving a false alarm of fire by the above means.

SECTION 96. It shall be unlawful for any person to obstruct any fire hydrant or cistern in such a manner as to hide it from view at any point, or hinder free access thereto by the apparatus of the Fire Department, or construct any area or other wall or thing so as to interfere in any manner with any hydrant below the level of the curb.

[AREA WALLS.]

The owner or owners, agent or agents, or the person or persons having control of any building shall build or cause to be built when requested to do so by the Chief Engineer of the Fire Department a substantial brick wall, for the protection of the hydrant bend, to be not less than eight (8) inches in thickness, to be built from the bottom of the basement to the sidewalk, said wall to be built in any shape or in any portion of the basement that the Chief of Fire Department may direct, said walls to be plastered on both sides with good cement plaster, so as to be perfectly water tight should the hydrant bend burst.

Whenever the Chief of the Fire Department determines that it is necessary that a hydrant should be erected, he shall give or cause to be given two (2) days' notice in writing to the owner or owners, agent or agents, person or persons, having control of any building where he determines said hydrant is needed to be placed. And the said owner or owners, agent or agents, person or persons, having control thereof, shall cause said wall to be built for the protection of their goods in case of break in the bend, within two (2) days after the serving of said notice; any damage done by the bursting of the hydrant bend or pipe shall be at the owner's risk.

[BLOCKADE OF STREETS DURING FIRE.]

SECTION 97. It shall be the duty of the police at the time of a fire to place ropes or guards across all streets, alleys and lanes on which shall be situated any building on fire, and at such other points as they may deem expedient and necessary, and they shall prevent any and all persons, except owners and occupants and employees of buildings endangered by the existing fire from entering within the lines designated by ropes or guards, save and except officers of the Fire Department and firemen, who shall be known by their badge, the Fire Marshal, Deputy Fire Marshal, Fire Marshal Police, and Fire Patrol, or such other person as may have permission of the officers of the Fire Department or Police Commissioners; and any person entering within the line designated by the ropes and guards, and refusing to go outside of such lines when directed to do so by any police officer or officer of the Fire Department; shall be deemed guilty of misdemeanor, and upon conviction thereof shall be punished as provided for in this Order.

[BREAKING BLOCKADE.]

SECTION 98. No person or persons shall break through or attempt to break through such blockade, or run over with any vehicle the line of hose in use at any fire.

[STEAM ENGINES TO HAVE RIGHT OF WAY.]

SECTION 99. All steam engines and other movable apparatus belonging to the Fire Department, Fire Marshal and Fire Patrol shall have the paramount right of way through all streets, lanes, alleys, places and courts of the City and County of San Francisco, when running or going to a fire, and such apparatus, together with all other vehicles contiguous thereto, excepting street cars, shall take and keep the right side of the street, unless the same be obstructed; all street cars in the vicinity of any such apparatus, going to a fire shall retard or accelerate their speed, as the occasion may require, in order to give the apparatus of the Fire Department, the Fire Marshal and the Fire Patrol the unobstructed use of the street for the time being.

SECTION 100. It shall be unlawful for any person having the control of any vehicle to permit the same to obstruct or delay the progress of the apparatus or other vehicles of the Fire Department, Fire Marshal or Fire Patrol while going to a fire or responding to an alarm of fire; and it shall be unlawful for any person or persons to in any manner obstruct the same while responding to an alarm of fire.

[INJURING APPARATUS PROHIBITED.]

SECTION 101. No person or persons shall willfully injure any enginehouse, hose, horse or horses, engine, carriage or other apparatus of the Fire Department in this city and county.

[REWARD FOR ARREST OF OFFENDERS.]

SECTION 102. The Mayor of this city and county is hereby authorized to offer a reward, not exceeding $250, for the arrest and conviction of any person or persons committing the misdemeanor described in the last section.

[PROHIBITING WATER BEING DRAWN FROM HYDRANTS—PROVISO.]

SECTION 103. No person shall open or in any way cause water to flow, or draw water from any of the hydrants erected or hereafter erected by the authorities of this city and county, or at their request by any corporation duly organized to supply said city and its inhabitants with water, except in case of fire (or for other necessary purposes for the benefit of the city), without a permit from the Chief Engineer or Assistant Chief Engineer of the Fire Department.

It shall be the duty of the Chief of Police to enforce the provisions of this section.

[CONSTRUCTION OF PROVISION OF PRECEDING SECTION.[

SECTION 104. The provisions of the preceding section shall not be so construed as to prevent the Spring Valley Water Works from opening the hydrants connected with their works therein described, or drawing their water therefrom at any time when the same are not actually used for fire purposes, provided the same shall not be used for the purpose of selling the water.

[PENALTY.]

SECTION 105. Any person who shall violate any of the provisions of Sections 82, 83, 84, 85, 86 of this Order shall be deemed guilty of a misdemeanor, and upon conviction thereof shall be punished as hereafter provided

Fine Calf Shoes to Order, $3.50
Fine Calf, Hand Sewed, $6.00

GEORGE POLLOCK

REPAIRING WHILE YOU WAIT

202 Powell Street,   Between O'Farrell and Geary Streets

---

in this Order; and it shall be the duty of all police officers to at once notify the Chief Engineer of the Fire Department upon their becoming cognizant of the violation of any of the provisions of the sections enumerated in this section.

[SMOKE STACKS AND CHIMNEYS.]

SECTION 106. Whenever in the judgment of the Board of Fire Wardens or upon the complaint of the majority of the residents adjacent thereto, any smoke stack, chimney flue or stove-pipe endangers the surrounding property by fire, or annoys the residents in the neighborhood with smoke, soot or cinders, the Fire Wardens shall cause the same to be abated, altered or improved as they may think most suitable for the protection of the surrounding property, and conducive to the comfort of the residents in the vicinity.

[MANUFACTURE OF GAS.]

SECTION 107. No person or persons, firm or corporation shall, in the City and County of San Francisco, without permit of the Board of Supervisors, erect any works or apparatus for the manufacture of gas. within the district bounded by the water front, Larkin, Bay, Devisadero, Ridley, Castro, Sixteenth, Center, Caroline and Channel streets.

[BOARD OF FIRE WARDENS.]

SECTION 108. The Board of Fire Wardens shall consist of the Chief Engineer, Assistant Chief Engineer, the Assistant Engineers, and the Fire Marshal, and any act done by a majority of said Board shall be deemed to be the act of the whole Board.

They shall organize by electing one of its members as Chairman and one Secretary. They shall hold regular monthly meetings, and other meetings during the month when occasion requires it. Special meetings may be called by any member of the Board (in writing), to transact business.

The Secretary of the Board shall notify in writing each member of the Board of any and all meetings.

[ARSON—REWARD FOR ARREST AND CONVICTION OF THE OFFENDERS.]

SECTION 109. Whenever a fire shall appear to have been caused by incendiarism, or when any bonfire shall have been kindled or fire shall have been set to a building or structure in violation of the provisions of this Order, the Mayor may, upon application of the Fire Marshal or at his discretion offer a reward of not more than $250 for the arrest and conviction of the offenders and the Mayor may at any time when in his opinion it appears expedient, offer a standing reward not to exceed $250 for the arrest and conviction of any person guilty of arson, or of any attempt of arson, and any reward which may become payable under the order of the Mayor, shall be paid out of the Treasury of the city and county.

[SHAVINGS, HAY, STRAW OR LITTER.]

SECTION 110. Subdivision 1. Each person in the City and County of San Francisco, making, using or having the charge or control of shavings, hay, straw, sacks, bags, litter or any other combustible waste or fragments, shall, at the close of each day cause the same to be securely stored or disposed of, so as to be safe from fire.

Subdivision 2. All receptacles for wastes, rags, paper and other substance liable by spontaneous combustion or otherwise to cause fire must be made of incombustible material.

[REMOVAL OF HAY, STRAW, ETC., RENDERED USELESS BY FIRE.]

The owner or any person having in his possession or under his control upon any premises within this city and county any hay, straw, or forage of any kind, bales of wool, cotton or paper, or other like substances, which have been rendered useless and unmerchantable by reason of any fire on said premises, shall within twenty-four hours after notice in writing from the Chief Engineer of the Fire Department so to do, remove from said premises all such hay, straw or other forage, or other substances above mentioned as may have been burned or rendered useless as aforesaid, and cause the same to be deposited in such place as may be designated by the Municipal Authorities for the deposit of debris, etc.

[GAS LIGHT IN SHOW WINDOWS.]

SECTION 111. All gas lights or burners in show windows, shall have a wire netting or screen over and around them: but this shall not apply to stationary gas reflectors in the upper portion of the windows.

[ASHES.]

SECTION 112. It shall be unlawful for any person or persons to deposit any ashes, cause the same to be deposited or placed, or to permit or suffer the same to be or remain in any wooden vessel or receptacle, or any vessel or receptacle composed or made of combustible material, but said ashes shall be placed and kept in some safe depository or receptacle of galvanized iron or other incombustible material, and not less than two inches from any woodwork or structure.

[DANGEROUS BUILDINGS, ETC.]

SECTION 113. Whenever in the judgment of the Board of Fire Wardens of this city and county any building, or any portion thereof, or any appurtenance thereto, or any structure, or any chimney, smokestack, stove, oven, furnace or thing connected with any building or upon any premises, is dangerous, defective or unsafe, the said Board shall cause the same to be torn down, altered, repaired or rebuilt, or such work to be done thereon as the said Board may deem necessary to render the same safe.

Any person, firm, company or corporation who violates, disobeys, omits, neglects or refuses to comply with the foregoing section or any of the provisions thereof, when requested or notified in writing to comply therewith, shall be deemed guilty of a misdemeanor and, upon conviction thereof, shall be punished as hereinafter provided in this Order.

[WOODEN BUILDINGS WITHIN THE FIRE LIMITS DAMAGED BY FIRE TO THE EXTENT OF 40 PER CENT OR MORE.]

When in the judgment of the Board of Fire Wardens any wooden building within the fire limits is damaged by fire to the extent of 40 per cent or more of its actual value, to be estimated above the line of the sidewalk in front of said building, the said Board shall immediately notify the owner or owners thereof or person having the control of the same, in writing, to remove the same forthwith, and the person receiving such notice shall, within 48 hours after receiving the same, comply with the requirements thereof.

In the event of a dispute as to the amount of damage caused by fire, between the owner or person having the control of such building and the

Board of Fire Wardens, said dispute shall be determined by arbitration of competent mechanics, said owner or person having control of the same to select one arbitrator, the Board of Fire Wardens the other; and in case the arbitrators so chosen cannot agree, they shall select a third and the decision of the majority shall be final and conclusive; all the expenses of the arbitration to be paid by the owner.

[BUILDINGS WITH INSUFFICIENT EGRESSES.]

Whenever, in the judgment of the Board of Fire Wardens, any building in this city and county is in a situation or condition to be dangerous to the lives or safety of the occupants, or persons frequenting the same, by reason of insufficient egresses or facilities for escape in case of fire, said Board shall forthwith notify the owner, agent, lessee or person having the control of said building, in writing, to supply, provide and equip the same with said facilities for escape as said Board may determine; and the person receiving such notice shall, within five days thereafter, comply with the requirements thereof.

[FIRE WARDENS TO STOP CONSTRUCTION OF CERTAIN BUILDINGS, ETC.]

The Fire Wardens shall have power to stop the construction of any building or the making of any alterations or repairs to any building within this city and county when the same is done in a reckless or careless manner, or in violation of any of the provisions of this Order, and to order in writing or by parole any and all persons in any way or manner whatever engaged in so constructing, altering or repairing any such building, to stop and desist therefrom, and the person or persons so ordered shall immediately comply therewith.

[UNOCCUPIED BUILDINGS TO BE SECURED.]

SECTION 114. Whenever any unoccupied building is not properly secured, the Fire Wardens or acting Assistant Engineers, or either of them, shall immediately visit the premises and notify the owner or person having control of the same, to forthwith secure the same, so as to prevent evil-disposed persons from gaining access thereto, and the persons so notified as aforesaid shall immediately comply therewith.

[WIRES PASSING THROUGH BUILDINGS.]

SECTION 115. All wires used for electric or other purposes, over six in number, placed in one bunch and passing through to the inside of any building, shall be inclosed and enveloped in a metal tube; and where the said metal tube passes through the bridging of any building the said bridging shall be made tight and flush on all sides, so as to prevent the passage of fire or smoke from one floor to another.

[PERMISSION TO ERECT TENT OR STEAM ENGINES OR BOILERS.]

SECTION 116. No cloth-covered or tent building or cloth-lined building shall be constructed or maintained east of Gough and Valencia streets and north of Twenty-sixth street, projected to the bay, without permission of the

---

George H. Tay Company

TINNERS AND PLUMBERS
TOOLS AND SUPPLIES

Hot Water, Hot Air and Steam Heaters and Radiators

610 to 620 BATTERY STREET
SAN FRANCISCO

Board of Supervisors, and after a copy of such permit has been filed in the office of the Chief Engineer and of the Fire Marshal, and for a time limited in such permit. No person or persons shall erect or cause to be erected, or shall maintain or use, within the City and County of San Francisco any cupola, furnace, or other appliance for melting iron or any other metal, or shall erect or cause to be erected, or shall maintain or use within the City and County of San Francisco any steam engine and boiler, or steam boiler, without permission from the Board of Supervisors; and no such permit to erect or use any steam engine and boiler, or steam boiler, shall be granted unless the person applying for the same shall file with the Clerk of the Board of Supervisors a certificate signed by the manufacturer or by a competent engineer, who shall also be a competent boiler inspector, of the soundness of the same at the date of the application for said permit. And the person or persons to whom such permit may be granted shall employ a competent person to attend to such engine and boiler, or steam boiler, who shall have a certificate of his competency signed by the said engineer; such certificate shall be filed in the office of the Chief Engineer. All cupolas, furnaces, engines and boilers, or steam boilers, must be constructed, erected and maintained to the satisfaction of the Chief Engineer of the Fire Department and the Fire Wardens. And all permits therefor may be revoked at the pleasure of the Board of Supervisors.

[GAS ENGINES.]

No gas engine shall be erected, maintained or used above the first story of any building, without first obtaining permission from the Board of Supervisors, and the approval of the Mayor.

SECTION 117. The Fire Wardens shall have full power in passing upon any question relating to the mode and manner of construction or materials used in the erection, alterations or repairs of any building or other structure provided for in this Order, and to make the same conform to the true intent and meaning of the several provisions thereof. They shall have discretionary power to vary or modify the provisions of this Order upon application therefor in writing in all cases of alterations of old buildings or the use of party walls belonging to different owners where the same cannot be taken down; and where there are practical difficulties in the way of carrying out the strict letter of this Order, so that the spirit of the Order is complied with, the public safety secured and substantial justice done; but no such deviation shall be allowed except a record of the same be kept by the said Board of Fire Wardens and a certificate issued to the party applying for the same.

[ENFORCEMENT OF PROVISIONS OF THIS ORDER.]

SECTION 118. The Chief Engineer of the Fire Department, Assistant Chief Engineer, the Assistant Engineers, the Clerk of the Fire Department, the Fire Commissioners and the Fire Marshal are directed to see that the provisions of this Order are enforced, and to that end are hereby empowered, whenever any complaint shall be made to them, or either of them, of the violation of any of the provisions of this Order, and they, or either of them, have reasonable grounds to believe that any of the provisions of this Order are being violated by any person, to enter on any premises or place, or go into any building about which complaint is made, or upon or in which they, or either of them, have reasonable grounds to believe that any of the provisions of this Order are being violated. And said officers are directed to make complaints in the Police Court against any person violating any of the provisions of this Order.

[HEIGHT OF FENCES.]

SECTION 119. No person owning, possessing, occupying or having the control of any premises or any real property, shall put, place, construct, erect, build, maintain, or suffer to be or remain thereon any fence, or division wall, or any framework, boards or material used as a fence, which shall exceed ten feet in height from the ground, or which shall exceed ten feet in height from the level of the street adjoining said premises or said real property, without first obtaining a permit so to do from the Board of Supervisors; but no such permit shall be granted unless the person applying therefor, and to whom such permit is granted, shall first obtain, and present to the Board of Supervisors, the written consent of the person or persons having ownership and possession of the adjoining premises affected thereby; provided, that where such fence or wall is constructed around a public garden, or place of resort where an admission fee is charged, no signature or consent of the adjacent owners shall be required.

[HEIGHT OF LUMBER PILES.]

SECTION 120. No person or persons, firm, company or corporation, shall within the City and County of San Francisco, place or pile, or cause to be placed or piled, any lumber or timber to a greater height than thirty-five feet, measuring in all cases from the line of the sidewalk to the highest point of said lumber or timber pile.

[PROVIDING FOR OFFICIAL BADGES OF THE FIRE DEPARTMENT, AND PASSES ISSUED TO PERSONS OTHER THAN MEMBERS THEREOF.]

SECTION 121. The Board of Fire Commissioners shall adopt an official badge for the Fire Department, the design and material of which shall be selected by them, and a copy of the same filed in the office of the Board of Supervisors.

Said Board of Fire Commissioners shall provide each member of the Fire Department with one of said badges, to be worn by them while on duty, on the outside of their outer garment, and on the left breast thereof.

No person shall falsely represent himself to be a member of the Fire Department of this city and county, or wear or use, or have in his possession, or under his control, any official badge of said Fire Department, unless he is a regular member thereof.

The Board of Fire Commissioners may, at the beginning of each fiscal year, issue passes to persons other than members of the Fire Department for the purpose of securing their admittance within the lines designated by ropes or guards at fires.

Not more than one hundred and fifty such passes shall be issued during any one fiscal year, and they shall expire at the end of each fiscal year. A record of the issuance of such passes shall be kept in the office of the Board of Fire Commissioners, with the date of issuance, the name of the person to whom issued, and the number of the pass. The Board of Fire Commissioners may, however, at any time, revoke and annul any and all such passes at its pleasure. Said passes shall not be transferable, and no person shall wear, or use, or have in his possession, or under his control, any such pass unless the same was issued to him by the Board of Fire Commissioners.

[PENALTY.]

SECTION 122. Any person, firm, company or corporation who violates, disobeys, omits, neglects or refuses to comply with, or who resists or opposes the execution of any of the provisions of this Order shall be deemed guilty of a misdemeanor, and upon conviction thereof shall be punished by a fine not exceeding five hundred dollars, or by imprisonment in the County Jail for not more than six months, or by both such fine and imprisonment; and every such person, firm, company or corporation shall be deemed guilty of a separate offense for every day such violation, disobedience, omission, neglect or refusal shall continue, and shall be subject to the penalty imposed by this section for each and every such separate offense; and any builder or contractor who shall construct any building in violation of any of the provisions of this Order, and any architect having charge of such building, who shall permit it to be so constructed, shall be liable to the penalties provided and imposed by this section.

[REPEALING CONFLICTING ORDERS.]

SECTION 123. Orders No. 2757, 2845 and 1917 of the Board of Supervisors of this city and county, and all Orders of said Board amendatory thereof, and all Orders or parts of Orders in conflict with any of the provisions of this Order are hereby repealed.

OFFICE SPECIALTY M'F'G CO.

MANUFACTURERS OF

Vault and Office Furniture
in Metal or Wood

29 New Montgomery Street   Grand Hotel Building
...San Francisco. Cal.

The Shannon Letter Filing Cabinet

Perfection of Speed and Security.

★

Rapid Roller Copier

Unerring Pressure. No Indexing of Copy Books.

Document Filing Cabinet

The Only Rational and Systematic Method of Filing Folded Papers.

★

System Reduced to Science

The Shannon Letter File is Used by Millions

★

Metal Roller Book Shelves

★

Schlicht's Ledger Indexes

★

The Card Index Cabinet is the Latest

★

Write or Visit Us

O. H. GREENEWALD, Pr.   D. H. BIBB, Vice Pr.   A. HEILBRONNER, Sec.

Golden Gate Lumber Co.

4 SUTTER ST., Cor. Sansome, SAN FRANCISCO, CAL.

(Agency California Lumber Co., Mills at Porter, Coos Bay, Or.)

YARDS and PLANING MILL at NORTH BEACH

Powell, Dupont, Stockton, Beach and North Point Streets

CUSHING·WETMORE·COMPANY
CONCRETE AND ARTIFICIAL STONE
508 CALIFORNIA ST
QUARRIES AT LOMBARD & WINTHROP STS
CRUSHED BLUE ROCK FOR SALE

MECHANICS' LIEN LAW
OF CALIFORNIA.

[CONSTITUTIONAL PROVISION.]

By Section 15 of Article XX. of our State Constitution, it is provided that: "Mechanics, material men, artisans, and laborers of every class, shall have a lien upon the property upon which they have bestowed labor or furnished material for the value of such labor done and material furnished, and the legislature shall provide, by law, for the speedy and efficient enforcement of such liens."—Cal. Const., Art. XX. Sec. 15.

[LIENS OF MECHANICS AND OTHERS UPON REAL PROPERTY UNDER THE PROVISIONS OF THE CODE OF CIVIL PROCEDURE.]

SECTION 1183—Code of Civil Procedure—Mechanics, material men, contractors, sub-contractors, artisans, architects, machinists, builders, miners and all persons and laborers of every class performing labor upon or furnishing materials to be used in the construction, alteration, addition to, or repair, either in whole or in part, of any building, wharf, bridge, ditch, flume, aqueduct, tunnel, fence, machinery, railroad, wagon-road, or other structure, shall have a lien upon the property upon which they have bestowed labor, or furnished materials, for the value of such labor done and materials furnished, whether at the instance of the owner or of any other person acting by his authority, or under him, as contractor or otherwise; and any person who performs labor in any mining claim or claims has a lien upon the same, and the works owned and used by the owners for reducing the ores from such mining claim or claims, for the work or labor done, or materials furnished, by each respectively, whether done or furnished at the instance of the owner of the building or other improvement, or his agent; and every contractor, sub-contractor, architect, builder, or other person having charge of any mining, or of the construction, alteration, addition to, or repair, either in whole or in part of any building or other improvement as aforesaid, shall be held to be the agent of the owner, for the purposes of this chapter. In case of a contract for the work, between the reputed owner and his contractor, the lien shall extend to the entire contract price, and such contract shall operate as a lien in favor of all persons, except the contractor, to the extent of the whole contract price; and after all such liens are satisfied, then as a lien for any balance of the contract price in favor of the contractor. All such contracts shall be in writing when the amount agreed to be paid thereunder exceeds one thousand dollars, and shall be subscribed by the parties thereto, and the said contract, or a memorandum thereof, setting forth the names of all the parties to the contract, a description of the property to be affected thereby, together with a statement of

BUILDING :: NEWS AND REVIEW

ESTABLISHED

AS A QUARTERLY IN 1879
AS A WEEKLY IN 1887
AS A MONTHLY IN 1880
AS A TRI-WEEKLY IN 1888

GEORGE H. WOLFE, Editor

FLOOD BUILDING   SAN FRANCISCO

As far as consistent with strict business principles, we give ADVANCE REPORTS of Building Projects before the Closing of Contracts, for the Special Use of Material Men, etc.

Published on Tuesdays, Thursdays and Saturdays ✣ $6.00 per Annum

the general character of the work to be done, the total amount to be paid thereunder, and the amount of all partial payments, together with the times when such payments shall be due and payable, shall, before the work is commenced, be filed in the office of the County Recorder of the county or city and county, where the property is situated, who shall receive one dollar for such filing; otherwise they shall be wholly void, and no recovery shall be had thereon by either party thereto; and in such case, the labor done and material furnished by all persons aforesaid, except the contractor, shall be deemed to have been done and furnished at the personal instance of the owner, and they shall have a lien for the value thereof. (Amendment approved March 15, 1887; Statutes and amendments 1887, 152; to take effect from and after its passage.)

The lien of mechanics and others on buildings and the land upon which they are erected as security for the amount due them for labor performed and material furnished, is the creation of Statute, being unknown either at common law or in equity, and the Statute creating it must be looked to, both for the right to such lien and the mode by which it can be secured.—98 Cal., 149; 97 Cal., 644.

The alteration of a building such as will change its form so that it may be considered a construction comes within the lien law.—24 Cal., 80. See 98 Cal., 374, 376.

A lien of a material man commences when the materials are ready for delivery at the place agreed on.—23 Cal., 208.

Sub-contractors may prevent the removal of a building by injunction when such removal would make their security insufficient.—33 Cal., 497.

Where specifications are referred to as annexed they become a part of the contract, and if not so annexed the contract and lien are void.—57 Cal., 61.

Services must be performed on the building sought to be made subject to the lien, otherwise they are not within the Statute.—40 Cal., 188.

The contractor must complete the contract to claim the benefit of the lien law, unless prevented by the other party.—31 Cal., 234-5; 48 Cal., 478.

An architect's certificate that laborers are paid concludes all parties if not obtained by fraud of owner.—54 Cal., 333.

A contract for extra work, if such condition is embodied in the contract may be verbal (54 Cal., 601) if the work conforms to the terms of the contract.—59 Cal., 1; 54 Cal., 601.

Lien is void if the law is not strictly complied with.—49 Cal., 337; 54 Cal., 218; 97 Cal., 644.

Where a contractor contracts to protect a building from liens the owner may retain enough to meet liens filed.—55 Cal., 179.

No foreclosure of a lien can be had until the debt is payable.—60 Cal., 439.

Material must have been furnished expressly by contract for the building sought to be charged.—99 Cal., 488.

A contractor's lien dates from commencement of work.—6 Cal., 295. See 23 Cal., 522; 44 Cal., 246-250; 61 Cal., 349.

An owner is liable only for amount due to contractor at date of, or subsequent to, service of notice.—62 Cal., 151; 64 Cal., 283; 65 Cal., 353; 67 Cal., 423.

A contractor for a building cannot recover damages for not being allowed to complete the building if the contract was not filed for record.—70 Cal., 221.

A mining superintendent is entitled to claim a lien on a mine if he performs manual labor.—70 Cal., 614.

A claim filed before the completion of a building cannot be enforced.—74 Cal., 273.

A material man who is not an original contractor must file his lien within thirty days after the completion of the building.—74 Cal., 432.

One who performs labor on a structure by request of a contractor is entitled to a lien.—75 Cal., 205.

Where a contractor furnishes a number of laborers he is entitled to a lien for the money due to him for their labor.—76 Cal., 578.

Materials must be actually used in a structure to entitle a material man to a lien.—80 Cal., 510; 83 Cal., 368.

One who supplies a mine with materials is entitled to a lien on the whole mine.—80 Cal., 510.

The amendment of 1887 makes homesteads liable to mechanics' liens filed after its passage.—81 Cal., 641.

A material man need not state in his lien how much has been furnished to each contractor separately where one who succeeds another assumes by consent all liabilities.—86 Cal., 617.

A material man's lien is limited to the amount of the contract price in the hands of the owner when the lien was filed.—86 Cal., 617.

Evidence to show that work sued for was not done in a workmanlike manner is admissible after a lienor introduces evidence to show that the labor was done in a good and workmanlike manner.—88 Cal., 146.

When 20 per cent is retained, the owner may deposit same in Court in case of contest between contractor and workmen or material men.—90 Cal., 631.

When the contract price of a structure exceeds One Thousand Dollars it must be written and recorded as provided by Section 1183 of the Code of Civil Procedure, and all payments of money must be made as stated therein.—88 Cal., 42.

No personal judgment can be recovered in an action to enforce a mechanics' lien as it is of the nature of a proceeding *in rem*. It is not a "claim" against an estate within the meaning of Subdivision 3 of Section 1880 of the Code of Civil Procedure.—88 Cal., 44.

Public buildings are not subject to a mechanics' lien. None can be enforced against a schoolhouse erected by a school district.—89 Cal., 114.

Where a party, in erecting a building, lets different contracts to various parties for the building of certain portions of it; these parties would be original contractors, and men employed by them would be entitled to file liens as laborers.

Papering or decorating a house is a proper subject matter of liens.—90 Cal., 375.

A material man, or a mechanic who furnishes materials to or does work for a contractor for the erection of a county building, upon giving written notice to the county of his claim, acquires as against the contractor, a prior right of payment of his claim from the unpaid portion of the contract price.—90 Cal., 543.

One furnishing materials which were neither to be used nor used in the construction of a building is not entitled to a lien.—90 Cal., 213.

Persons contracting with an owner of a factory, to manufacture at their own shop the boiler, engine, feed-pipes and necessary attachments, and deliver them finished and complete and properly set them in the building, are material men. The work done by them on the premises of the owner, in placing them in position, did not convert them into contractors for the erection of the building or any part of it.—91 Cal., 140.

In case a contractor abandons his work and a new contract is made by owner, those claiming lien under abandond contract must file their liens within thirty days from time work ceased under unfinished contract.—102 Cal., 324.

A painter who contracts with the owner to paint a building and furnish the necessary materials therefor, is an original contractor. If his contract provides for payment of part of the contract price in land it does not render the contract void.—See Section 1184.—92 Cal., 255.

A description in a claim of lien of the property sought to be charged is sufficient if it enables a party familiar with the locality to identify the premises.—94 Cal., 205.

Where a building contract provides that the contractor shall do the work contracted for according to certain drawings and specifications referred to in the contract as being "hereto annexed," the drawings and specifications are an essential part of the contract, and they should be filed in the Recorder's office, and a failure so to do destroys the validity of the contract.—94 Cal., 229. Specifications, etc., must be filed with memorandum of contract.—102 Cal., 443.

An owner or contractor can file either the contract, or a memorandum; if he files the contract, he must file the whole of it, including the drawing and specifications, if they were made a part thereof; the memorandum must contain all the matters required by the Statute to be stated therein.—94 Cal., 229.

The memorandum filed can have no higher force than the contract itself, if the contract fails to comply with the requirements of the Statute, the memorandum will also fail.—94 Cal., 229.

In an action to foreclose a lien under Sections 1183 and 1184 of the Code of Civil Procedure, where the claimants sue for materials furnished, at the special instance and request of the owner, the contract with the original contractors being void, it is not necessary the complaint should set out the original contract and allege its invalidity; the plaintiff may show such matters in evidence.—94 Cal., 558.

Under Section 1183 of the Code of Civil Procedure the failure to file the contract or memorandum containing the statements required by the statute renders the contract wholly void for all purposes.—94 Cal., 229; 97 Cal., 644; 98 Cal., 149.

The reasonable value of work done and materials furnished in the erection of a building is recoverable, although their value exceeds one thousand dollars. And a recovery is not defeated either by the fact that the implied contract for reasonable value was not recorded, or that the work and materials were done and furnished in pursuance of a written contract which was not filed for record in accordance with the Statute.—95 Cal., 390.

A minor's guardian cannot subject the property of the ward to a mechanics' lien, for work done and materials furnished for the erection or repair of a building, the property of the ward, without first obtaining an order of the court, authorizing the guardian to make the contract.—96 Cal., 484.

The right of a laborer or material-man to create a lien under the mechanics' lien law is personal, and cannot be assigned.—97 Cal., 254.

SECTION 1184. No part of the contract price shall, by the terms of any such contract, be made payable, nor shall the same, or any part thereof, be paid in advance of the commencement of the work, but the contract price shall, by the terms of the contract, be made payable in installments at specified times after the commencement of the work, or on the completion of specified portions of the work, or on the completion of the whole work; provided, that at least twenty-five per cent of the whole contract price shall be made payable at least thirty-five days after the final completion of the contract. No payment made prior to the time when the same is due, under the terms and conditions of the contract, shall be valid for the purpose of defeating, diminishing, or discharging any lien in favor of any person, except the contractor, but as to such liens such payments shall be deemed as if not made, and shall be applicable to such liens, notwithstanding that the contractor to whom it was paid may thereafter abandon his contract, or be or become indebted to the reputed owner in any amount for damages or otherwise, for non-performance of his contract or otherwise. As to all liens, except that of the contractor, the whole contract price shall be payable in money, and shall not be diminished by any prior or subsequent indebtedness, offset, or counterclaim in favor of the reputed owner and against the contractor; no alteration of any such contract shall effect any lien acquired under the provisions of this Chapter. In case such contracts and alterations thereof do not conform substantially to the provisions of this Section, the labor done and materials furnished by all persons except the contractor, shall be deemed to have been done and furnished at the personal instance and request of the person who contracted with the contractor, and they shall have a lien for the value thereof. Any of the persons mentioned in Section eleven hundred and eighty-three, except the contractor, may at any time give to the reputed owner a written notice that they have performed labor or furnished materials, or both, to the contractor, or other person acting by the authority of the reputed owner, or that they have agreed to do so, stating in general terms the kind of labor and materials, and the name of the person to or for whom the same was done or furnished, or both, and the amount in value, as near as may be, of that already done or furnished, or both, and of the whole agreed to be done or furnished, or both. Such notice may be given by delivering the same to the reputed owner personally, or by leaving it at his residence or place of business, with some person in charge, or by delivering it to his architects, or by leaving it at their residence or place of business, with some person in charge, or by posting it in a conspicuous place upon the mining claim or improvement. No such notice shall be invalid by reason of any defect of form, provided it is sufficient to inform the reputed owner of the substantial matters herein provided for, or to put him upon inquiry as to such matters. Upon such notice being given, it shall be the duty of the person who contracted with the contractor to, and he shall, withhold from his contractor, or from any other person acting under such reputed owner, and to whom by said notice the said labor or materials, or both, have been furnished, or agreed to be furnished, sufficient money due or that may become due, to such contractor or other person, to answer such claim, and any lien that may be filed therefor for record under this chapter, including counsel fees not exceeding one hundred dollars in each case, besides reasonable costs provided for in this chapter (Amendment approved March 15, 1887; Statutes and Amendments 1887, 152; to take effect from and after its passage).

Where a contractor abandons a contract before completion, the owner cannot complete the work at his expense without giving notice required by the the contract.—48 Cal., 478.

Payments made by contractor to material men must be applied to materials furnished the building and not to an open account.—54 Cal., 640.

One who performs labor for a contractor must give notice of this claim in some way to the owner of the property before he has paid the contractor in full for the building or improvements which the contractor is employed to construct.—76 Cal., 508.

Where a contract is invalid, material men and laborers are deemed employed directly by the owner, though they cannot recover a judgment against him personally.—81 Cal., 170; 81 Cal., 640.

Where a building contract is void, by reason of failure to record, it is only so between the parties. It does not effect the right of material men or laborers to a lien.—78 Cal., 193.

A notice of lien need not contain an itemized account, nor state the value of labor performed, or materials furnished.—81 Cal., 144.

Contracts for a price over one thousand dollars are void unless recorded; and if void, sub-contractors, laborers and material men may enforce their liens without regard to what is due to the contractor.—81 Cal., 641; 81 Cal., 170.

Notice to the owner is not requisite unless there is a valid contract between the contractor and owner.—81 Cal., 170.

The amendments of 1887 to Sections 1183 and 1184 of the Code of Civil Procedure do not effect contracts where the price is less than one thousand dollars.—82 Cal., 42.

Section 1184 of the Code of Civil Procedure applies only where contracts are in excess of One Thousand Dollars.—86 Cal., 22.

Whether a contract is recorded or not the owner must, on notice, withhold from the contractor sufficient money to pay the material man's claim.—87 Cal., 589.

Neglect of the owner to retain for thirty-five days after the completion of the work and contract, and to pay over 25 per cent. of the contract price, renders him liable to those entitled to that extent, less any lawful credits.—90 Cal., 590.

A laborer or material man must file his claim therefor in the Recorder's office within the time limited by the Statute.—94 Cal., 229.

Where a contract is void there is neither a "contract" nor an "original contractor," and a laborer or material man, in order to perfect his lien, cannot file his claim therefor until after the actual completion of the building, or until after there had been a cessation from labor for thirty days upon the unfinished building.—94 Cal., 229.

SECTION 1185—The land upon which any building, improvement, or structure is constructed, together with a convenient space about the same, or so much as may be required for the convenient use and occupation thereof, to be determined by the court on rendering judgment, is also subject to the lien, if, at the commencement of the work, or of the furnishing of the materials for the same, the land belonged to the person who caused said building, improvement or structure to be constructed, altered or repaired, but if said person owned less than a fee-simple estate in such land then only his interest therein is subject to such lien. (Amendment, approved March 24, 1874; Amendments 1873-4, 351; took effect July 1, 1874.)

A lessee's estate is subject to a mechanic's lien, and may be sold to satisfy it.—36 Cal., 623; 80 Cal., 275.

A lessee cannot bind his lessor by a mechanics' lien unless the lessor has by some act made his estate liable.—36 Cal., 623.

The amount of land subject to a lien for work done or materials furnished for a structure thereon is an issuable fact, to be determined by the Court where presented by the pleadings. 94 Cal., 205.

"The land upon which a building is erected, together with a convenient space about the same," is construed to mean such space or area of land as is necessary to the enjoyment of the building, for the purpose for which it was constructed, and the uses to which it is put must determine the quantity of land necessary to the convenient use and occupation of the building.—98 Cal., 285.

A race track and training stables, grand stands, corrals and other improvements belonging to an agricultural park association and situated upon its fair grounds tract, is not necessary to the convenient use and occupation of a building erected for a hotel, club house and saloon upon such fair grounds tract, and cannot be made subject to a lien for the erection of such building.—98 Cal., 285.

SECTION 1186—The liens provided for in this chapter are preferred to any lien, mortgage, or other incumbrance which may have attached subsequent to the time when the building, improvement, or structure was commenced, work done, or materials were commenced to be furnished; also to any lien, mortgage or other incumbrance of which the lienholder had no notice, and which was unrecorded at the time the building, improvement or structure was commenced, work done, or the materials were commenced to be furnished.

SECTION 1187—Every original contractor, within sixty days after the completion of his contract, and every person, save the original contractor, claiming the benefit of this chapter, must within thirty days after the completion, of any building, improvement or structure, or after the completion, alteration, addition to, or repair thereof, or the performance of any labor in a mining claim, file for record with the county recorder of the county in which such property, or some part thereof, is situated, a claim containing a statement of his demand, after deducting all just credits and offsets, with the name of the owner or reputed owner, if known, and also the name of the person by whom he was employed, or to whom he furnished the materials, with a statement of the terms, time given, and conditions of his contract, and also a description of the property to be charged with the lien; sufficient for identification, which claim must be verified by the oath of himself or some other person; any trivial imperfection in the said work, or in the construction of any building, improvement, or structure, of the alteration, addition to, or repair thereof, shall not be deemed such a lack of completion as to prevent the filing of any lien; and in case of contracts the occupation or use of the building, improvement, or structure, by the owner, or his representative, or the acceptance by said owner or his agent of said building, improvement, or structure shall be deemed conclusive evidence of completion, and cessation from labor for thirty days upon any unfinished contract or upon any unfinished building, improvement or structure, or the alteration, addition to, or repair thereof, shall be deemed equivalent to a completion thereof, for all the purposes of this chapter. (Amendment, approved March 15, 1887; Statutes and Amendments 1887, 152; to take effect from and after its passage.)

A material man who has filed no lien for materials furnished a contractor, is not entitled to a personal judgment against the owner of the building.—74 Cal., 625.

A building erected in part only is held to be completed when it was the original purpose of the owner to erect it in part only, or when having proceeded to erect it in part, he abandoned his design to finish it.—74 Cal., 432.

Where the original contract is entire, a material man's lien need not be filed until the completion of the contract.—80 Cal., 510.

Where a contract between the owner and a contractor for the erection of a building is void, because not filed before the work is commenced, a claim of men for labor or materials may be filed at any time within thirty days after the actual completion of the building, irrespective of its previous acceptance and occupancy by the owner.—94 Cal., 205.

The time of completion of a building is a question of fact for the Trial Court to determine.—94 Cal., 205.

A valid contract between the owner and original contractor is necessary to establish conclusive evidence of completion of a building, by occupation, use or acceptance as provided in Section 1187 of the Code of Civil Procedure, —91 Cal., 229.

Cessation of labor for thirty days, to bring it within the meaning of Section 1187 of the Code of Civil Procedure, must be a *bona fide* cessation and such that will carry some charge of notice to a careful person. 96 Cal., 332.

A laborer's lien must be filed within the time required by law to make it valid.—76 Cal., 508.

A material man's lien need not be filed until the contract is completed, where the original contract is entire.—80 Cal., 510.

Where the right of a person depends upon performance within a definite number of days, it is necessary to allege and prove that the performance was made within the time required by law. "On or about" would be too indefinite an expression in an allegation that plaintiff had filed his notice of lien "on or about" a certain time.—89 Cal., 88.

A valid recorded contract, where the price is more than one thousand dollars, is not rendered void by the fact that a final payment is to become due thirty days after completion of a building instead of thirty-five days, as required by Section 1183 of the Code of Civil Procedure. 90 Cal., 579.

SECTION 1188.—In every case in which one claim is filed against two or more buildings, mining claims, or other improvements owned by the same person, the person filing such claim must at the same time designate the amount due to him on each of such buildings, mining claims, or other improvements; otherwise the lien of such claim is postponed to other liens. The lien of such claimant does not extend beyond the amount designated, as against other creditors having liens, by judgment, mortgage or otherwise, upon either of such buildings or other improvements, or upon the land upon which the same are situated.

SECTION 1189—The recorder must record the claim in a book kept by him for that purpose, which record must be indexed as deeds and other conveyances are required by law to be indexed, and for which he may receive the same fees as are allowed by law for recording deeds and other instruments.

SECTION 1190—No lien provided for in this chapter binds any building, mining claim, improvement, or structure for a longer period than ninety days after the same has been filed, unless proceedings be commenced in a proper court within that time to enforce the same; or, if a credit be given, then ninety days after the expiration of such credit; but no lien continues in force for a longer time than two years from the time the work is completed, by any agreement to give credit.

Notwithstanding the insolvency of a debtor, action must be brought within ninety days.—63 Cal., 122.

SECTION 1191—Any person who, at the request of the reputed owner of any lot in any incorporated city or town, grades, fills in, or otherwise improves the same, or the street or sidewalks in front of or adjoining the same, or constructs any areas, or vaults, or cellars or rooms, under said sidewalks, or makes any improvements in connection therewith, has a lien upon said lot for his work done and materials furnished. (Amendment, approved March 15, 1887; Statutes and Amendments, 1887, 152; to take effect from and after its passage).

SECTION 1192—Every building or other improvement mentioned in section eleven hundred and eighty-three of this code, constructed upon any lands with the knowledge of the owner, or the person having or claiming any interest therein, shall be held to have been constructed at the instance of such owner or person having or claiming any interest therein, and the interest owned or claimed shall be subject to any lien filed in accordance with the provisions of this chapter, unless such owner or person having or claiming an interest therein shall, within three days after he shall have obtained knowledge of the construction, alteration, or repair, or the intended construction, alteration, or repair, give notice that he will not be responsible for the same, by posting a notice in writing to the effect, in some conspicuous place upon said land, or upon the building or other improvement situated thereon. (Amendment approved March 30, 1874; Amendments 1873-4, 410; took effect sixtieth day after passage.)

<small>An owner or claimant who knowingly allows buildings, or improvements on land, without giving notice that it is without his consent, will be held to have acquiesced therein.—41 Cal., 583.</small>

SECTION 1193—The contractor shall be entitled to recover upon a lien filed by him, only such amounts as may be due to him according to the terms of his contract, after deducting all claims of other parties for work done and materials furnished, as aforesaid; and in all cases where a lien shall be filed, under this chapter, for work done or materials furnished to any contractor; he shall defend any action brought thereupon at his own expense, and during the pendency of such action, the owner may withhold from the contractor the amount of money for which lien is filed; and in case of judgment against the owner or his property upon the lien, the said owner shall be entitled to deduct from any amount due or to become due by him to the contractor the amount of such judgment and costs, and if the amount of such judgment and costs shall exceed the amount due by him to the contractor, or if the owner shall have settled with the contractor in full he shall be entitled to recover back from the contractor any amount so paid by him, the said owner, in excess of the contract price, and for which the contractor was originally the party liable. (Amendment, approved March 30, 1874; Amendments 1873-4, 411; took effect sixtieth day after passage.)

SECTION 1194—In every case in which different liens are asserted against any property, the Court in the judgment must declare the rank of each lien, or class of liens, which shall be in the following order, viz.:

    1. All persons performing manual labor in, on, or about the same.
    2. Persons furnishing materials.
    3. Sub-contractors.
    4. Original contractors.

And the proceeds of the sale of the property must be applied to each lien, or class of liens, in the order of its rank; and whenever, in the sale of the property subject to the lien, there is a deficiency of proceeds, judgment may be docketed for the deficiency in like manner and with like effect as in actions for the foreclosure of mortgages. (Amendment, approved March 18, 1885; Statutes and Amendments 1885, 145.)

A mechanics' lien is subordinate to a prior recorded mortgage, and such mortgagee need not give notice of non-responsibility for cost of improvement required of claimants of interests by Section 1192 of the Code of Civil Procedure.—66 Cal., 193.

A mortgagee executed after the time when materials were commenced to be furnished is subordinate to the lien of the material man.—87 Cal. 619.

SECTION 1195 Any number of persons claiming liens may join in the same action, and when separate actions are commenced the Court may consolidate them. The Court must also allow, as a part of the costs, the money paid for filing and recording the lien, and reasonable attorney's fees in the Superior and Supreme Courts, such costs and attorney's fees to be allowed to each lien claimant whose lien is established, whether he be plaintiff or defendant, or whether they all join in one action or separate actions are consolidated. (Amendment, approved March 18, 1895; Statutes and Amendments 1885, 146.)

SECTION 1196—Whenever materials shall have been furnished for use in the construction, alteration, or repair of any building or other improvement, such materials shall not be subject to attachment, execution, or other legal process, to enforce any debt due by the purchaser of such materials, except a debt due for the purchase money thereof, so long as in good faith the same are about to be applied to the construction, alteration or repair of such building, mining claim, or other improvement. (Amendment, approved March 30, 1874; Amendments 1873-4, 412; took effect sixtieth day after passage.)

SECTION 1197—Nothing contained in this chapter shall be construed to impair or affect the right of any person to whom any debt may be due for work done or materials furnished to maintain a personal action to recover such debt against the person liable therefor. (Amendment, approved March 24, 1874; Amendments 1873-4, 351; took effect July 1, 1874.)

SECTION 1198—Except as otherwise provided in this chapter, the provisions of Part II of this code are applicable to and constitute the rules of practice in the proceedings mentioned in this chapter.

SECTION 1199—The provisions of Part II of this code, relative to new trials and appeals, except in so far as they are inconsistent with the provisions of this chapter, apply to the proceedings mentioned in this chapter.

SECTION 1200—In case the contractor shall fail to perform his contract in full or shall abandon the same before completion, the portion of the contract price applicable to the liens of other persons than the contractor shall be fixed as follows: From the value of the work and materials already done and furnished at the time of such failure or abandonment, including materials then actually delivered or on the ground, which shall thereupon belong to the owner, estimated as near as may be by the standard of the whole contract price, shall be deducted from payments then due and actually paid, according to the terms of the contract and the provisions of sections eleven hundred and eighty-three and eleven hundred and eighty-four, and the remainder shall be deemed the portion of the contract price applicable to such liens. (New Section, approved March 18, 1885; Statutes and Amendments 1885, 146.)

A lien filed within thirty days for materials used on a flume after the company took possession and control and completed it, the contractor having abandoned the work before completion, is valid.

The company by its action "occupies," "uses" and "accepts it" within the meaning of the Code of Civil Procedure—88 Cal., 20.

In an action to enforce liens for labor and materials furnished after the abandonment of a contract by the contractor, he need not be made a party to the action—94 Cal., 49.

An "occupation" or "acceptance" of a building by the owner is not created by the employment of a painter as keeper who lives in the building while painting it, after the contractor has abandoned the work.—96 Cal., 332.

The abandonment of work upon a building, by a contractor, before its completion does not necessitate the filing of a lien within thirty days thereafter, where the owner goes on with the work, and does not "occupy" or "accept" the building.—96 Cal., 332.

SECTION 1201—It shall not be competent for the owner or contractor, or either of them by any term of their contract, or otherwise, to waive, affect, or impair the claims and liens of other persons whether with or without notice, except by their written consent, and any term of the contract to that effect shall be null and void. (New section approved March 18, 1885; Statutes and Amendments 1885, 146.)

SECTION 1202—Any person who shall wilfully give a false notice of his claim to the owner, under the provisions of section eleven hundred and eighty-four shall forfeit his lien. Any person who shall wilfully include in his claim filed under section eleven hundred and eighty-seven, work or materials not performed upon or furnished for the property described in the claim, shall forfeit his lien. If the owner and his contractor shall directly or indirectly conspire to or agree that the written contract filed shall appear to show the contract price to be less than it really is, and it shall accordingly so show, then such contract shall be wholly void and no recovery shall be had thereon by either party thereto and in such case the labor done and materials furnished by all persons, except the contractor, shall be deemed to have been done and furnished at the personal instance of the owner, and they shall have a lien for the value thereof. (New section approved March 18, 1885; Statutes and Amendments 1885, 146.)

SECTION 1203—Every contract required to be filed under the provisions of this chapter shall be accompanied by a good and sufficient bond in an amount equal to at least twenty-five per cent. of the contract price, which said bond shall be filed at the same time and in the same manner as herein provided for the filing of such contract, or memorandum thereof. Said bond shall, by its terms, be made to inure to the benefit of any and all persons who perform labor for, or furnish materials to the contractor, or any person acting for him, or by his authority; and any such person shall have an action to recover upon said bond, against the principal and sureties, or either of them, for the value of such labor or materials, or both, not exceeding the amount of the bond; but such action shall not affect his lien, nor any action to foreclose the same, except that there shall be but one satisfaction of his claim, with costs and counsel fees. Any failure to comply with the provision of this section shall render the owner and contractor jointly and severally liable in damages to any and all material men, laborers, and sub-contractors entitled to liens upon the property affected by said contract. (New section approved March 23, 1893. Statutes and Amendments 1893, 202.)

CERTAIN LIENS FOR SALARIES AND WAGES.

SECTION 1204—In all assignments of property made by any person to trustees or assignees, on account of the inability of the person at the time of the assignment, to pay his debts, or in proceedings in insolvency, the wages and salaries of the miners, mechanics, salesmen, servants, clerks, laborers employed by such person who renders services or performs work to the amount of one hundred dollars each, and for services rendered within sixty days previously, are preferred claims, and must be paid by such trustees or assignees before any other creditor or creditors of the assignor. (Amendment approved March 9, 1893. Statutes and Amendments, 1893, 97.)

SECTION 1205—In case of the death of any employer the wages of each miner, mechanic, salesman, clerk, servant, laborer or other person who renders services or performs work, for services rendered within the sixty days next preceding the death of the employer, not exceeding one hundred dollars, rank in priority next after the funeral expenses, expenses of the last sickness, the charges and expenses of administering upon the estate, and the allowance to the widow and infant children, and must be paid before other claims against the estate of the deceased person. (Amendment approved March 9, 1893. Statutes and Amendments, 1893, 97.)

SECTION 1206—In cases of executions, attachments, and writs of a similar nature, issued against any person except for claims for labor done, any miners, mechanics, salesmen, servants, clerks and laborers, or any other person who renders service or performs work, who have claims against the defendant for labor done or work performed, may give notice of their claims, and the amount thereof, sworn to by the person making the claim, to the creditor and the officer executing either of such writs, at any time before the actual sale of property levied on or in the event of a levy upon money, at any time before the transfer of such money under execution; and, unless such claim is disputed by the debtor or a creditor, such officer must pay to such person out of the proceeds of the sale, or in the event of a levy on money, out of such money, the amount each is entitled to receive for services rendered within the sixty days next preceding the levy of the writ not exceeding one hundred dollars. If any or all of the claims so presented and claiming preference under this section are disputed by either the debtor or a creditor, the person presenting the same must commence an action within ten days for the recovery thereof, and must prosecute his action with due diligence or be forever barred from any claim or priority of payment thereof; and the officer shall retain possession of so much of the proceeds of the sale or money as may be necessary to satisfy such claim until the determination of such action; and in case judgment be had for the claim, or any part thereof, carrying costs, the costs taxable therein shall likewise be a preferred claim, with the same rank as the original claim. (Amendment approved March 9, 1893. Statutes and Amendments, 1893, 87.)

SECTION 1207—The debtor or creditor intending to dispute a claim presented under the provisions of the last section shall, within ten days after receiving notice of such claim, serve upon the claimant and the officer executing the writ, a statement, in writing, verified by the oath of the debtor, or the person disputing such claim, setting forth that no part of said claim, or not exceeding a sum specified, is justly due from the debtor to the claimant for services rendered within the sixty days next preceding the levy of the writ. If the claimant brings suit on a claim which is disputed in part only, and fail to recover a sum exceeding that which was admitted to be due, he shall not recover costs, but costs shall be adjudged against him. (New section, approved March 7, 1883; Statutes and Amendments, 1883, 47.)

No Matter

We Can Please You

Whether your Printing amounts to much or little; whether it's

Cards, Stationery, Catalogues
OR
SOUVENIRS

L. H. Cosper & Co.   216 Eddy Street
                          San Francisco

Telephone Main. 5440

FRANK COGHLAN
PLASTERER

BOX 91
BUILDERS' EXCHANGE
New Montgomery and Mission

Box 234 and 205 st.
SAN FRANCISCO

873 HARRISON STREET, OAKLAND

M. BRENNAN & SON

Box 297,
BUILDERS' EXCHANGE

BUILDERS

40 New Montgomery St.   SAN FRANCISCO

W. N. MILLER.   J. W. HAMILTON.

Miller & Hamilton

... MANUFACTURERS OF ...

Mouldings, Brackets, Frames, Doors, Sash and Blinds

Sawing, Planing, Sizing and all kinds of general Mill Work.

Hardwood Finish for Buildings, Store and Bank Fixtures a Specialty.

TELEPHONE MAIN 5256

413 and 415 Mission Street.   SAN FRANCISCO., CAL.

Telephone No. 5369   Box 125, Builders' Exchange

RALSTON IRON WORKS

H. RALSTON, Proprietor

Manufacturer of all kinds of

Architectural and Ornamental Iron Work

VAULTS, FIRE ESCAPES, CRESTINGS,

DOORS, SHUTTERS, BOLTS AND STEEL CEILING

222 and 224 Howard Street,   SAN FRANCISCO, CAL.

Steel and Wrought Iron Beams, Columns, Girders, Etc.

Improved Vault Construction, Sidewalk Lights, Fire and Burglar Proof Illuminating Roofs and Partitions, Ventilators, Etc.

Architectural and Fine Iron Work

For Buildings

JACKSON'S PATENT
IRON STAIRWAYS

Are in General Use Throughout the United States

✻✻✻✻

JACKSON'S PATENT TIES FOR CONCRETE CONSTRUCTIONS

Made in part of Cheap, Worn Out Railway Rails

Possess the Great Desideratum of Having

Fully Three Times the Holding Power to the Concrete Compared to the Best Concrete Tie Known

SEND FOR CIRCULAR TO KNOW WHAT SIZE TIES TO USE.

✻✻✻✻

228 and 230 First Street
5 and 7 Tehama Street   SAN FRANCISCO

Computations Made as to the Strength of any Iron or Steel Building or Bridge Construction

REFERENCE ABSTRACT

TO FOREGOING LIEN LAW

Mechanics' Lien—Who entitled to, on what property, contracts, recording of, etc. See Sec. 1183, p. 137.

Contract—Terms of payment, alteration, notice to owner of contractor's delinquency and effect. See Sec. 1184, p. 141.

Land—What interest in and amount subject to lien. See Sec. 1185, p. 143.

Effect of Lien—As to mortgage or other incumbrances, etc. See Sec. 1186, p. 144.

Claim of Lien—Time for filing, statement of claim and property, where recorded, verification, effect of cessation of work. See Sec. 1187, p. 144. See Sec. 1200, p. 147.

Liens Upon Two or More Pieces of Property—Necessary statement and failure to comply with. See Sec. 1188, p. 145.

Record—When and how indexed. See Sec. 1189, p. 145.

Time of Continuance of Lien—When suit must be commenced to foreclose lien. See Sec. 1190, p. 145.

Lien for grading, filling, or improving lot or street or making cellar vault or room under sidewalk, etc. See Sec. 1191, p. 145.

Work done, but not at Instance of Owner—When lien exists and what owner must do to prevent. See Sec. 1192, p. 146.

Lien of Contracts—What amount due, deducting amount due subcontractors and others. See Sec. 1193, p. 146.

Priority of liens and order of payment. See Sec. 1194, p. 146.

Consolidating action, costs, attorney's fees. See Sec. 1195, p. 147.

My Motto is "Moderate Prices Consistent with Good Tailoring."

Charles Adams,

Merchant Tailor . .

1384 Market Street
Opp. CENTRAL PARK

San Francisco

KENNEY AND WELLS

1110 BROADWAY, OAKLAND

PARQUET FLOORS
WOOD CARPET
MOORISH & EGYPTIAN
FRETWORK & GRILLES

Box 319, Builders' Exchange

Tel. Main 1882   422 Sutter St., SAN FRANCISCO

REFERENCE ABSTRACT—Concluded.

Materials furnished when exempt from attachment, execution, etc. See Sec. 1196, p. 147.

Personal action aside from lien. See Sec. 1197, p. 147.

Owner and contractor cannot make contract impairing right of others to liens. See Sec. 1201, p. 148.

Effect of filing false contract or giving false notice. See Sec. 1202, p. 148.

Bond—Requisites of filing of, who entitled to benefit, effect on lien, effect of failure to file. See Sec. 1203, p. 148.

LIENS FOR SALARIES AND WAGES.

Persons preferred on assignment for benefit of creditors. See Sec. 1204, p. 149.

Same against estates. See Sec. 1205, p. 149.

Same in cases of executions and attachments. See Sec. 1206, p. 149.

How above claim of lien is disputed and contested. See Sec. 1207, p. 150.

Telephone Main 5440   Residence 640? Castro Stree

R. J. PAVERT

CONTRACTOR AND BUILDER

OFFICE BUILDERS EXCHANGE

Cor. of Mission and New Montgomery Sts

San Francisco

FORM FOR MECHANIC'S LIEN

STATE OF CALIFORNIA, }
.................County of.............................} ss.

.... }
                        vs.   } MECHANIC'S
                                    ....   } LIEN.

    NOTICE IS HEREBY GIVEN, that...
of the.....................County of...
of th... certain building... or structure... and now upon th... certain lot... and
parcel... of land situate in the............. County of................of........................,
and sought to be charged with this lien and described as follows, to wit :......
....
    That...............................the name... of the owner..........of said
premises, and cause said building... or structure... to be.................................
    That.......................................the name... of the contractor...., who on
the............day of..........18...., as such contractor.................. entered into a
contract ....with said.................under and by which.......................
and the following is a statement of the terms, time given, and condition
of said contract, to wit :—
....
    That said contract has been fully performed on the part of said..............
............................and the same was completed, and the.............said building...
or structure... finished on the......day of........ ....., 18.... and .... days have
not elapsed since the same was completed, and said building... or structure...
finished.
....
    That the amount of the contract price for said......................furnished
as aforesaid, is................ ....Dollars, in United States Gold Coin.
....
    That..............paid on................said contract price, and that the
sum of...................Dollars, in Gold Coin of the United States, is still due
and owing thereon to said..after deducting all just
credits and offsets.
    WHEREFORE, said..................claim.. the benefit of the law to liens
of Mechanics and others upon real property, to wit: Chapter II, Title IV,
Part III, of the Code of Civil Procedure.

STATE OF CALIFORNIA, } ss.
.................County of................................}
    ....being duly sworn, depose.. and say...That.....
the person... named as..............in the foregoing Claim of Lien; That.....
he...ha...read the same and know...the contents thereof, and that the same
is true, and that the contents (among other things), a corrected statement
of........demand after deducting all just credits and offsets

    Subscribed and sworn to before me, }
this ....day of...............18... }

Telephone WEST 585.

JOHN TUTTLE

Teamster and Plasterers' Supplies

516 Haight Street. San Francisco

Box 79, Builders' Exchange, New Montgomery and Mission.

Telephone MAIN 1752

Charles M. Depew

PLANING MILL COMPANY

General Mill Work
Ship and Steamboat Work
Planing, Sizing and Resawing

Office and Factory
229-233 Berry St., Bet. 4th and 5th

BOX 19, BUILDERS' EXCHANGE, SAN FRANCISCO

Telephone—MISSION 1

A. B. MAGUIRE

Wholesale and Retail Dealer in

Lime, Laths, Plaster, Cement, Hair, Nails, Fire Clay, Fire Brick,

HAY, GRAIN, WOOD AND COAL,

Coke and Charcoal.

YARD, Nos. 2230-32-34 Folsom Street, Near 20th — San Francisco

COAL IN BULK 2240 LBS., DELIVERED FROM WHARF

Telephone MAIN 5110

BUILDERS' EXCHANGE Box No.

INSURANCE PROMPTLY ATTENDED TO.

CHAS. M. SORENSEN

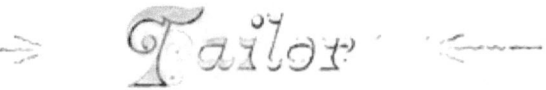

Tailor

422 Post Street • • • San Francisco

Members Builders' Exchange.

ALPHABETICALLY ARRANGED.

Box No.

Abrahamson, P.; patent ventilators..................123
Ackerson & Patterson; contractors and builders..................343
Adams, John G.; contractor and builder..................270
Alameda Brick & Tile Co.; brick..................170
Ambrose, William F.; concrete and artificial stone..................356
Anderson Bros.; contractors and builders..................128
Architectural Iron Works; (O'Connell & Lewis)..................17
Arizona Sandstone Co.; building stone..................326
Artistic Decoration Co..................337

Bassett Bros.; contractors and builders..................6
Bass-Hueter Paint Co.; paints, oils and varnishes..................136
Barry, James; mason and builder..................118
Bateman Bros.; contractors and builders..................236
Bay City Iron Works..................266
Beck, Adam; mason and builder..................11
Bell, Frank C.; contractor and builder..................14
Bennett Bros.; hardware..................320
Black, E. H.; painter..................102
Boyd, Robert; mason and builder..................77
Brady, M. V.; mason and builder..................34
Brady, O. E.; mason and builder..................360
Brennan, D. J.; mason and builder..................51
Brennan, M. & Son; carpenters and builders..................297
Brennan, & Fraser; plasterers..................158
Britt, James E.; plumber..................36
Brode, R.; iron works..................295
Burden & Helm; masons and builders..................260
Burnham, Stanford Co.; planing mill..................28
Burrell, E. H.; building material..................146
Burt, W. J.; house mover..................296
Butler, Thos.; mason and builder..................255
Butler, Wm. A.; mason and builder..................
Butterworth, Thos. C.; art glass..................371

California Sandstone and Contracting Co...................230
California Art Glass Works..................63
California Electrical Works..................223
California Mills; planing mill..................300
Campbell, Alex.; contractor and builder..................105
Campbell & Pettus; contractors and builders..................184
Carle, Silas; contractor and builder..................
Cartwright, D. S.; teaming..................10
Central Lumber & Mill Co.; lumber and planing mill..................345
Chatham, Wm.; contractor and builder..................62
Chisholm, C.; contractor and builder..................44
Christy, Chas.; contractor and builder..................276
Clark, N., & Sons; terra cotta, etc..................209
Clawson, L. E., & Co.; patent chimneys..................66
Coghlan, Frank; plasterer..................91
Commary, Wm. T.; contractor and builder..................
Concannon & Shay; contractors and builders..................24
Conlin & Roberts; metal roofers..................90
Cowell, H., & Co.: lime, cement, fire, brick, etc..................7
Crighton, Peter; contractor and builder..................339
Crocker, Wm.; planing mill..................12

Cronan, Wm.; Eagle Sheet Metal Works..26
Currie & Loomer; contractors and builders..227
Currie, Robert; contractor and builder..143
Cushing-Wetmore Co.; concrete and artificial stone........................222
Curry, J. M.; stone dealer..35

Daniels, Gus. V.; painter and decorator...85
Davies E.; plasterer...42
Davis, Geo., & Son; house movers...293
Davis, R. O.; carpenter and builder..201
Day, Thos. H., & Sons; contractors and builders...............................131
Degan, Patrick; stone contractor..366
DeGear, J. D.; galvanized iron..259
Depew, Chas. M.; planing mill..19
Diggins Bros.; street contractors, concrete stone............................176
Dillon, David; teamster and contractor..139
Donovan, M. J.; painter...121
Donnelly, E.; teaming and grading..39
Dougherty, J. P.; plumber..351
Douglass, Chas.; carpenter..125
Doyle, R., & Son; carpenters and builders.......................................142
Duffy, Bros.; plumbers...243
Dunbar, Wm.; mason and builder..364
Dunham, Carrigan & Hayden Co.; hardware.......................................4
Dunlop, Chas.; plasterer...59
Dwyer, L. J.; painter and decorator...197
Dyer Bros.; Golden West Iron Works..64

Elam, Thos.; carpenter and builder...202
Electrical Maintenance Co.; construction and repair work...............350
Excelsior Mill Co..72

Feely, M. J.; contractor and builder..180
Fennall, M., & Son; masons and builders...58
Field, Wm. J.; contractor and builder...89
Flanagan, L. G.; lime and cement...53
Flint, J. A., & Co.; tiles, etc..234
Foley, Michael; grading and teaming..254
Forderer Cornice Works; patent sky lights, roofing, etc................164
Fortin Brick Co...98
Foster, John; contractor and builder...330
Fraser, J. P; painter and decorator...50
Fuller, W. P. & Co; paints, oils and glass..333
Furness, John; contractor and builder...152

Geary, James; contractor and builder..275
Geier, Frank A.; Market Street Planing Mills...................................252
Gillespie, G. G.; carpenter and builder..352
Giletti, Secondo; artificial stone...308
Gillogley, Geo.; teaming..324
Gladding, McBean & Co.; arch. terra cotta.....................................162
Golden Gate Lumber Co.; lumber and planing mill............................
Golden West Iron Works (Dyer Bros.)..64
Gonyeau, John B.; contractor and builder.......................................194
Goodman, Geo.; artificial stone, etc...334
Granniss J. G., & Co.; steam heating, etc......................................331
Grant, W. J.; contractor and builder..84
Gray Bros.; artificial stone and concrete work.................................86
Griese, Carl; artificial stone and concrete work..............................231
Griffin P.; contractor and builder..103
Guilfoy, James; metal roofer..370

Hammond, Philip; metal roofer..43
Hanavan, J. H.; mason and builder..49
Hansen, A.; planing mill...3
Hansen, F. L.; contractor and builder...108
Hansen, M., & Co.; planing mill..187

Harmon Lumber Co.; lumber...... Box 314
Harrison, Fred; mason and builder...... 309
Haustein, H.; tiles...... 82
Hayes, John T.; contractor and builder...... 167
Healy, M. J.; stone contractor...... 220
Henon & Son; mason and builders...... 45
Henzel, Ed. F., & Co.; electricians...... 375
Herring, R.; mill work...... 70
Hinchman & Co.; planing mill...... 283
Hindes, Edward B., & Co.; patent blinds...... 174
Hock, T., & Son; masons and builders...... 232
Hogan, Ed.; plumber...... 84
Hoffman, V.; masons and builders...... 9
Holmes, H. T., Lime Co.; lime, cement, etc...... 268
Hooper & Co. lumber
Howell Tiling Co...... 303
Huber, Frank; sash, blinds and doors...... 342
Hurlbut, R. P.; builder...... 156

Ickelheimer, Samuel & Bro.; plumbers...... 353
Ingerson & Gore; contractors and builders...... 37

Jacks, Henry; contractor and builder...... 267
Jackson, A.; contractor and builder...... 200
Jackson, P. H., & Co.; illuminating tiles...... 27
Jessee, Geo. R.; stair builder...... 102
Jordan D., & Son; masons and builders...... 57
Jackson, W. E.; curbing...... 304
Joshua Hendy Machine Works...... 188

Keatinge, Leonard & Ransome; concrete and twisted iron...... 13
Kelleher, M.; house raiser and mover...... 23
Kendall, A.; Pacific Coast Lumber and Mill Co...... 52
Kennedy, J.; contractor and builder...... 65
Kenney & Wells; inlaid floors...... 368
Keefe, J. H.; painter and decorator...... 199
Kent, S. M.; contractor and builder...... 190
Kern, F. W.; contractor and builder...... 225
Kilpatrick, D.; stone contractor...... 265
Kittredge, E. H. & Co.; sash, doors and blinds...... 204
Klatt, F.; contractor and builder...... 277
Knowles, Wm.; contractor and builder...... 150
Knox & Cook; contractors and builders...... 244
Kronnick, Fred G.; contractor and builder...... 373
Kuss, P. N.; painter, decorator and wood finisher...... 307

Lewis, D.; stair builder...... 226
Lang, Geo. R.; contractor and builder...... 214
Larsen, H. H.; mason and builder...... 33
Leahy, D.; plasterer...... 344
Leprohon, P.; steam and hot water heating...... 239
Liebert, J. G.; mason and builder...... 32
Linden, W.; contractor and builder...... 229
Lindsay, J. R., & Co.;
Llewellyn, R.; Columbia Foundry...... 182
Logan, J. F.; adjuster and builder...... 21
Lucas & Co; (Golden Gate Plaster Mills) calcined plaster...... 31
Lynch, M. C.; contractor and builder...... 274

Maguire, A. B.; lime, laths, plaster, cement, etc...... 263
Maguire James A.; manufacturer's agent...... 120
Mahoney Bros.; builders
Mallon, John; art glass...... 93
Maloney, P.; contractor and builder...... 224
Martland, Grindell & Simpson; electricians...... 269
Mason, Chas.; contractor and builder...... 228

Market St. Planing Mill............Box 252
McBain, John; contractor and builder............323
McCarthy, John; mason and builder............168
McClure, H. N.; teaming and grading............311
McClure, P. L.; water............161
McCann, R.; builder............75
McDonald, D. A.; Enterprise Planing Mill............127
McDonald, John A.; contractor and builder............369
McElroy, A.; contractor and builder............211
McFarland Bros.; planing mill............322
McGilvray, John D.; stone contractor............340
McGowan, M.; mason and builder............17
McInerny, James; contractor and builder............365
McKay, D.; stone setter............
McKee, John; stair builder............262
McLachlan, T. M.; contractor and builder............92
McLeod, J. C.; plastering and brickwork............94
McMahon, Henry; stair builder............113
McMurray, J. P.; plaster decorations............78
McPhee & Groliere; stone contractors............256
Mennie, Alex; plasterer............146
Miller, Adam; carpenter and builder............54
Miller, J. W.; mason and builder............208
Miller & Hamilton; planing mill............110
Mills, A. T.; mason and builder............95
Mitchell, R.; mason and builder............74
Moore, C. Parker; contractor and builder............80
Moore, G. Howard; contractor and builder............358
Morehouse, C. C.; plasterer............301
Morehouse, J. J.; plasterer............97
Miller, Jas.; Oakland Art Pottery Works............133
Mulcahy, J.; mason and builder............55
Muller, W. A.; carpenter and builder............235
Mulville, D. F.; plasterer............76
Munster, John H.; carpenter and builder............212
Murray, R. M.; carpenter and builder............30
Mussey, John; contractor and builder............302

Niehaus, Edward F. & Co.; hardwood lumber............205
Niehaus Bros., planing mill............20
Nutting, C.; iron, etc............104

O'Brien, Jas. J.; carpenter and builder............107
O'Connell & Lewis; architectural iron works............47
Ogle, John; contractor and builder............215
O'Sullivan, D.; mason contractor............40
O'Sullivan, J.; mason contractor............310

Pacific Refining & Roofing Co.............346
Pacific Coast Door Co.............237
Pacific Lumber Co.............
Paff, Chas.; carpenter............216
Palace Hardware Co.; builders' hardware............292
Paraffine Paint Co., roofers, building paper............144
Patent Brick Co.; brick............172
Pavert, R. J.; contractor and builder............281
Peacock & Butcher, masons and builders............122
Petersen Brick Co., original red pressed brick............68
Petersen, H. M. & Co.; concrete............245
Phillips, J. P. M.; stone dealer............46
Pleace, Henry; mason and builder............299
Pool Jas. R.; house mover and raiser............217
Powers, Daniel; carpenter and builder............141
Preston & McKinnon; lumber dealers............348

Rae, James; stone contractor..Box 56
Ralston Iron Works; Architectural Iron Work..........................175
Raymond Granite Co.; contractors for stone work.....................165
Reichley Geo.; contractor and builder......................................189
Reigle & Jamieson; machine white washing.............................240
Remillard Brick Co.; pressed stock and common brick................278
Rice, Richard; plumber..253
Richardson & Gale; masons and builders...................................328
Riley & Loane; masons and builders..329
Ringrose, R.; mason and builder... 18
Ritter Lumber Co..247
Robinson & Gillespie; contractors and builders..........................211
Rocklin Granite Co.; granite work.. 68
Rosenbaum, F. H.; glass... 96
Ruffino & Bianchi; marble..219

Sacramento Transportation Co.; patent and stock brick.............332
Sanborn, A. I.; stairbuilder...185
San Francisco Lumber Co...
San Francisco Novelty and Plating Works..................................291
San Francisco Planing Mill; Wm. Crocker................................. 12
San Joaquin Brick Co.; brick...288
San Jose Brick Co.; brick.. 5
Santini, L.; plaster decorations...318
Saunders, J. S. W.; contractor and builder...............................250
Schroeder, Wm.; art glass... 63
Schuster, Bros.; patent chimneys..196
Scott & Van Arsdale Lumber Co...193
Sessions, M. P.;..
Sibley, L. B.; teamster, grading, etc...................................336
Sinnott, R.; carpenter...166
Smilie Bros.; carpenters... 16
Smith, J. W.; carpenter.. 71
Smith & Young; building supplies.......................................374
Snell, E. L.; lime and plaster..101
Snook, W. S. & Son; plumbers..372
Soule Bros.; carpenters.. 61
Steiger, A., Sons; architectural terra cotta..........................134
Steinman, F. V.; carpenter..279
Stevens, F. M.; patent chimneys.. 15
Stoddard & Barber; planing mill... 87
Stratton, Jno. S.; house mover..362
Sullivan, J. F.; painter and decorator.................................. 1
Sullivan, Tim.; carpenter.. 83
Sutton & Johnston; stone contractors..................................... 38
Sweeney, G. C.; plumber..135

Tay, Geo. H., Co.; plumbers supplies..................................321
Thornton, W. E.; stone contractor..338
Tobin, J. R.; plasterer..173
Towle & Broadwell..298
Trotter, John; contractor and builder.................................251

Tucker and Maxwell; street contractors..Box 347
Tuttle, John; teamster, plasterers' supplies.................................... 79

Union Lumber Co.; lumber..335
Union Pressed Brick & Terra Cotta Co..140

Vance, R. A.; plumber..233
Vogler, J. F.; glazier..185
Vulcan Iron Works..284

Wagner, Henry F.; painter and decorator......................................312
Wagner, J.; mason and builder.. 41
Wagner J. Ferd; mason and builder..181
Walker, George H.; carpenter...367
Walsh, Patrick J.; glazier...287
Warren, C. A.; grading...272
Washington Street Planing Mill... 48
Watson, W. C.; plasterer...100
Wersen, L. H.; mason and builder...315
Western Granite & Marble Co..316
Western Iron Works...171
White Bros.; carpenters..257
White Bros. (hardwood lumber)..
Whittle H.; mason and builder.. 60
Wickersham, W. H.; contractor and builder....................................271
Williams, F. A.; contractor and builder......................................178
Wilcox, J. R.; carpenter...195
Wilson Bros. & Co.; lumber...354
Williamson, H; plumber...280
Wilson, W. F.; plumber...238
Wilson, James A.; mason and builder..221
Wilson, J. H.; mason and builder...294
Wilkie, Andrew; planing mill...305
Woods, F. N. & Co.; paints...361
Worden, S. G.; carpenter...106
Wright, F. W.; builders' hardware..357
Worrel, C. R.; mason and builder... 2
West Coast Wire Works..

Yates & Co.; paints..349

ADMISSION CARDS
FROM OAKLAND EXCHANGE.

Anderson & Grieg; contractors and builders 248
Cameron & McDonald; contractors and builders.....................................137
Kellett, Samuel,; plaster decorations..285
Ingler & Atkinson; millmen...359
Jones, H. E.; contractor and builder... 67
O'Leary, P. J.; plasterer..
Leiter & Prugh; contractor and builder... 8
Peterson, G. A.; painter...264
Gardiner & Boyden; contractors and builders......................................154
Davis, D. L.; contractor and builder...282

THE BUILDERS' ASSOCIATION.
OF
CALIFORNIA

New Montgomery and Mission Sts.   San Francisco, California

Officers

STEPHEN R. DOYLE, President.

M. J. FEELY..........Vice President   JOHN T. HAYES............Secretary
M. C. LYNCH..........Fin. Secretary   P. GRIFFIN....................Treasurer

Executive Committee

JAS. McINERNY, Chairman.

S. H. KENT,   DANIEL POWERS,   ROBERT CURRIE,
    A. JACKSON,   J. W. FISH,   R. O. DAVIS.

Constitution

ARTICLE I.

NAME.

SEC. 1. This Association shall be known as THE BUILDERS' ASSOCIATION OF CALIFORNIA.

OBJECTS.

SEC. 2. Its objects shall be to encourage a more intimate acquaintance and cultivate a feeling of friendship among its members; to make them better acquainted with the wants and necessities of the building business; to arbitrate and settle disputes, if any arise among the members, and generally to advance and protect their business interests as contracting builders.

ARTICLE II.

MEMBERSHIP.

SECTION 1. Any carpenter residing and doing business as a general contractor and builder in the State of California, and who has announced his willingness to join this Association, shall be eligible to membership upon the payment of the fee as provided in this Constitution and the By-Laws.

SEC. 2. Each application for membership must be presented in writing and recommended by one member of the Association, with names of two references attached.

Such application shall be referred to a committee of three for investigation, who shall report at the next regular meeting, and upon receiving th affirmative vote of three-fourths of the members present shall be declared elected. The member so elected shall be notified to appear at the next meeting, and be introduced to the Association, and be required to sign the Constitution, By-Laws and Agreements.

PRIVILEGED MEMBERSHIP.

SEC. 3. Any member in good standing, temporarily retiring from the building business, may, by the affirmative vote of two-thirds of the members present at a regular meeting of the Association, have his dues remitted during the time of such retirement. Such member shall be designated as a "privileged member." He must make application on blank form furnished by the Association. One of the conditions of said form shall be an agreement that the said "privileged member" shall not estimate on any plans, nor enter into any contract for the construction or repair of any building or other structure, nor transact any business as a Carpenter and Builder, until first giving notice to the Association to place his name on the Roll of Active Members. Said Privileged Member shall have no voice nor vote in the Association, nor shall he have any interests in the funds or property thereof.

HONORARY MEMBERSHIP.

SEC. 4. Any person who has been identified with this Association in such a manner as in the judgment of the members renders his membership and co-operation desirable, may be elected an honorary member, upon two weeks' written notice to the members, by a three-fourths vote of all the members present at a regular meeting, and shall be entitled to the free use of the rooms of the Association, and shall be permitted to address the Association, but shall have no vote therein.

ARTICLE III.

MEETINGS.

SECTION 1. The regular meetings shall be held at least once a month upon the day and hour fixed in the By-Laws, and in the City of San Francisco.

SPECIAL MEETINGS.

SEC. 2. Special meetings may be called by the President (and in his absence by the Vice President) at his discretion, and shall be called by him at the written request of the Executive Committee or of five other members.

SEC. 3. The President shall state the object of the special meeting in the call therefor; and no business shall be transacted, except such as appertains to the business specified.

ADJOURNED MEETINGS.

SEC. 4. Adjourned meetings may be held at any time by authority of a majority vote of a quorum at a regular meeting, notice being given of such meeting as provided in the By-Laws, stating the business for which the meeting is to be held; and no other business shall be transacted thereat, except such as is stated in the notice.

ARTICLE IV.

QUORUM.

SECTION 1. Seven members shall constitute a quorum for the transaction of business at all meetings.

ARTICLE V.

FEES, DUES AND VOTES.

SECTION 1. Each individual member shall pay an admission fee of not less than Five Dollars, which fee shall accompany the application for membership.

In the event of an application being rejected, the admission fee shall be returned.

SEC. 2. The dues to be paid by each member shall not be less than Twenty-Five Cents per month, payable in advance.

ARTICLE VI.

OFFICERS AND THEIR DUTIES.

SECTION 1. The elective officers shall be a President, a Vice President, a Recording Secretary, a Financial Secretary, a Treasurer and an Executive Committee of seven members.

SEC. 2. The appointed officers shall be such as are prescribed in the By-Laws.

SEC. 3. Four members of the Executive Committee shall at all times be residents of the City and County of San Francisco. Four members of said committee shall constitute a quorum thereof.

SEC. 4. The President shall preside at the meetings, preserve order, see that the rules and laws are enforced, sign all drafts for money voted by the Association, appoint all committees, unless otherwise ordered or provided for, and have the care and custody of all bonds which may be required of the other officers.

He shall see that all other officers and committees perform their respective duties, and shall report any neglect or delinquency forthwith to the Association. He shall not speak upon any question, except one of order, without calling the Vice President, or in his absence some other member, to the chair.

He shall vote only upon applications for membership, or upon questions requiring a two-thirds vote, except to give the casting vote when the members are equally divided. He shall, at the commencement of his term, appoint a Finance Committee consisting of three members not having charge of the Association Funds, and perform such other and further duties as may be imposed by the By-Laws.

SEC. 5. The Vice President shall, during the absence or inability of the President to act, perform all the duties of that officer. He shall preside when called upon by the President, and perform such other duties as may be imposed upon him by the laws or rules.

SEC. 6. The Recording Secretary shall keep correct minutes of the proceedings of the Association, file and preserve all papers and documents belonging thereto, conduct the correspondence, draw and attest all drafts for moneys voted, and perform all other duties usually devolving upon a secretary, or which may hereafter be imposed by law or rule.

SEC. 7. The Financial Secretary shall keep correctly the accounts between the Association and its members and others, in proper books to be provided for that purpose. He shall collect and receipt for all money due from any source, and pay the same to the Treasurer at each meeting, when practicable, but at least once each month, taking his receipt for the same. He shall report at the first stated meeting in each month the amount of all moneys received during the preceding month, and the source from which received, together with the amount paid out and for what paid. His books and accounts shall be kept in such a manner that the financial condition of the Association and the state of each account can be determined at any time. He shall render the Finance Committee all the facility required in the examination of his accounts, and upon retiring from office deliver to his successor, or other person designated by the Association, all money, books, papers or other property belonging thereto.

SEC. 8. The Treasurer shall receive and receipt for all money received by him as such and deposit the same, or all amounts in his hands exceeding Fifty Dollars in some bank designated by the Association or the Executive Committee, in his name as Treasurer of The Builders' Association of California, with the distinct understanding that the said account shall be transferred to his successor in office, upon notice from the Association, through

P. GRIFFIN
Contractor and Builder

BOX 103

OFFICE: Builders' Exchange
New Montgomery and Mission Streets

TEL. MAIN 5110

WHITE BROTHERS

Importers of and Dealers in

Hard Wood Lumber

Oak and Teak Ship Plank and Timber

Mahogany, Primavera and Spanish Cedar

Quartered Oak, Walnut, Cherry, Poplar, Ash, Etc.

HARDWOOD FLOORING IN OAK AND MAPLE
DOOR STOCK AND VENEERS

Southeast Cor. Spear and Howard Streets, San Francisco

PALACE HARDWARE CO.
Builders' and Cabinet Hardware
Tools, Cutlery and Novelties

603 MARKET STREET
SAN FRANCISCO, CAL.
GRAND HOTEL BLOCK

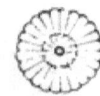

Agents for
P. & F. CORBINS LOCKS
COBURN TROLLEY HANGERS
BOMMER SPRING BUTTS
ATWOOD SASH LOCKS, Etc.

TELEPHONE 752

the President and Secretary thereof, stating the person who has been elected to succeed him.

The money when so deposited shall be paid out by said bank only upon drafts or checks, signed by the President, attested by the Secretary and countersigned by the Treasurer.

The Treasurer shall keep a correct account of all moneys received, deposited and paid out, and render a correct report thereof, at the first stated meeting in each month.

Upon retiring from office he shall deliver to his successor or such person as the Association shall designate, all money, books, papers and property in his hands belonging thereto.

SEC. 9. The Executive Committee shall have and exercise a general supervisory care over the affairs of the Association, and the Chairman or a quorum of the Committee, shall have, and is hereby vested with power to fine any member of this Committee for non-attendance at a called meeting of the Committee, which fine shall not be less than One Dollar, nor more than Five Dollars, provided notice of forty-eight hours be given. Members of the Executive Committee shall be exempt from monthly dues. They shall designate the bank in which the funds of the Association shall be deposited, unless the same shall have been done by a vote of the Association, and require the officers to change the same when in their judgment the safety thereof requires it. They shall hear, examine into, and if possible settle all disputes between members, when they can do so to the satisfaction of all parties concerned; otherwise report the facts, testimony, and their conclusions thereon, to the Association, for their action.

All amendments to the Constitution and By-Laws or Rules, and all agreements to be entered into by and between the members affecting the building business, shall be referred to them to examine and report thereon before action.

SEC. 10. The President, Vice President and Secretary shall constitute a Committee. If any two thereof shall report a member of this Association, as in their opinion sufficiently accused of acts of a character demanding investigation, it shall be their duty to report the accused to the Executive Committee, who shall take the necessary steps to investigate and report to the Association, as provided in Section 5 of By-Laws.

ARTICLE VII.

ELECTIONS.

SECTION 1. The regular election for officers of the Association shall be held annually at the regular meeting in December of each year, and they shall be installed at the regular meeting in January following their election.

SEC. 2. The election shall be by ballot; and the majority of all the votes cast shall be necessary to elect, except where there is only one nominee for an office, when the election may be by acclamation.

SEC. 3. The time and manner of making nominations and matters pertaining to the qualifications, etc., of officers may be provided for by the By-Laws.

ARTICLE VIII.

FUNDS.

SECTION 1. The money of the Association shall be kept in one General Fund.

SEC. 2. Rent, salaries and other necessary current expenses may be paid by a majority vote of a quorum at any regular meeting. But no money shall be otherwise appropriated or paid out in amounts exceeding Twenty-Five Dollars for any one purpose, except by resolution signed and introduced by a member, which shall be laid over at least one week and then passed by a two-thirds vote of the members present.

ARTICLE IX.

AMENDMENTS AND BY-LAWS.

SECTION 1. Any amendments to this Constitution must be proposed by a member at a regular meeting, each section proposed to be amended written out in full as it will read when amended. Such proposition shall then be laid over for two weeks, and when acted on must receive the affirmative vote of two-thirds of the members present, *except* as provided in Section 2 of this Article.

SEC. 2. By-Laws, not in conflict herewith may be adopted from time to time as the Association shall determine, and may be repealed or amended as provided in said By-Laws. But no By-Laws or Rules shall be passed abridging the right of any member to carry on or transact his business in such manner as he shall deem just and proper, unless such law or rule shall have received the affirmative consent of at least three-fourths of all the members of this Association. Due notice of the passage of any such By-Law or Rule shall be given to each member in writing at least two weeks before the same shall take effect and be in force.

This section shall not be repealed except by a three-fourths vote of all the members of the Association.

By-Laws.

MEETINGS.

SECTION 1. The regular business meetings of this Association shall be held on the second Monday of each month in the City and County of San Francisco, at 1:30 o'clock P. M., excepting on legal holidays.

NOTICE OF MEETINGS.

SEC. 2. Notice of all special or adjourned meetings shall be given either by postal card or by advertisement in two or more daily papers of the City and County of San Francisco. The notice must state the nature of the business to be transacted thereat.

ADMISSION FEE AND DUES.

SEC. 3. The fee for admission to membership shall be Twenty-Five Dollars. The dues shall be Twenty-Five Cents per month, payable in advance; but the following shall be exempt from paying said dues, to wit: the President, Vice President, Recording Secretary, Financial Secretary, Treasurer, and the seven members of the Executive Committee.

Any member of this Association entering into co-partnership with any person or persons, not members of this Association, or the representative of any firm becoming a member hereof, shall be held responsible to the Association for the observance of the Constitution, By-Laws, Agreements and Rules hereof, by and upon the part of such co-partnership, but no membership shall be created except as provided in Article II of the Constitution.

Only in case of co-partnership heretofore existing between members of this Association, may any member thereof represent said firm herein upon the payment of single dues, as provided in this Section.

The title to all property of this Association is vested in the Association as a body, and no individual interest therein shall ever be created or recognized. Therefore, when the representative of any firm in this Association shall cease to be a member hereof, neither the co-partners nor surviving partners shall have any claim upon the Association nor the property thereof. Neither shall the heirs or assignee of any member have any claim upon the property of this Association.

PENALTY FOR NOT PAYING.

SEC. 4. Any member who shall be in arrears for six months' dues, shall be notified by the Financial Secretary, and if he fails to pay the same, or such part thereof as shall bring him less than three months in arrears, during the space of one month thereafter, he shall be suspended from all the rights and privileges of membership, and so notified with a copy of this Section within thirty days from date of suspension; or any member who shall fail to pay any fine within thirty days from the day such fine shall have been levied, shall be suspended from all the rights and privileges of membership, and so notified. A member suspended, as herein provided, may be reinstated upon the payment of such delinquent Dues or Fines, together with Dues for the time he shall have been suspended, and upon receiving the affirmative vote of three-fourths of the members present at a regular meeting of this Association.

SEC. 5. Any member of this Association who shall be accused of willful violation of this Constitution and By-Laws, or a breach of contract, or of any proceeding inconsistent with just and equitable principles of trade, first having been duly tried by the Executive Committee (or by a Special Committee duly appointed in case the Executive Committee or any member thereof are disqualified from acting), and duly convicted by their report and a vote of the Association, shall be fined, suspended or expelled, as shall be adjudged by a two-thirds vote of the members present.

CHARGES.

SEC. 6. Any person desiring to bring charges against a member of this Association, shall reduce the same to writing, specifying clearly and explicitly the nature of the same, with time, place and circumstances connected therewith, and signed by him and delivered to the Association or Executive Committee.

COPY SERVED.

SEC. 7. A copy of the charges shall be immediately served upon the member against whom they are made, by the Recording Secretary or some person selected by him or by the Executive Committee, and at least five days' notice given him of the time and place of trial. If the accused refuse or neglect to stand trial, the Committee shall report him guilty of contempt, and the punishment shall be expulsion.

TESTIMONY, ETC.

SEC. 8. The testimony shall be taken in writing by the committee and signed by the witness. The committee may adjourn from time to time; and a quorum may proceed at any meeting.

DUTIES OF COMMITTEE.

SEC. 9. When testimony is all in on both sides, they shall consider the same, and see if they can settle the matter to the satisfaction of all parties. If they fail to do this, they shall report the testimony, together with their conclusions thereon, to the Association for their action and decision.

ACTION OF THE ASSOCIATION.

SEC. 10. The Association shall then proceed to take action thereon, and may have the testimony read, if desired by either party. During the reading and discussion of the testimony, both parties shall be entitled to be present and to be heard. But when the Association proceeds to act thereon, all parties interested shall be excluded from the room.

PENALTY AND MANNER OF FIXING.

SEC. 11. If the Association find the accused guilty, it shall forthwith proceed to fix the penalty, first voting upon expulsion. If two-thirds of the members vote in favor of that penalty, the member shall stand expelled. If not, the next vote shall be upon suspension. If two-thirds of the members vote in favor of suspension, that shall be the penalty; and the Association

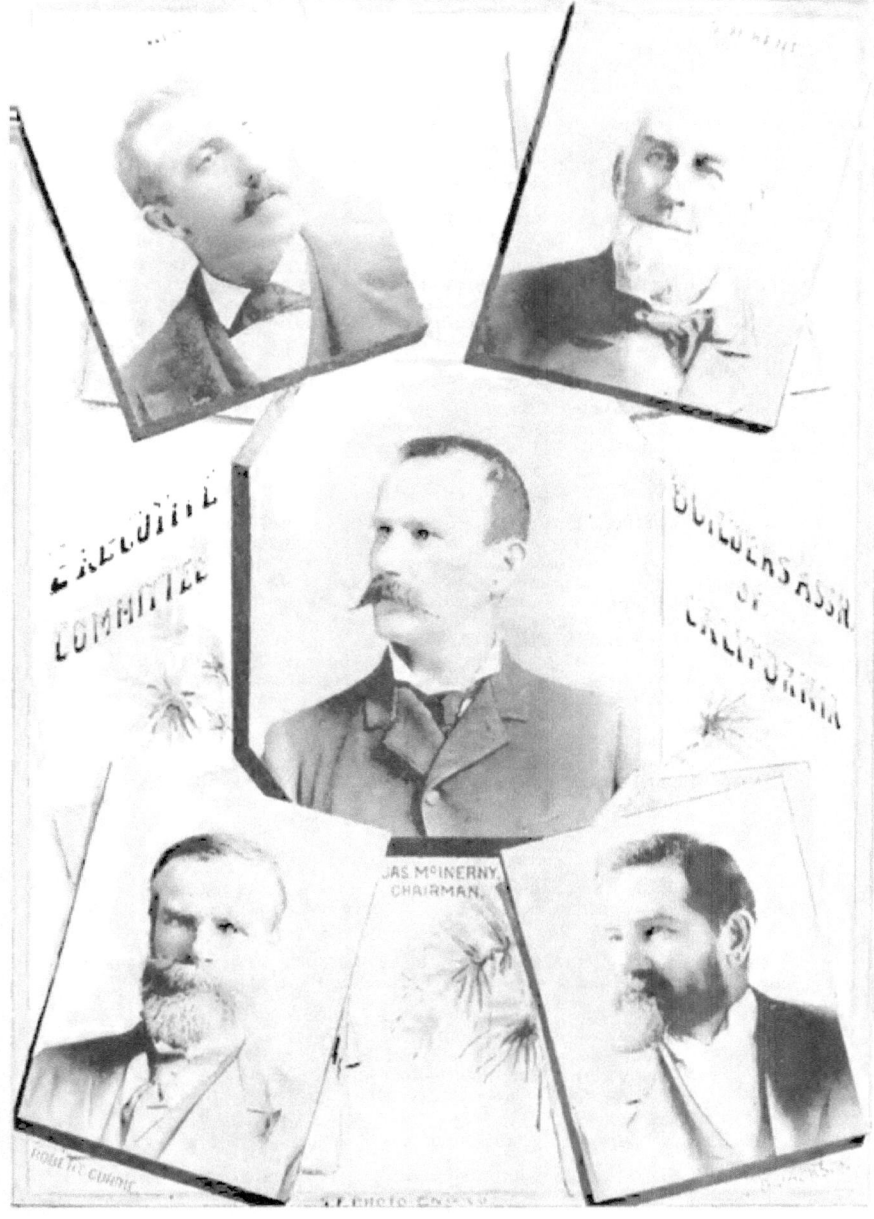

shall proceed to fix the time or duration thereof by vote, which time shall not exceed six months. If two-thirds of the members do not vote in favor of suspension, the penalty shall be a fine, and the Association shall then proceed to fix the amount of the fine (unless the same shall have been previously fixed in the By-Laws for like offenses), which may be done by a majority vote, but shall in no case exceed the sum of Two Hundred Dollars, except that any member convicted of a violation of his agreement with the other members in regard to the signing of contracts, shall be fined not less than Two Hundred and Fifty (250) Dollars nor more than One Thousand (1,000) Dollars, and that he stands suspended until said fine is paid.

SERGEANT-AT-ARMS.

SEC. 12. The President in his discretion, or when directed by the Association, shall appoint a Sergeant-at-Arms to serve during his pleasure, who shall have charge of the room, furniture, etc. He shall serve papers when required by the Association or by the Executive Committee, assist in preserving order at the meetings, and perform such other duties as may be required of him by the Association or the presiding officer thereof.

FINANCE COMMITTEE.

SEC. 13. The Finance Committee shall examine and audit all demands against the Association, examine and report upon the books of the officers at the end of each term, and at such other times as the Association may require.

SPECIAL COMMITTEES.

SEC. 14. The President may appoint a special committee of investigation at any time he may deem the same necessary, or when required by vote of the Association; said committee shall consist of one or more members, who shall examine and report upon the matter referred to them.

He shall also appoint a committee of one on the first meeting in February of each year to serve for a term of one year, whose duty it shall be to confer with a similar committee from the Lumber Dealers' Exchange and the San Francisco Chapter of A. I. A. in regard to the consideration of any laws or amendments that may be introduced into the legislature or municipal body affecting the Building Business.

BONDS.

SEC. 15. The Association may at any time require its officers who have the charge of collection of its funds to give bonds for the faithful discharge of their duties, which bonds (when required) shall be made payable to the President in trust for and for the benefit of the Association.

CLERK, PAY OF OFFICERS.

SEC. 16. The Association may employ a clerk to take charge of its rooms, who may also act as Secretary, or it may assign either of its Secretaries to that duty.

It may pay any of its officers or employees for their services such sums as it may from time to time determine by By-Law or Rule.

NOMINATIONS.

SEC. 17. Nominations for officers shall be made at the regular meeting in November of each year, but nominations may be made on the night of election, if the nominees all decline or if ordered by a two-thirds vote of the members present.

AMENDMENTS.

SEC. 18. These By-Laws may be repealed or amended in any manner not in conflict with Section 2 of Article IX of the Constitution, by designating the section proposed to be repealed, or by writing out in full the section proposed to be amended as it will read when amended, such proposition being signed by the member offering the same, the proposition being first laid over for one meeting and adopted by a two-thirds vote of the members present.

The following agreements numbered from 1 to 6 inclusive, have all been signed by more than three-fourths of all the members of this Association, and are, therefore, in full force and effect, and must be strictly complied with by all members.

I.

For a violation of the following agreement there is a fine of not less than two hundred and fifty dollars.

CONTRACT AGREEMENT.

ARTICLES OF AGREEMENT, made and entered into this 31st day of May, 1887, by and between the undersigned CARPENTERS AND BUILDING CONTRACTORS, doing business in the State of California.

We, and each of us, do hereby agree to and with each other, that we or either of us will not for ourselves, or by any representative for us, enter into or sign any form of contract except that adopted by The Builders' Association of California in regular session.

And it is further agreed, that this agreement shall not be held to include contracts let by the United States, State of California or Municipal work when the official blanks are used.

II.

BOND AGREEMENT.

Resolved, That the members of said Association will not give any bond or guarantee for performance of any contract for more than one-fourth of the contract price thereof; *provided,* that this resolution or rule will not be binding on the members of this Association, when the above rule would, if adhered to, have the effect of barring out our members in favor of some other handicraft or person not members of our Association.

III.

AGREEMENT NOT TO PATRONIZE MEN WHO VIOLATE AGREEMENTS ENTERED INTO WITH THIS ASSOCIATION.

Resolved, That the members of this Association will not trade with or otherwise patronize in their business as builders, any material man, sub-contractor or other person or firm of persons connected with the building business who may or does hereafter violate any written agreement entered into with this Association, until said person or firm has made due apology and reparation to this Association, either by fine or otherwise for so doing, and has been excused therefor by the vote of the Association.

IV.

AGREEMENTS NOT TO FIGURE AGAINST SUSPENDED OR EXPELLED MEMBERS.

We, the undersigned, members of the Builders' Association of California, do hereby agree with each other, and with said Association, that we will not estimate upon any plan, or upon any job of work, or put in any bid for same, when any person who has been expelled for cause from said Builders' Association either estimates or bids upon the same.

We further agree that if, after we have estimated or bid upon any job of work, we shall ascertain that the bid of any expelled member of said Association has been received thereon, we will at once withdraw our bid, and refuse to contract for said job of work.

We also further agree that we will refuse to estimate upon work in the office, or that is to be done under the superintendence of any architect who allows any expelled member of said Builders' Association to estimate or bid upon work in his office, or that is under his control, after he has been notified of the expulsion of said member.

This agreement does not refer to or include work that by virtue of any law of this State or the United States is open to public competition.

V.

RULE 1.

Under no circumstances shall bids be submitted *both* as a whole and in separate parts. When bids are invited both ways, then those invited to bid shall decline to do so until the owner shall elect which way he prefers to do the work.

RULE 2.

After bids are received, any bidder whose bid is not the lowest, who shall make another bid or make any false representations in order to secure the contract for himself, shall be considered guilty of unbusinesslike conduct, and such action shall be deemed good cause for expulsion.

VI.

ARTICLES OF AGREEMENT, made and entered into this 31st day of May, 1892, by and between the undersigned, CARPENTERS AND BUILDING CONTRACTORS, doing business in the State of California.

CLAUSE FIRST.

We, and each of us, do hereby agree to and with each other, that we will not either estimate, bid upon, or contract to do, a job of work of any kind upon which there has been, or is to be, any competition whatever, where the owner or any other person, except ourselves, either furnishes, or reserves the right to furnish, either by himself, his agent or other person, any of the material which enters into, or forms a part of, said job of work, which is, or is to be, the subject of such contract: PROVIDED, that when an OWNER at the time of taking estimates on, or entering into a contract for, the erection or repair of a building or other structure, is for himself, and not as an agent or employee of another,—in reality actually engaged in the manufacture or sale of any material required in the construction or repair of such building or other structure, the subject of such contract, and reserves the right to furnish such material only,—competition therefor will not be deemed a violation of this agreement: Provided further, that this agreement shall not be held to include contracts let or work done by the United States or the State of California.

CLAUSE SECOND.

It is also further understood and agreed, by and between all the parties thereto, that we or either of us shall not contract to become responsible for the care or preservation of any portion of a building or other structure, or job of work, or for any material furnished for, or put therein by the owner, or by any other contractor, or other person except ourselves, or those employed by us, nor for any loss thereof or damage thereto, except loss or damage only occurring from the acts or negligence of ourselves, or persons in our immediate employ, or under our immediate direction and control.

CLAUSE THIRD.

And we do each and all of us hereby further agree, that we will not become interested, either directly or indirectly, in any contract in violation of these Articles of Agreement, nor will we advise or consent to the signing of any such contract, by any other person.

CLAUSE FOURTH.

And we do hereby, each one for himself, solemnly declare that we have signed this agreement without any mental or other reservation whatsoever; and we do hereby pledge to each other our solemn word of honor, faithfully to keep inviolate all and singular the conditions of the foregoing agreement.

MEMBERS
OF
THE BUILDERS' ASSOCIATION
OF CALIFORNIA

Ackerson	88 Flood Bldg.
Adams, John G.	761 Haight street
Anderson Bros.	1221 Nebraska street
Bassett, James G.	726 Twentieth street, Oakland
Bateman Bros.	1912 Pacific avenue
Behrens, H.	24 Rutledge street
Brennan Bros.	337 Eddy street
Campbell, Alex	40 New Montgomery street
Campbell, James	230 Seventh street
Carle, Silas	Sacramento, Cal.
Chatham, William	943 Mariposa street
Christy, Charles	Euclid avenue, Berkeley
Coady, Charles	1424 Point Lobos avenue
Cochran, James	908 Minna street
Cogswell, James	San Francisco
Commary, William	Devisadero & McAllister
Crighton, Peter	100 Baker street
Currie, Robert	1308 Grove street
Currie & Loomer	421 Twenty-eighth street
Davis, R. O.	623 Tennessee street
Day, J. G. & I. N.	Oregon
Day, Thomas H., & Sons	1012 Devisadero street
Douglass, Charles	1120 Hampshire street
Doyle, R. S., & Son	2810 Howard street
Dunn, John J. (Privileged)	2026 Golden Gate avenue
Elam, Thos.	511 Sanchez street
Freely, M. J.	910 Page street
Fish, J. W.	326 Valley street
Foster, John	3716 Jackson street
Furness, John	8 Steiner street
Geary, James	2324 Sutter street
Gillespie, G. G.	1318 Devisadero street
Gonyeau, J. B.	124 Seventh avenue
Gorman, M. J.	1540 Seventeenth street
Grant, Wm. J.	301 Jones street
Griffin, P.	114 Ridley street
Hansen, F. L.	515 Thirty-third street, Oakland
Hayes, John T.	2637 Mission street
Hicks, R. B.	1347 Alabama avenue
Ingerson & Gore	40 New Montgomery street
Jack, W. R.	913 Ellis street
Jacks, H.	313 Twenty-first street
Jackson, A.	12 Middle street
Kent, S. H.	711 Leavenworth street
Kern, F. W.	Santa Clara and Hampshire streets
Klahn, Aug.	5 Chenery street
Klatt, F.	1201 Treat avenue

MEMBERS OF THE BUILDERS' ASSOCIATION.

Knowles, Wm .... 40 New Montgomery street
Knox & Cook .... 1218 Cypress street, Oakland
Kreger, W. B. (Honorary) .... 560 Mission street
Kronnick, Fred G. .... 1429 Washington street

Lang, G. R. .... 14th street and 14th avenue, Oakland
Lawson, A. (Privileged) .... 943 Fourteenth street
Linden, Wm. .... 433 Jersey street
Logan, J. F. .... Bryant avenue, bet. 25th and 26th streets
Lynch, M. C. .... San Mateo

Macdonald, A. .... 1405½ Ellis street
Mahoney Bros .... Crocker Building
Maloney, P. .... 1620 Lincoln street, Oakland
Mason, C. M. .... 235 Seventh street
Massey, John .... 729 Army street
Mayder, J. W. .... 1616 Fulton street
McBain, John .... Menlo Park
McCann, R. .... 217 Waller street
McDonald, J. A. .... 620 Ellis street
McElroy, A. .... 715 McAllister street
McInerny, Jas. .... 152 Hancock street
McKay, J. H. .... 2408 Washington street
Miller Adam .... 2424 Folsom street
Mitchell, Thos. F. .... 1324 Utah street
Moore, G. H. .... 221 Front street
Muller, W. A. .... S. W. cor. Twenty-second and York street
Munster, J. H. .... 2140 O'Farrell street

O'Brien, Jas. J. .... 1524 Golden Gate avenue
Ogle, John .... Twenty-fourth and Kansas street

Paff Bros .... 1322 Jackson street
Pavert, R. J. .... 640½ Castro street
Pluns, Wm. .... Menlo Park
Powers, Daniel .... 1216 Scott street

Quinn, Chas. .... 133 Oak street

Reichley, Geo. .... 734 Hermann street
Rohling, Henry .... Palmer, opposite Sanchez

Sanchez, R. P. .... 653 Capp street
Saunders, J. S. W. .... 411 Lyon street
Sinnot, Richard .... 1321 Guerrero street
Smilie, Robt. .... 1125 E. Third avenue, Oakland
Smith, J. W. .... 924 Page street
Soule Bros .... 9 Pond street
Steinmann, F. V. .... 810 Jessie street
Sullivan, T. .... 201½ Laskie street
Sweeney, Daniel .... 110 Hyde street

Trost, Robt. .... 433 Twenty-ninth street
Trotter, John .... 105 Hollis street, Oakland

Walker, Geo. H. .... 2130 Union street
White Bros. .... 15 Delong avenue
White, O. E. .... 879 Seventeenth street
Wickersham, W. H .... 1125 York street
Wilcox, J. R. .... 608 Willow avenue
Williams, F. A. .... 35 Lapidge street
Worden, E. G., & Son .... Berkeley, Cal
Worden, S. G. .... 307 San Jose avenue

Zwierlein, C. .... 1612 Grove street

SAN FRANCISCO   SAN JOSE   PALO ALTO

Mangrum & Otter

27 New Montgomery Street
and 110-112 Jessie Street

PACIFIC COAST AGENTS

MAGEE FURNACE COMPANY

Designers, Inventors and Manufacturers
of Highest Grades of

Cooking, Heating and Ventilating Apparatus

Examine our Famous . . .

MAGEE CHAMPION and MAGEE BOSTON HEATER FURNACES

. . . For Warming Dwellings, Halls, Churches
. . . School Houses and Public Buildings

MAGEE MYSTIC GOLDEN WEST AND PURITAN RANGES

Tin, Agate, White and Enameled Ware
and all kinds of Kitchen Ware

SAN FRANCISCO   SAN JOSE   PALO ALTO

A. M. DeSOLLA, President
T. DEUSSING, Gen'l Manager
W. H. BACKLEY, Secretary

DeSolla-Deussing Company

Sole Agents for Kennedy & Morrison's

Magnesia Sectional Steam Pipe and Boiler Covering

It Has No
Equal
.·.
Can Be Put On
By Anyone

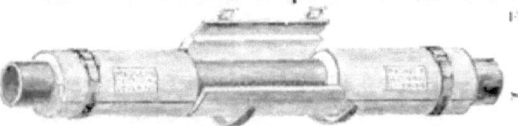

ESTIMATES
GIVEN
.·.
Personal
Supervision of
Work

ABSOLUTELY FIRE-PROOF AND NON HEAT CONDUCTING

Office and Salesroom, No. 2 California Street, San Francisco, Cal.

Telephone Private

Box 232, Builders' Exchange   Telephone, Main 5110

T. HOCK & SON

MASONS & BUILDERS

Office, 400 Kearny Street

Residence, 610 Devisadero Street   San Francisco

Established in 1872

D. F. Mulville

Plasterer

20 Fair Oaks St.

Bet. 21st and 22d   San Francisco

**Prompt Attention Given
to Repairing**

MEMBER OF BUILDERS' EXCHANGE
Cor. New Montgomery and
Mission Sts.

Box 76

SAN FRANCISCO ARCHITECTS

Armitage, Wm. H. .... 321 Phelan Building

Babson, Seth .... 408 California Street
Ball, R. C. .... 107 St. Ann's Building
Banks, W. O. .... 126 Kearny Street
Barnett, A. J. .... 103 Flood Building
Bayless, W. H. .... 2216½ Mission Street
Berger, G. A. .... 126 Kearny Street
Bestor, H. T. .... 408 California Street
Bordwell, Geo. A. .... 318 Pine Street
Brady, J. P. .... 116 Tenth Street
Brown, A. Page .... Crocker Building
Brown, B. Allen .... 99 Donohoe Building
Bugbee & Gash .... 431 California Street
Burns, Howard .... 61 Columbian Building

Cahill, B. J. S. .... 89 Donohoe Building
Cebrian, J. C. .... 328 Montgomery Street
Clark, J. J. .... 70 St. Ann's Building
Clinch, B. J. .... 126 Kearny Street
Colley, C. J. .... 67 Flood Building
Comstock, N. A. .... 91 Donohoe Building
Copeland & Pierce .... 126 Kearny Street
Coxhead & Coxhead .... 120 Sutter Street
Curlett, Wm. .... 307 Phelan Building
Curtis, J. M. .... 126 Kearny Street
Cuthbertson, W. J. .... 103 Flood Building

Daley, Robt. H .... 2121 Post Street
Day, Clinton .... 222 Sansome Street
Depierre, Emile .... 334 Kearny Street
Devlin, C. J. I. .... Supreme Court Building

Evans, W. S. .... Bush and Stockton Streets
Everett, Oliver .... 126 Kearny Street

Geddes, Chas. .... 415 Montgomery Street
Guilfuss, H. .... 120 Fulton Street

Hamilton, W. H. .... 409 California Street
Hatherton & Ross .... 916 Market Street
Havens & Toepke .... 55 Flood Building
Henrikson, B. E. .... 124 Post Street
Herold, R. A. .... 343 Phelan Building
Hess, H. .... 431 Pine Street
Hermann & Swain .... 120 Sutter Street

John, Emil .... 14 Grant Avenue

Kenitzer & Barth .... 501 California Street
Kidd, J. T. .... Market and Taylor Streets
Kollofrath, E. .... 58 Flood Building
Kraft, J. E. .... 41 Academy of Sciences

1873   1895

P. LEPROHON
—— Dealer in ——

BOILERS For .... Steam and Hot Water Heating

RADIATORS, RADIATOR VALVES, AIR VALVES,
DAMPER REGULATOR, AUTOMATIC WATER FEEDERS.

56 Eighth Street = = = **San Francisco, Cal.**

BOX 78, BUILDERS' EXCHANGE   TEL. MAIN—5110

J. P. McMURRAY
Formerly of KELLETT & McMURRAY

DESIGNER and MANUFACTURER of Plaster Decorations

STAFF and PLASTIC RELIEF

314 O'FARRELL St., Near Mason.   SAN FRANCISCO

RESIDENCE: BOX 76, BUILDERS' EXCHANGE
826 FOURTEENTH ST., OAKLAND   OAKLAND

J. C. McLEOD
Contractor For

PLASTERING and BRICK WORK

BOX 94, BUILDERS' EXCHANGE   San Francisco
New Montgomery and Mission

DENNIS JORDAN   Residence, 800 Fulton St.   PETER JORDAN

D. JORDAN & SON
Masons and Builders

Box 57   Office:
TEL. MAIN—5110   BUILDERS' EXCHANGE

San Francisco - - Cal.

Kraetzer, H. J.	2201 Geary Street
Laist & Schwerdt	Spreckels Building
Laver & Mullany	93 Flood Building
Lemme, Emil S.	67 Flood Building
Lillie, W. H.	28-29 St. Ann's Building
Littlefield, J. H.	126 Kearny Street
Lutgens, A. C.	125 Phelan Building
Lyon, M. J.	120 Sutter Street
Macy, H. C.	208 Kearny Street
Mahoney & Ryland	7 Flood Building
Marion, M. J.	526 Mission Street
Marquis, John	230 Kearny Street
Martens & Coffee	20 Academy of Sciences
Mathisen & Howard	523 Montgomery Street
McDougall, B. & Son	330 Pine Street
Merritt, H. P.	214 Pine Street
Mitchell, H. D.	126 Kearny Street
Mooser, W.	14 Grant Avenue
Newsom, Jos. C.	819 Market Street
Newsom, Samuel	Mills Building
Newsom, J. J. & T. D.	431 California Street
O'Brien, Smith	126 Kearny Street
Oakey, A. F.	Spreckels Building
Pare, Aime	420 Montgomery Street
Patton, Wm.	Mills Building
Pelton, J. C.	216 Bush Street
Percy & Hamilton	Hobart Building
Pissis & Moore	307 Sansome Street
Polk, W.	220 Post Street
Portois, Peter	519 Montgomery Street
Rabin, F. P.	504 Kearny Street
Reid Bros	Spreckels Building
Robertson, C. F.	74 Donohoe Building
Rousseau, C. M.	Spreckels Building
Rowlatt, H. B.	Mills Building
Salfield & Kohlberg	339 Kearny Street
Schetzel, M. P.	88 St. Ann's Building
Schultz, Henry A.	94 Flood Building
Schweinfurth, A. C.	229 Crocker Building
Shea & Shea	26 Montgomery Street
Smith & Freeman	206 Sansome Street
Stone & Cahill	89 Donohoe Building
Sutton, Albert	Stock Exchange Building
Swain, Edward R.	227 Crocker Building
Townsend & Wyneken	515 California Street
Vogel, E. J.	12 Montgomery Street
Welsh, M. J.	37 Donohoe Building
Welsh, T. J.	95 Flood Building
Wharff, W. H.	1839 Green Street
White, R. H.	104 Flood Building
Wieland & Binder	316 Phelan Building
Wilson, C. R.	315 Phelan Building
Winterhalter, W.	318 Phelan Building
Wolfe, J. E.	29 Flood Building
Wood, F. B.	214 Pine Street
Wright & Sanders	418 California Street

JAMES J. O'BRIEN

Carpenter × and × Builder

Box 107
BUILDERS' EXCHANGE.

CORNER NEW MONTGOMERY AND MISSION STS.
SAN FRANCISCO

TELEPHONE, MAIN 519

Box No. 14
TELEPHONE, MAIN 519

RESIDENCE
1810 GREEN STREET

FRANK C. BELL

Successor to FARRELL & BELL

Carpenter . and . Builder

CORNER NEW MONTGOMERY AND MISSION STS.
SAN FRANCISCO

TELEPHONE, MAIN 519

G. G. GILLESPIE

× Carpenter and Builder ×

1318 Devisadero Street

Member of the BUILDERS' EXCHANGE
Box No. 14

New Montgomery and Mission streets

C. A. INGERSON
Claremont Ave., East Oakland

C. A. GORE
751 Market Street, Oakland

INGERSON & GORE

Contractors and Builders

Public and Private Buildings Erected at any Point on the Pacific Coast

TELEPHONE MAIN 519

OFFICE BOX 17 BUILDERS' EXCHANGE
New Montgomery and Mission Streets

CLASSIFIED BUSINESS DIRECTORY

Architects
Brown, B. Allen .... 59 Donohoe Bldg
Lutgens, A. C. .... 125-127 Phelan Bldg
Schulze, Henry A .... 93 Flood Bldg
Swain, Edward R. .... 227 Crocker Bldg

Architectural Iron Work
Golden West Iron Works .... 117-119 Beale
Jackson, P. H. & Co .... 228-230 First
O'Connell & Lewis sw cor Kearny & Francisco
Ralston Iron Works .... 222-224 Howard

Architectural Terra Cotta
Gladding, McBean & Co. ..... 1358-1360 Market
Steiger, A. Sons .... 206 Market
Clark, N. & Sons .... 17-19 Spear

Art Glass
Butterworth, Thos C .... 225-227 Tenth
California Art Glass Works .... 103 Mission

Artificial Stone
Ambrose, W. F. .... 10 New Montgomery
Cushing-Wetmore Co. .... 408 California
Gillett, S. .... 10 New Montgomery
Goodman, Geo .... 307 Montgomery
Gray Bros. .... 316 Montgomery
Griese, Carl
Jackson, P. H. & Co. .... 228-230 First
Keatinge, Leonard & Ransome ... 661 Market

Asphalt Paints
Pacific Refining & Roof Co. ... 153 Crocker Bldg
Smith & Young (see page 90) .... 723 Market

Attorneys-at-Law
Cobb, Wm. H. .... 137 Montgomery

Banks
California Title Insurance & Trust Co Mills B

Bell Hangers
Hetty, Louis B. .... 124-126 Eddy

Blue Print Paper and Blue Prints
Smith & Young (see page 90) .... 723 Market

Boiler Compounds
De Solla Deussing Co. .... 2 California

Boiler Covering
De Solla Deussing Co. .... 2 California

Boots and Shoes—Repairing, Retail Dealers and Manufacturers
Level, A. .... 638 Market
Pollock, Geo .... 202 Powell

Brick—Manufacturers and Dealers
Clark, N. & Sons .... 17-19 Spear
Gladding, McBean & Co. ... 1358-1360 Market
Patent Brick Co.
Peterson Brick Co. (Orig. red) pressed } 10 N. Mont'g Brick infl's
Remillard Brick Co. .... Berry n Fifth
Sacramento Transportation Co. Third & Berry
San Joaquin Brick Co .. Berry bet 6th and 7th

Brick Preservation and Brick Wash
Smith & Young (see page 90) .... 723 Market

Building Papers
Pacific Refining & Roofing Co .. 152 Crocker B
Paraffine Paint Co .... 116 Battery
Smith & Young (see page 90) .... 723 Market
Wright, J. W. .... 727 Market

Building News
Building News and Review .... Flood Bldg
(Geo H Wolfe)

Burglar Alarms
Hetty, Louis B. .... 124-126 Eddy

Cement
Cowell, Henry & Co .... 213-215 Drumm
Gray Bros. .... 316 Montgomery
Holmes, H. T. Lime Co. .... 22 Sacramento
Louis & Co. .... 215 Main
Maguire, A. B. .... 2520-2524 Folsom
Remillard Brick Co. .... Berry, near Fifth
Snell, E. J. .... 46 Hayes
Spreckels, J. D. & Bros. Co .... 325 Market
Tuttle, John .... 546 Haight
Wolff, Wm. & Co. .... 727-729 Market

Cement—Roofing
Smith & Young (see page 90) .... 723 Market

Chimney Pipe and Tops
Clark, N. & Sons .... 17-19 Spear
Clawson, L. E. & Co .... 1200 Market
Conlin & Roberts .... 728-730 Mission
Crowan, Wm .... 1215 Market
Forderer Cornice Works .... 226 Mission
Gladding, McBean & Co ..... 1358-60 Market
Hammond, Philip .... 318 Larkin
Steiger, A. Sons .... 206 Market
Stevens, F. M. .... N E cor. Larkin & Market

Chimney Hood—(Clawson's Patent)
Smith & Young (see page 90) .... 723 Market

Chimneys Patent
Clawson, L. E. & Co .... 1200 Market
Conlin & Roberts .... 728-730 Mission
Stevens, F. M. .... N E cor. Larkin & Market

Concrete
Ambrose, Wm. F. .... 10 New Montgomery
Cushing-Wetmore Co. .... 408 California
Gillett, S. .... 10 New Montgomery
Goodman, Geo .... 307 Montgomery
Gray Bros. .... 316 Montgomery
Griese, Carl .... 118 Stanyan
Jackson, P. H. & Co. .... 228-230 First
Keatinge, Leonard & Ransome ... 661 Market

Contractors and Builders
Ackerson & Patterson .... 38 Flood Bldg
Anderson Bros. .... 107 McAllister
Bassett, T. F. & Bros .... Tennessee & Alameda Co
Bell, Frank C. .... 1830 Geary

MANGRUM & OTTER
27 NEW MONTGOMERY STREET

Mangrum & Otter

Contractors for

All Classes of Buildings Warmed and Ventilated by the most Improved System... Heating of Homes a Specialty

27 NEW MONTGOMERY STREET

Magee Furnace Co.
Pacific Coast Agents

Contractor and Builder

BUILDERS' EXCHANGE
New Montgomery and Mission Sts.

943 MARIPOSA ST. San Francisco, Cal.

ROBERT KNOX
1218 Cypress Street

1807 Polk Street

KNOX & COOK

CONTRACTORS & BUILDERS

BUILDERS' EXCHANGE
Oakland

BUILDERS' EXCHANGE
San Francisco

BOX 89 Telephone—MAIN 5110

Contractor and Builder

BUILDERS' EXCHANGE   New Montgomery and Mission Sts.

Wm. J. Field Tel.—MAIN 5110

BOX 89
BUILDERS'
EXCHANGE
New Montgomery
and
Mission Sts.

 Contractor and Builder
417
Powell Street.

CLASSIFIED BUSINESS DIRECTORY 187

Get Your Estimates For Heating of MANGRUM & OTTER
27 NEW MONTGOMERY STREET

Heating and Ventilating OF ALL KINDS
MANGRUM & OTTER ... 27 New Montgomery Street

Contractors — Continued

Brennan, M. & Son........875 Harrison, Oakl'd
Currie, Robert.................... 1308 Grove
Chatham, Wm .... 993 Mariposa
Day, Thos. H. & Sons .... 1012 Devisadero
Doyle, R. & Son .... 2840 Howard
Elam, Thos .... 511 Sanchez
Field, W. J......................... 417 Powell
Foster, John .... 736 Jackson
Furness, John .... 8 Stone
Gillespie, G. G. .... 1308 Devisadero
Grant, W. J. .... 848 Mission
Griffin, P. .... 111 Ridley
Hansen, F. L. ...... 515 Thirty third, Oakland
Hayes, John I .... 2637 Mission
Ingerson & Gove .... 40 New Montgomery
Jacks, Henry .... 315 Twenty first
Jack, Wm. R .... 918 Ellis
Kent, S. H .... 711 Leavenworth
Klatt, F. .... 40 New Montgomery
Knowles, Wm .... Alameda
Knox & Cook .... 40 New Montgomery
Logan, J. F. .... 2719 Bryant ave.
McDonald, John A .... 918 Ellis
McInerny, Jas .... 152 Hancock
McLachlan, T. M .... 329 Twentieth
Munster, John H .... 2110 or Farrell
Moore, G. H .... 721 Front
Muller, W. A .... 22d and York
O'Brien, Jas. J .... 1521 Golden Gate ave.
Pavert, R. J. .... 690 Castro
Powers, Daniel .... 2164 Scott
Reichley, Geo .... 551 Hermann
Trotter, John .... 165 Hollis, Oakland
Wickersham, W. H .... 1225 York
Williams, F. A .... 40 New Montgomery

Door Checks and Springs

Maguire, James A. (Bardsley)... 131 Sansome
Morrell, Frank D. (Norton) ..... 207 Mission

Doors, Sash and Blinds

Central Lumber and Mill Co. ...... 19-26 Tenth
Depew, Chas. M. .... 229 233 Berry
Doe, B. and J. S .... 16 Market
Hansen, A .... Berry near Sixth
Hansen, M. & Co .... 241-251 King
Hinds, Edw. B. & Co. (inside sliding blinds) .... 411 Mission
Huber, Frank .... 565 Brannan
Scott & Van Arsdale Lumber Co. 5th & Brannan

Drain and Sewer Pipe

Clark, N. & Sons .... 17-19 Spear
Gladding, McBean & Co .... 1358-60 Market
Steiger, A. Sons .... 206 Market
Montague, W. W. & Co .... 309-317 Market

Draying

Cartwright, D. S .... 101 Main
Dillon, David .... 40 New Montgomery
Gillogley, G. & R .... Channel, bet. 4th and 5th
Sibley, L. B .... 40 New Montgomery

Electricians

Electrical Maintenance Co. 40 New Montgomery
Henzel, Edw. F. & Co ..... 40 New Montgomery
Hetty, L. B. .... 126 Eddy

Electric Light Wiring

Electrical Maintenance Co. 40 New Montgomery
Henzel, Edw. F. & Co ..... 40 New Montgomery
Hetty, L. B. .... 126 Eddy

Electrical Supplies

Henzel, Edw. F. & Co ..... 40 New Montgomery
Hetty, L. B. .... 126 Eddy

Electrical Work

Electrical Maintenance Co. 40 New Montgomery
Henzel, Edw. F. & Co ..... 40 New Montgomery
Hetty, L. B. .... 126 Eddy

Elevators

Pettitt, J. G., Elevator Works ... 325 Mission

Engineers Electrical

Henzel, Edw. F. & Co ..... 40 New Montgomery
Hetty, L. B. .... 126 Eddy

Fire Brick and Fire Clay

Clark, N., & Sons .... 17-19 Spear
Cowell, H., & Co .... 211-215 Drumm
Gladding, McBean & Co ...... 1358-60 Market
Holmes, H. T. Lime Co .... 22 Sacramento
Remillard Brick Co .... Berry near 5th
Steiger, A. Sons .... 206 Market

Fire Escapes

Golden West Iron Works ..... 117-119 Beale
Jackson, P. H. & Co .... 228 230 First
Ralston Iron Works .... 222-224 Howard

Flooring — Tile and Hardwood

Kenney & Wells .... 122 Sutter

Fretwork — Artistic and Carved

Kenney & Wells .... 122 Sutter

Furnaces

Mangrum & Otter ..... 27 New Montgomery
Montague, W. W. & Co .... 309-317 Market
Tay, Geo. H. Co .... 604-606 Battery

Galvanized Iron

Montague, W. W. & Co .... 309-317 Market
Tay, Geo. H. Co .... 604-606 Battery

Galvanized Iron Cornices

Conlin & Roberts .... 728-730 Mission
Cronan, Wm .... 1295 Market
Forderer Cornice Works ...... 221-226 Mission
Hammond, Philip .... 515 Larkin
Oakland Metal Works 838 Webster st., Oakl'd

Glass Bending

Butterworth, Thos. C .... 225-227 Tenth
Cal. Art Glass Bending and Cutting Works, 116 Mission

Glass Bevelers

Butterworth, Thos. C .... 225-227 Tenth
Cal. Art Glass Bending and Cutting Works 116 Mission
Fuller, W. P. & Co .... cor. Pine and Front

Box 350   Tel. Main 5110

JOHN FOSTER
CONTRACTOR ✦ AND ✦ BUILDER

BUILDERS' EXCHANGE

New Montgomery and Mission Street

Residence, 3710 Jackson Street

Box 358, Builders' Exchange

G. H. MOORE
Contractor and Builder

Office, 221 FRONT STREET

Telephone, Front 9   Room 5

Jobbing Promptly Attended To

R. Doyle & Son   Tel. Main 5110

CARPENTERS AND BUILDERS

Box 142
BUILDERS' EXCHANGE
40 New Montgomery St.

Jobbing of All Kinds Attended To

Residence, 1216 Treat Avenue

A. HANSEN

Scroll Sawing, Planing, Shaping

Mill Work of All Kinds

All Kinds of House Finish Made to Order

PACIFIC PLANING MILL

Sash, Doors and Blinds

Turning, Brackets and Mouldings

Telephone, South 65

Box 3 Builders' Exchange

BERRY STREET, near Sixth, San Francisco, Cal.

CLASSIFIED BUSINESS DIRECTORY

GET ESTIMATES FOR HEATING OF ALL KINDS
From MANGRUM & OTTER, 27 New Montgomery St.

Glass—Plate and Window
Ammerup, G. .... 1311 Market
Bass-Hueter Paint Co .... 18-22 Elis
Butterworth, Thos. C .... 225-227 Tenth
Cal. Art Glass Bending and Cutting Works .... 163-165 Mission
Fuller, W. P. & Co .... cor. Pine and Front
Merchant & Nickels .... 16 Third

Glassware
Maguire, Jas. A .... 130 Sansome

Glaziers
Butterworth, Thos. C .... 225-227 Tenth
Schroeder, Wm. .... 163-165 Mission
Vogler, J. F. .... 10 New Montgomery

Grading
Sibley, L. B. .... 10 New Montgomery
Tuttle, Jno. .... 516 Haight

Granite
Raymond Granite Co. .... Tenth & Channel
Rocklin Granite Co. .... 10 New Montgomery
Western Granite and Marble Co. ..... 10 New Montgomery

Grill Work—Wood
Kenney & Wells .... 122 Sutter

Grill Work—Iron
Golden West Iron Works .... 117-119 Beale

Hangers—Duplex
Maguire, Jas. A .... 130 Sansome

Hardware—Building
Osborn, R. F. & Co .... 751 Market
Palace Hardware Co .... 603 Market
Wright, F. W. .... 727 Market

Hats and Caps
Herrmann, C. & Co. [Incorp.] .... 328 Kearny

Heating and Ventilating
Cronan, Wm .... 1213-1215 Market
Gramm, J. G. .... 10 New Montgomery
Leprohon, P. .... 56 Eighth
Mangrum & Otter .... 27 New Montgomery
Montague, W. W. & Co .... 309-317 Market
Tay, Geo. H. Co. .... 610-620 Battery

House Raisers and Movers
Davis, Geo. & Son .... 31 South Park
Kelleher, Mathew .... 2055 Folsom

MATHEW KELLEHER
HOUSE RAISER
2055 Folsom St., bet 16th and 17th

STEEL Screws of 50 tons, Power for raising Iron, Stone or Brick Buildings. Estimates given on Brick or Wooden Foundations.

Builders' Exchange—Box 23
New Montgomery St., San Francisco

Pool, J. R. .... 1202 Mission

Illuminating Tiles
Jackson, P. H. & Co. .... 228-230 First

Inlaid Floors
Kenney & Wells .... 122 Sutter

Inside Sliding Blinds
Charles Edw. R. & Co. .... 111 Mission

Iron Crestings
Golden West Iron Works .... 117-119 Beale
Jackson, P. H. & Co .... 228-230 First
Ralston Iron Works .... 222-224 Howard

Iron Doors, Shutters, Etc.
Golden West Iron Works .... 117-119 Beale
Jackson, P. H. & Co .... 228-230 First
Ralston Iron Works .... 222-224 Howard

Iron Foundries
Architectural Iron Works ...... S. W. cor. Francisco & Kearny
Golden West Iron Works .... 117-119 Beale
Jackson, P. H. & Co .... 228-230 First
Ralston Iron Works .... 222-224 Howard

Lath—Metalic
Maguire, James A. .... 130 Sansome
Smith & Young [see page 90] .... 724 Market

Laundries
San Francisco Towel Co .... 116 Davis

Lime
Cienega Lime Co. [E. L. Snell, Agt] ..... 16 Hayes
Cowell, Henry, & Co .... 211-215 Drumm
Holmes, H. T. Lime Co .... 22 Sacramento
Lucas & Co. .... 215-17 Main
Maguire, A. B. .... 2850-54 Folsom
Snell, E. L. .... 16 Hayes
Tupper, O. M. [Cienega Lime Co] ..... San Jose
Tuttle, Jno. .... 516 Haight

Liquors—Wholesale
Blumenthal, M. & Co .... 658 Mission

Liquors—Retail
Walsh, Thos. J .... 620 Mission

Loans—On Real Estate
Cal. Title, Insurance and Trust Co. .. Mills Bldg

Locks
Osborn, R. F. & Co .... 751-753 Market
Palace Hardware Co .... 603 Market
Wright, F. W. .... 727 Market

Lumber
Central Lumber and Mill Co .... 25-26 Tenth
Golden Gate Lumber Co .... 1 Sutter
Niehaus, Edward F. & Co .... 561-46 Brannan
Pac. Coast Lumber & Mill Co .... 10 New Montg'y
Scott & Van Arsdale Lu. Co ..... 5th & Brannan
Union Lumber Co. .... 22 Market
White Bros .... S. E. cor. Spear and Howard

Lumber—Hardwood
Niehaus, Edward & Co .... 561-46 Brannan
White Bros .... N. E. cor. Spear and Howard

Mantels
Clawson, L. E. & Co .... 1330 Market
Montague, W. W. & Co .... 309-317 Market
Tay, Geo. H. & Co .... 610-620 Battery

Mangrum & Otter Have the BOSTON HEATERS AT 27 New Montgomery Street

J. F. LOGAN

Builder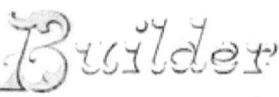

RESIDENCE:
2719 Bryant Ave.
Bet. 25th and 26th Sts.

OFFICE:
Builders' Exchange
New Montgomery, Cor. Mission

BOX 141   TEL.—MAIN 5110

DANIEL TOWER

Carpenter and Builder

RESIDENCE:
SAN FRANCISCO

OFFICE:
New Montgomery and Mission Sts.

Box 131   TEL. MAIN 5110

THOS. H. DAY & SONS

Contractors and Builders

Office:
BUILDERS' EXCHANGE
New Montgomery and Mission Sts.

RESIDENCE:
1012 Devisadero Street.

Box 108   Telephone—MAIN 5110

F. L. Hansen

Contractor and Builder

Residence:
515 33d St., Oakland
Telephone

Office:
Builders' Exchange
New Montgomery and Mission Sts., S. F.

Marble Work

Healy, M. J. .... 10 New Montgomery
Raymond Granite Co. .... Tenth and Channel
Rocklin Granite Co. .... 10 New Montgomery
Vermont Marble Co. .... 214-250 Brannan
Western Granite and Marble Co. ...... 10 New Montgomery
Smith & Young (Serpentine) ...... 725 Market

Masons and Builders

Beck, Adam .... 308 Mission
Brady, M. V. .... 10 New Montgomery
Brady, O. F. .... 10 New Montgomery
Butler, Thos. .... 10 New Montgomery
Fennell, M. & Son .... 10 New Montgomery
Hanavan, J. H. .... 2402 Seventeenth
Harrison, Fred. .... 10 New Montgomery
Hock, T. & Son .... 910 Divisadero
Hodman, Victor .... 10 New Montgomery
Jordan, D. & Son .... 801 Fulton
Leibert, John G. .... 10 New Montgomery
McGowan, M. .... 1616 Hayes
Miller, J. W. .... 234 Eighteenth
O'Sullivan, D. .... 10 New Montgomery
Peacock & Butcher .... 10 New Montgomery
Wilson, Jas. A. .... 10 New Montgomery
Wilson, J. H. .... 10 New Montgomery

Mill Work

Central Lumber and Mill Co. .... 20-26 Tenth
Depew, Chas. M. .... 229-233 Berry
Doe, B. & J. S. .... 44-46 Market
Golden Gate Lumber Co. .... 4 Sutter
Hansen, A. .... Berry, near Sixth
Hansen, M. & Co. .... 234-254 King
Huber, Frank .... 563 Brannan
Pacific Coast Lumber and Mill Co. ...... Second and Grove, Oakland
Scott & Van Arsdale Lumber Co. ..... Fifth and Brannan

Millwrights

Pettit, J. G. .... 525 Mission

Mortar Stains

Smith & Young (see page 90) ...... 725 Market

Mouldings

Central Lumber and Mill Co. .... 20-26 Tenth
Depew, Chas. M. .... 229-233 Berry
Hansen, A. .... Berry, near Sixth
Hansen, M. & Co. .... 234-254 King
Huber, Frank .... 563 Brannan
Miller & Hamilton .... 413-415 Mission
Pacific Coast Lumber and Mill Co. ...... Second and Grove, Oakland
Scott & Van Arsdale Lumber Co. ..... Fifth and Brannan
Smith & Young (see page 90) ...... 725 Market

Office Furniture

Office Specialty Mnfg. Co. .... 29 New Montgomery

Painters

Daniels, Gus. A. .... 10 New Montgomery
Dwyer, L. J. .... 1230 Utah
Keefe, J. H. .... 517 Sutter
Kuss, P. N. .... 122 Sutter
Merchant & Nickels .... 16 Third
Sullivan, J. P. .... 10 New Montgomery
Wagner, Henry F. .... 616 California

Paints, Oils, etc.

Ammerop, G. .... 1311 Market
Bass Hueter Paint .... 18-22 Ellis
California Paint Co. .... 22 Jessie
Fuller, W. P. & Co. ...... S. W. cor. Front and Pine
Kuss, P. N. .... 122 Sutter
Merchant & Nickels .... 16 Third
Pac. Refining and Roofing Co. 155 Crocker Bldg
Paraffine Paint Co. .... 136 Battery
Smith & Young (see page 90) ...... 725 Market

Paint Works

California Paint Co. .... 22 Jessie
Fuller, W. P. & Co. ...... S. W. cor. Front and Pine
Pac. Refining and Roofing Co. 151 Crocker Bldg
Paraffine Paint Co. .... 136 Battery

Pipe—Sewer

Clark, N. & Sons .... 17-19 Spear
Clawson, L. E. & Co. .... 1310 Market
Gladding, McBean & Co. .... 1358-1360 Market
Steiger, A. Sons .... 236 Market
Stevens, F. M. N. E. cor. Larkin and Market

Planing Mills

Central Lumber & Mill Co. .... 20-26 Tenth
Depew, Chas. M. .... 229-233 Berry
Doe, B. & J. S. .... 44-46 Market
Golden Gate Lumber Co. .... 1 Sutter
Hansen, M. & Co. .... Berry, near Sixth
Hansen, M. & Co. .... 234-254 King
Miller & Hamilton .... 413-415 Mission
Scott & Van Arsdale Lumber Co. 5th & Brannan

Plaster

Cowell, Henry, & Co. .... 211-213 Drumm
Holmes, H. T. Lime Co. .... 22 Sacramento
Lucas & Co. (Manufrs.) .... 215 Main
Maguire, A. B. .... 230-34 Folsom
Snell, E. L. .... 16 Hayes
Tuttle, Jno. .... 546 Haight

Plaster Decorations

Lucas & Co. .... 215 Main
McMurray, J. P. .... 314 O'Farrell
Santini, L. .... 10 New Montgomery

Plasterers

Broman & Fraser .... 10 New Montgomery
Coghlan, Frank .... 1113 Hampshire
Davies, E. .... 10 New Montgomery
Dunlop, Chas. .... 10 New Montgomery
McLeod, J. C. .... 10 New Montgomery
Morehouse, J. J. .... 10 New Montgomery
Mulville, D. F. .... 29 Fair Oaks
O'Sullivan, D. .... 10 New Montgomery
Tobin, J. R. .... 10 New Montgomery

Plumbers' Materials

Buddy, Jos. .... 575 Mission
Montague, W. W. & Co. .... 301-17 Market
Tay, Geo. H. Co. .... 616-620 Battery

Charles Lyons

London Tailor

1212 TO 1218 MARKET ST.
Bet. Taylor and Jones

302 KEARNY STREET 908 MARKET STREET
In the Evening Post Bldg. Bet. Powell and Stockton

SAN FRANCISCO, CAL.

Printers and Publishers

Cosper, L. H., & Co. .... 216 Eddy
Hammond, J. D. .... 1037 Market

Real Estate

Alum Rock Orchard Co. .... 401 California

Roofers

Conlin & Roberts .... 728-730 Mission
Cronan, Wm .... 1213 Market
Forderer Cornice Works .... 224-226 Mission
Hammond, Philip .... 318 Larkin
Oakland Metal Works 8?8 Webster, Oakland
Pacific Refining & Roofing Co. 151 Crocker Bld
Paraffine Paint Co. .... 116 Battery

Roofing Materials

Maguire, Jas. A. .... 130 Sansome
Montague, W. W., & Co. .... 309-317 Market
Pacific Refining & Roofing Co. 151 Crocker Bld
Paraffine Paint Co. .... 116 Battery
Smith & Young (see page 90) .... 723 Market

Sanitary Appliances

Budde, Jos. .... 575 Mission

Shingle Stains

Smith & Young (see page 90) .... 723 Market

Sidewalks

Ambrose, W. F. .... 916 Hayes
Cushing-Wetmore Co. .... 568 California
Goodman, Geo. .... 307 Montgomery
Gray Bros. .... 316 Montgomery
Griese, Carl .... 1318 Stanyan
Keatinge, Leonard & Ransome ..... 604 Market

Skylights

Conlin & Roberts .... 728-730 Market
Cronan, Wm .... 1213-1215 Market
Forderer Cornice Works .... 224-226 Mission
Hammond, Philip .... 318 Larkin
Jackson, P. H., & Co. .... 228-230 First
Oakland Metal Works 8?8 Webster, Oakland

Stone Contractors

Cal. Sandstone & Cont'g Co. .. 10 New Mont'ry
Healy, M. J. .... 10 New Montgomery
Raymond Granite Co. ..... Tenth and Channell
Rocklin Granite Co. .... 10 New Montgomery
Western Granite & Marble Co. 10 New Mont.

Street Contractors

Diggins Bros. .... 10 New Montgomery
Gray Bros. .... 316 Montgomery

Tailors

Adams, Chas. .... 1384 Market
Bridge, H. S., & Co. .... 622 Market
Lyons, Chas. 1212-1218 Market, 908 Market
                                    302 Kearny
Reid, John .... 507 Market
Sorensen, Chas. M. .... 122 Post

Terra Cotta—Manufacturers

Clark, N. & Sons .... 17-19 Spear
Gladding, McBean & Co. .... 1358-1390 Market
Steiger, A. Sons .... 206 Market

Tiles

Clark, N., & Sons .... 17-19 Spear
Cowell Henry, & Co. .... 211-215 Drumm
Gladding, McBean & Co. .... 1358-1390 Market
Montague, W. W. & Co. .... 309-317 Market

Tools Mechanics

Osborn, R. F., & Co. .... 751-753 Market
Palace Hardware Co. .... 605 Market
Wright, F. W. .... 727 Market

Towel Companies

San Francisco Towel Co. .... 116 Davis

Varnishes

Ahnbruster, G. .... 1314 Market
Bass-Hueter Paint Co. 18-22 4-ths
Fuller, W. P., & Co. ..... S.W. cor. Front & Pine
California Paint Co. .... 22 Jessie
Merchant & Nickels .... 16 Third
Pacific Refining & Roofing Co. 151 Crocker Bld

Ventilators

Conlin & Roberts .... 728-730 Mission
Cronan, Wm .... 1213-1215 Market
Jackson, P. H., & Co. .... 228-230 First
Mangrum & Otter .... 27 New Montgomery
Montague, W. W. & Co. .... 309-317 Market

Water Closets

Budde, Jos. .... 575 Mission

THE ALUM ROCK...
ORCHARD COMPANY

(INCORPORATED)

* 200 Acres of Fruit *
* Land in Tracts of *
* 5 Acres or More *

WITHIN 6 MILES OF SAN JOSE
SANTA CLARA COUNTY

Price $200.00 per Acre

Payable as Follows

$5.00 per acre when papers are delivered.
$5.00 per acre in 30 days after
$5.00 per acre in 60 days after
$5.00 per acre in 90 days after

Balance to be paid at the rate of $5.00 per acre, each month, giving purchaser 64 months in which to pay the principal

For further particulars call or address

S. SLESINGER, Secretary and Attorney
401 California Street

MANGRUM & OTTER — 27 New Montgomery Street

BOSTON HEATERS

GET ESTIMATES FOR HEATING OF ALL KINDS FROM MANGRUM & OTTER, 27 New Montgomery Street

Home Industry
JOSEPH BUDDE
Manufacturer of Sanitary Appliances
Factory and Showroom, 575 MISSION STREET

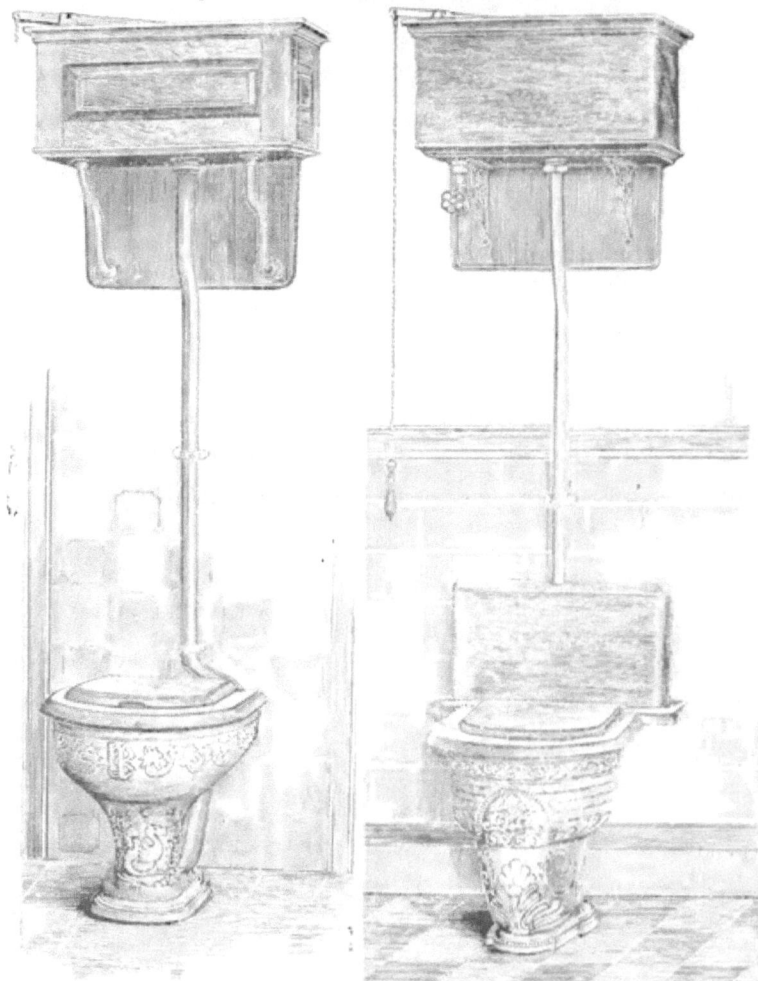

The No. 1 Cyclone Closet

With Tank, seat, Nickel Plate Flush Pipe and Brackets attached, is the most elegant design ever offered to the trade. Its method of operation is the same as that of any other Closet, but the design and finish are far superior. This Closet requires no trap beneath it. Size of Tank, 11 x 20 x 12 inches; capacity, 12 gallons. Tank lined, zinc or copper.

The Favorite Closet

As shown above, is the largest of its size, holds the most water in the Bowl. Fitted up with Noiseless Tank, either Grecian or Beaded Design, seat to match; Nickel Plated Flush Pipe and Brackets; and is sold as cheap as a Common Closet. Size of Tank, 18 x 10 x 10 inches. Capacity, 8 gallons.

www.ingramcontent.com/pod-product-compliance
Lightning Source LLC
Chambersburg PA
CBHW020241170426
43202CB00008B/181